Dr. Bob Kellemen knows that God has calle[d] participants in the ministry community tha[t] Bob also knows that it is not enough to gi[ve] to commitment—they must also be biblically trained. Equip[ping] of Christ for personal ministry has been Bob's lifework. This practical, step-by-step equipping manual is the mature fruit of that lifelong commitment.

—**Paul Tripp,** Founder and President of Paul Tripp Ministries; Author of *Instruments in the Redeemer's Hand*

So many of us long to see our churches equipped to minister the blessings of God's Word to one another . . . and yet somehow it seems all too easy to get bogged down in the "how." Bob Kellemen has given the church a tremendous resource—outlining not only the "how" but also the "why" and most importantly the "who." This is a resource that will revolutionize the way your church does ministry and will give you the resources you need to offer practical help from a many-membered body serving one another and their community.

—**Elyse Fitzpatrick,** Author of *Counsel from the Cross*

This is a must-read book for every person who longs to see their church be more effective at helping people grow and handle the issues of everyday life. It is intensely biblical with a model that flows right out of the pages of Scripture. But it is equally practical. You will be encouraged and equipped to be a person who . . . encourages and equips. My friend Bob Kellemen has done a masterful job at helping us all think about how to be truly effective in the culture in which Christ has placed us.

—**Steve Viars,** Senior Pastor, Faith Baptist Church, Lafayette, Indiana; Author of *Putting Your Past in Its Place*

Equipping Counselors for Your Church is an excellent resource for both individual leaders and also group discussion. The insight gained from years of experience by Dr. Kellemen and by the twenty-four best-practice churches is evident throughout the book. This is the book for you if you want to launch a biblical counseling ministry or want your church's current counseling ministry to move to a place of increased effectiveness. Use *Equipping Counselors for Your Church* to help you identify the issues and solutions in your situation.

—**Randy Patten,** Executive Director, National Association of Nouthetic Counselors

Bob Kellemen—trainer and coach extraordinaire—has a simple goal: he wants to see your church's one-on-one ministry transformed. The way he does that is by giving clear, practical instruction along with a huge package of supplies and tools. And when you follow his coaching you'll be surprised to find that the result is not so much Bob's system as it is an equipping model that is specific to your church.

—**Ed Welch,** Faculty Member of CCEF; Author of
When People Are Big and God Is Small

This is the book we needed years ago at Mars Hill Church to help us rethink our counseling ministries. By God's grace we ended up with something like what Dr. Kellemen envisions—but save yourself the trouble we endured and let Bob's wisdom guide you strategically through the process. In fact, join me; I'll be using this book to rethink it all over again.

—**Mike Wilkerson,** Pastor of Biblical Living, Mars Hill Church,
Seattle, Washington; Author of *Redemption: Freed by Jesus
from the Idols We Worship and the Wounds We Carry*

Dr. Kellemen has produced a landmark book that fills a significant vacuum in the biblical counseling literature: a comprehensive work that not only offers an exceptional overview of biblical counseling, but also provides a wise, strategic, and thoughtful guide outlining the essentials of developing a robust counseling ministry within the local church. *Equipping Counselors for Your Church* has the potential to influence a massive paradigm shift in how ministry is exercised in the body of Christ both now and in future generations.

—**Jeremy Lelek,** President, Association of Biblical Counselors

Bob Kellemen knows equipping biblical counselors from A to Z. He has done a tremendous job of structuring a step-wise strategy to develop the lay counselors in your church. In his humble style, Bob has gathered the best leaders of local church counseling ministries and done the work of benchmarking for you. This is a book that you will reference often as you help the hurting and equip the saints for the work of soul care in your church.

—**Garrett Higbee,** Executive Director of Biblical Soul Care Ministries,
Harvest Bible Chapel, Elgin, Illinois

Bob Kellemen's *Equipping Counselors for Your Church* is a desperately needed gift to pastors and church leaders for helping the church to envision, enlist, equip, and empower the saints for the work of ministry. Bob's seasoned, insightful, and humble experience emerges in each chapter and is also reflected in his detailed appendices. I highly recommend this work whether you are just starting out or have been in the trenches for years. I was personally encouraged and challenged in addition to coming away with many ideas that I will use to assess my own ministry.

—**Robert K. Cheong,** Pastor of Care and Counseling, Sojourn Community Church, Louisville, Kentucky

Dr. Bob Kellemen is a born encourager, coach, and equipper. His vision and enthusiasm are contagious! Bob has thought carefully about how to foster effective counseling of those struggling with sin and suffering in the context of the local church, and how to encourage informal disciple-making among all members. The result is this comprehensive resource, which will take your congregation through envisioning your unique counseling ministry; enlisting, equipping, and leading counselors; and administering your program. Whether you are a pastor, a ministry leader, or a church member who's already caught the biblical counseling vision, there's something in this manual for you. Read it and dare to dream.

—**Laura Hendrickson,** Psychiatrist; Biblical Counselor; Author of *Will Medicine Stop the Pain?*

Dr. Kellemen's book fills a long-standing gap in Christian counseling and church-based ministry literature. It is an excellent resource for church leaders or counselors who are looking for practical biblical guidance, which includes instructions and all the necessary nuts and bolts for developing the one-on-one personal ministry component in their church's spectrum of care. It is marvelously comprehensive and systematic, while at the same time flexible enough to apply to a variety of church personalities.

—**Sam R. Williams,** Associate Professor of Counseling, Southeastern Baptist Theological Seminary

This is a remarkable book. Bob Kellemen has accomplished the seemingly impossible task of combining sound Christian theology, informed biblical counseling principles, and practical training procedures into a guidebook for developing a counseling ministry in the local church. He walks you through each step and shows you how to make counseling ministry unique to your church—not borrowed and artificially applied, but intrinsic to the God-given vision and biblical mission of the local body of believers. The result is a thoroughly biblical book that provides rich material for ministers, seminary students, and people interested in developing caregiving ministries. This book is a must for anyone interested in counseling and the church.

—**Ian F. Jones,** Chair of Pastoral Counseling, Baptist Community Ministries, New Orleans Baptist Theological Seminary

I am alarmed at how many people in our ever-increasing multiethnic urban society faithfully attend Bible-believing churches with successful external appearances while living in unbelievable personal and family dysfunction! Bob Kellemen's call for and guidance toward a revolution of humble biblical counselors within the church is a timely resource for an urgent need.

—**A. Charles Ware,** President, Crossroads Bible College, Indianapolis; Author of *Darwin's Plantation: Evolution's Racist Roots*

Do you ever wish someone would help you better envision, understand, organize, and implement personal ministry in your local church? If so, this book is for you. After interacting with twenty-four ministry leaders, Dr. Bob Kellemen serves as your personal coach, giving you insight on how to better serve the body of Christ. As you seek to serve those God has called you to help grow and maneuver through the challenges of life, this book will help you understand, plan, develop, and implement authentic and lasting personal ministry in your church.

—**Kevin Carson,** Pastor, Sonrise Baptist Church, Ozark, Missouri

EQUIPPING
COUNSELORS
for
YOUR CHURCH

EQUIPPING COUNSELORS
for
YOUR CHURCH

THE **4E** MINISTRY TRAINING STRATEGY

Robert W. Kellemen

PUBLISHING

P.O. BOX 817 • PHILLIPSBURG • NEW JERSEY 08865-0817

Printed in the United States of America

ISBN: 978-1-59638-381-4

Contents

Foreword

As a pastor who has served in the same church for over twenty years, I hold up and preach the Bible not only as God's timeless truth, but as practical truth for every day. If you have been in ministry for very long, you know that there are some knots that can only be untied in a more personal time of sharing God's Word one on one. Historically the problem has been twofold: most pastors are not well equipped and their time is very limited. The other issue is that Christian counselors coming out of many seminaries and Bible colleges have been taught and bought by the therapeutic culture.

Those who would counsel representing Christ and His church need to get back to the sufficiency and relevance of Christ and the Word in counseling. We need to complement solid Bible teaching from the pulpit with strong biblical counseling in the office. Church staff members also need to equip non-vocational counselors to meet the needs of the church body.

That is why I could not be more excited about Bob Kellemen and *Equipping Counselors for Your Church*. Bob's thorough research and benchmarking only confirms what our elders and staff found as we recently searched the country for the best leaders and models for a solid biblical counseling ministry. This is hard work, and it will take an army of well-equipped soldiers to address the issues of people today. However, we don't just need more biblical counselors; we need gifted equippers and those who can train and mobilize the troops. *Equipping Counselors for Your Church* does not teach you how to develop a great counseling center in your church, but how to help your church become a full-orbed center for counseling.

Bob has made it his life's mission to equip the saints for ministry. He is a counselor's counselor and someone who has gathered the best practices in biblical counseling for over two decades. He is a champion for what some call the "every person ministry" of speaking the truth in love. It's about time someone gave us a careful and biblical blueprint of how to develop an excellent biblical counseling ministry in our churches.

As the senior pastor of a growing, multi-campus church, I know the staff will never be enough to meet the needs of our congregation. We increasingly depend on the amazing servant volunteers that we call non-vocational counselors. They may serve as small-group leaders, as ministry leaders, or as formal counselors in our Biblical Soul Care ministries, but they are the backbone of care for our people at Harvest Bible Chapel.

Bob is leading the charge with several other key pastors and biblical counseling leaders who have started the Biblical Counseling Coalition. This book comes on the heels of a new day for biblical counseling in the church. I could not think of a better resource to put into the hands of those who want to know what to do next. You will want this resource on your shelf as you partner with many others in returning godly counsel to our churches, our homes, and our hearts to equip the saints for the work of ministry.

I am personally encouraged by the men and women like those mentioned in this book. They understand that the church is the place God intended for counseling. They understand that counseling and discipleship are on the same continuum and that we should be ready to help our people in the family of God. They understand that secular care leaves our people wanting and confused.

In this book you will find a thoughtful step-by-step approach to beginning or growing a counseling ministry in your church. Bob has spent time with the best equippers in the country and has done the work of condensing a mountain of extremely helpful information on these pages. I am particularly struck by his humility as he highlights many of his peers and their models as helpful examples of care in the church. You don't have to do the time-consuming work of benchmarking your ministry or coming up with forms and procedures because they are all here.

Do yourself a favor and learn from the best. Make the course corrections now and enjoy the fruitfulness of fulfilling the Great Commission as you teach your people to love and obey God's Word.

James MacDonald
Senior Pastor, Harvest Bible Chapel
Author of *When Life Is Hard*

Acknowledgments

The year was 1973 and I was fourteen. My older brother, Rick, began dating a Baptist girl, and if you date a Baptist girl you attend a Baptist church. Rick, being the *older* brother, informed me that if he had to go to church each week, then so did I. That, from the human side of the equation, was how God sovereignly arranged for me to begin attending Grace Baptist Church in Gary, Indiana. Within a year, I surrendered my life to Christ as my Savior.

During my high school years at Grace Baptist, my life intertwined with three individuals, without whom this book would never have been written. The first was Senior Pastor Bill Goode (who is now home with Christ). Though I didn't know it at the time, it was during these very years that Pastor Goode was instrumental in the launch and early development of what now has become known as the modern nouthetic biblical counseling movement. Pastor Goode's commitment to equipping counselors for the local church has stayed with me these forty years.

At Grace Baptist I also met and was discipled by our youth pastor, Ron Allchin. Pastor Ron not only ministered to me, but reached out to my family in many ways. Though the Lord led Pastor Ron to another church during my high school years, we always stayed in contact. Today, Dr. Ron Allchin equips biblical counselors around the nation and the world. He was a model for me as a youth; he remains an example for me now.

A third influential person from Grace Baptist was Steve Viars. Steve and I actually met years earlier in the neighborhood when I was in second grade and he was in first grade. So our paths go way back, to say the least. Steve and I grew up (though some might question that about us), and we journeyed together to Baptist Bible College and to Grace Theological Seminary. Steve is now the senior pastor at Faith Baptist Church in Lafayette, Indiana—one of the premier churches in the world where you can be equipped as a biblical counselor. Steve's real-life, best-practice approach to equipping counselors has richly influenced my own ministry.

Who, other than God, would have thought that Rick's dating a Baptist girl would lead to Bob's writing *Equipping Counselors for Your Church*? All I know is that this book would not be in your hands without the shaping influence of Bill Goode, Ron Allchin, and Steve Viars. It is with gratefulness to Christ that I dedicate *Equipping Counselors for Your Church* to Bill, Ron, and Steve.

Introduction

WANT TO CHANGE LIVES?

During the early days of television, two shows dominated the airwaves. One aired on Tuesday nights and the other on Sunday evenings. Initially the more popular of the two shows was *The Texaco Star Theatre* hosted by Milton Berle. It was originally designed along the lines of the old-fashioned vaudeville variety hour with a host highlighting a half-dozen guests each week. However, little by little, Milton Berle became the star. As the format changed, the accent gradually focused increasingly on Berle himself. There were fewer guest acts, and Berle began to dominate each show. In just eight years, the show ran out of steam. *No one person is talented enough to carry any show, or any ministry, for more than a short time.*

The other show, *The Ed Sullivan Show*, experienced a very different fate. If any show in the history of television could be called an institution, it would be *The Ed Sullivan Show*. Every Sunday night for more than two decades, this show brought an incredible variety of entertainers into homes. Sullivan's show continued as a major hit for fifteen years longer than Berle's show.

Unlike Milton Berle, Ed Sullivan never wavered from his original format. *He was the host who called other people to center stage.* Numerous performers made their television debut on his show: Walt Disney, the Beatles, Elvis Presley, Bob Hope, Dean Martin, Jerry Lewis, and hundreds more. Though Ed Sullivan died soon after the last run of his show, his legacy outlives him.

Are You like Milton Berle or Ed Sullivan?

God calls Christian leaders to be like Ed Sullivan, not like Milton Berle. If we are like Milton Berle, and the spotlight increasingly focuses on us and our individual ministry, then biblically we are missing God's mark as equippers. If we fail to focus on equipping, then we selfishly treat God's people like children who have never grown up spiritually.

God wants us to be like Ed Sullivan—a host who calls others to center stage by equipping them to fulfill their calling. When we focus on equipping, we leave an other-centered legacy of loving leaders.

Allow me to introduce you to several modern-day Ed Sullivan-like church leaders. I currently provide 4E consulting for each of these leaders, and they represent well the readers I picture as I write this book.

Pastor Eric is planting a church. He and the eight families ministering with him are passionate about launching a church from the ground up—a church where every member is equipped to speak the truth in love. They want biblical counseling to be the DNA of their congregation.

Jan has been a volunteer women's ministry director in her church for over a decade. She wants to train a dozen women in biblical counseling. She envisions some of them using their training to be more effective small-group leaders—relating truth to life. Others she foresees providing biblical counseling to the growing number of women who seek her help.

Randy and Monica serve together on a ministry launch team that's so new they don't have a ministry name yet. Randy is an elder, seminary student, and youth pastor; Monica is a volunteer ministry leader. The leadership team in their church of two hundred wants them to launch a counseling ministry. As Monica put it when she e-mailed me, "We don't want another *program*. We want a *ministry* that saturates our whole church with equipped one-another ministers."

John is the senior pastor of a large church, and his wife Rachel has two degrees in counseling. They called me to ask, "Bob, do you help churches to do course corrections and relaunches? Five years ago we tried to launch a biblical counseling ministry, but it was too program-focused. Could you help us figure out how to do it more relationally this time?"

I have written this book for people like Eric, Jan, Randy, Monica, John, and Rachel. People like *you*—pastors, ministry leaders, women's ministry directors, elders, deacons, church planters, and students. I have written this book because I am convinced that you want to be an Ed Sullivan, not a Milton Berle. I know that you are passionate about equipping God's people for every-member ministry as disciple-makers—as biblical counselors. I want to be part of the process of equipping you to equip others (2 Tim. 2:2).

Changing Lives with Christ's Changeless Truth

The people I consult with are hungry for a comprehensive, real-world approach to equipping God's people for one-another ministry. Like you, they want to empower others for the personal ministry of the Word—as biblical counselors, caregivers, spiritual friends, elders, deacons, small-group leaders, disciplers, or mentors. *Leaders want to change lives.* However, for most church leaders, the training process can seem overwhelming—vision-casting confusion, change-management struggles, recruiting headaches, quality-of-care matters, training material questions, supervisory difficulties, legal issues, and other legitimate, complex concerns often derail the equipping process.

My purpose in writing *Equipping Counselors for Your Church* is to assist leaders like you in equipping people confidently, wisely, lovingly, and biblically. I want this book to be like a personal conversation with your private consultant—coming alongside you, walking step-by-step, hand-in-hand, to equip you to fulfill your Ephesians 4:11–16 calling to empower the body of Christ to change lives with Christ's changeless truth.

As I speak in churches about one-another ministry, God's people share with me their rejection of the old model where the pastoral staff hoarded the ministry. They are clamoring to be unleashed and mobilized for the personal ministry of the Word. *God's people want to change lives.* They care, but they feel ill-equipped to care like Christ. They want to know what to do after the hug. They know the Bible says they are competent to counsel (Rom. 15:14), but they also know that the Bible calls them to be equipped to speak the truth in love (Eph. 4:11–16).

So my second purpose in writing is to launch a revolution in every-member ministry. This book's *4E Ministry Training Strategy* offers a twenty-first-century, best-practice manual for Christ-centered, church-based, comprehensive, compassionate, and culturally informed mobilization of the priesthood of all believers. It assists churches to become places not simply *with* biblical counseling ministries, but *of* biblical counseling. My goal is not the production of yet another program or yet another ministry on the sidelines. My goal is the promotion of a congregation-saturated mindset of every-member ministry, which will result in an entire congregation passionate about and equipped to make disciples.

The 4E Ministry Training Strategy: Passing the Baton of Ministry

It's a nice goal, right? But we both know that you've "been there, done that." You've heard the promises before. Lots of theoretical talk, but little practical, real-world, biblical help. You are tired of equipping approaches that promise much but deliver little. If you are like the people I consult with, then you are ready for an approach to equipping that is comprehensive, simple to implement, and relationship-oriented, rather than program-focused.

Some equipping approaches are like straitjackets with a one-size-fits-all model. *The 4E Ministry Training Strategy* provides practical principles that you can personally, relationally, and uniquely apply in your specific ministry setting. By reading best-practice case studies from two dozen churches with a wide diversity of ethnic, demographic, and denominational backgrounds, you will be able to design a simple process for *your* church.

Some equipping approaches offer piecemeal advice that addresses aspects of equipping, but lacks a comprehensive strategy to move from launch to leaving a legacy of loving leaders. *The 4E Ministry Training Strategy* moves you through the four stages that every ministry launch must tackle to establish ministries built to last and to grow ministries from good to great. Its biblical and practical focus will empower you to:

- Envision God's ministry.
- Enlist God's ministers for ministry.
- Equip godly ministers for ministry.
- Employ/Empower godly ministers for ministry.

Like you, I dread seeing effort expended on programs that don't launch or don't last. This is why I have focused the past quarter-century on answering questions such as these: How do we pass the baton of ministry? How do we effectively disciple the body of Christ for one-another ministry in the church and to the community? How do we disciple disciple-makers? How do we equip biblical counselors for the local church?

After launching biblical counseling ministries in three significantly different churches, after over a dozen years of training hundreds of pastors, counselors, and ministry leaders in the seminary setting, and after a decade of consulting with churches, I am ready to answer those questions in writing. To paint for you the big picture of the training skills this book will help you to hone, imagine with me passing the ministry baton in a four-lap relay.

Lap One: Envisioning God's Ministry—Core Values

I understand that some of you have spent countless hours in relatively unproductive vision-catching/casting training. We will see why such sessions often fall flat and fall short of producing lasting congregational change. Chapter one will show how to saturate the entire congregation with a passion for and equipping in one-another ministry. Chapters two through four will model how to facilitate relationship-building gatherings that excite people about mutually developing a powerful *Mission, Vision, Passion,* and *Commission* Statement (MVP-C Statement) that results in a practical ministry action plan.

In a sentence, here is what you will learn in lap one (envisioning God's ministry): *How to jointly create church-wide and ministry-specific*

MVP-C Statements that nourish the compassion, conviction, and connection needed to launch flourishing training ministries. You will learn to discern if you are running in the right direction—core values. It does no good to equip people for the wrong purposes for your church and community. That's why we need to learn the ministry mindset shift that changes everything. It is why we need clarity about God's calling.

Lap Two: Enlisting God's Ministers for Ministry—Connected People

I understand that some of you have launched ministries with great expectations, but then experienced crushing resistance. Even the best-laid plans can face bumps in the road, and even the best-prepared runners can stumble when jostled by other participants. Chapter five will address this with strategies that many training curriculums omit—relational change management (consensus building) and biblical conflict resolution. I also understand that some of you have spent countless hours in relatively non-relational recruiting. Chapter six will describe how to move from "panicked recruiting of warm bodies to a program," to relational enlisting of like-minded, committed servant-leaders connected to a captivating vision.

In a sentence, here is what you will learn in lap two (enlisting God's ministers for ministry): *How to mobilize ministers by nurturing a family and building a team prepared for change, skilled in conflict resolution, and connected to the MVP-C Statement.* You will learn how to ensure that the right people are running the right lap in the relay race—connected people. It does no good to launch a ministry if the congregation is not passionately involved. That is why we need a connected congregation.

Lap Three: Equipping Godly Ministers for Ministry—Coached People

I understand that some of you have spent wasted hours in somewhat disorganized training. Chapters seven through ten will demonstrate how to unite the 4Cs of equipping creatively and biblically. These four chapters will explain how to equip the head (content/truth), the heart (*c*haracter/love), and the hands (*c*ompetence/skills) in the context of the home (*c*ommunity/relationship).

In a sentence, here is what you will learn in lap three (equipping godly ministers for ministry): *How to apply transformational training strategies that comprehensively address the 4Cs of biblical content, Christlike character, counseling competence, and Christian community.* You will learn to ensure that every race participant is a skilled runner—coached people. It does no good, and potentially much harm, to send ill-equipped people into the personal ministry of the Word. That is why we need clear biblical counseling equipping goals, objectives, curriculum, materials, strategies, and methods.

Lap Four: Employing/Empowering Godly Ministers for Ministry—Comprehensive Strategy

I understand that some of you experience a spontaneously negative reaction to words like "organizing," "administrating," and "programs." It all sounds, and often is, so non-relational. I get it. That is why chapters eleven and twelve will map out organizing the organism and administrating the ministry. These chapters will equip you for *relational* leadership that leaves a legacy of loving leaders.

In a sentence, here is what you will learn in lap four (employing/empowering godly ministers for ministry): *How to oversee the ongoing organizing of the organism for God's glory by leading ministries that are built to last, that grow from good to great, and that leave a legacy of loving leaders.* You will learn to discern if the runners are running on all cylinders—comprehensive strategy. It does no good and wastes valuable time to envision, enlist, and equip, only to stop short of the ongoing administering of the ministry. You have these trained folks; now what do you do with them? How do you equip people in a caring way that builds community? How do you become a community as you impact your community?

"These Are Your Grandbabies!"

Sister Ellen Barney is the First Lady (senior pastor's wife) of a large, predominantly African-American church near Baltimore, Maryland. She has implemented the *4E Ministry Training Strategy* for over a decade to equip over a thousand women in her LEAD (Life Encouragers And Disciplers) Ministry.

They do it up big! Their graduation ceremonies are better than those of many colleges. I remember the first time Sister Ellen invited me to be their commencement speaker. As she introduced me, she looked over the crowd of more than fifty graduates and said, "These are your grandbabies, Dr. Kellemen! You trained me and I trained them!" Now, years later, as Sister Ellen has trained trainers who train others, she tells me, "Dr. Kellemen, these are your great-great-grandbabies!"

Do you want to be a spiritual grandparent—discipling disciple-makers? Do you want to pass the baton of ministry? Do you want to change lives? Keep reading.

The 4E Ministry Training Strategy

Want to Change Lives?

I. Envisioning God's Ministry: 2 Timothy 1:6–7
   A. More than Counseling: Catching God's Vision for the Entire Church
   B. Examining Heart Health: Diagnosing Congregational and Community Fitness
   C. Dreaming God's Dream: Jointly Crafting Your *MVP-C* Statement
      1. *Mission* Statement: Your God-Given Ministry Calling and Purpose
      2. *Vision* Statement: Your Unique Ministry Dream, DNA, and Fingerprint
      3. *Passion* Statement: Your Captivating Ministry Identity and Imprint
      4. *Commission* Statement: Your Strategic Ministry MAP—Ministry Action Plan

II. Enlisting God's Ministers for Ministry: 2 Timothy 2:2
   A. Shepherding the Transformation: Cultivating a Climate for Ongoing Ownership
      1. Preparing the Congregation for Change: Relational Change Management
      2. Building Bridges and Breaking Down Barriers: Biblical Conflict Resolution

24

B. Mobilizing the Ministers: Nurturing a Family and Building a Team
   1. Conducting Christ's Opus: Saturating the Congregation with One-Another Ministers
   2. Calling People to Connection: What People Need to Know about Your Ministry
   3. Matching the Right People to the Right Ministry: What You Need to Know about Ministers

III. Equipping Godly Ministers for Ministry: Ephesians 4:11–16; Romans 15:14
   A. Competent to Counsel: The Résumé of the Biblical Counselor
      1. Biblical Content: How to Change Lives with Christ's Changeless Truth—Head
      2. Christlike Character: How to Be like Christ—Heart
      3. Counseling Competence: How to Care like Christ—Hands
      4. Christian Community: How to Grow Together in Christ—Home
   B. Mapping Our Focused Curriculum: Core Proficiencies of Competent Biblical Counselors
   C. Transformational Training Strategies and Methods: Equipping Competent Biblical Counselors

IV. Empowering/Employing Godly Ministers for Ministry: Matthew 22:35–40; 28:18–20
   A. Orchestrating Ministries for God's Glory: Organizing the Organism
      1. Launching Ministries Built to Last: Administrating Ministries
      2. Leading Ministries from Good to Great: Mentoring/Supervising Ministers
      3. Leaving a Lasting Legacy of Loving Leaders: Passing the Baton of Ministry
   B. Practicing Ethical and Legal Wisdom in Ministry: Caring Carefully

PART 1
Envisioning God's Ministry

When my daughter, Marie, was young, we played *How Much Do I Love You?* I'd say, "I love you as big as this room." Marie would respond, "I love you as big as this house." I'd answer back, "I love you as big as this city!" Marie would counter, "I love you as big as the world!" Not to be topped, I'd reply, "I love you as big as the solar system!" Marie would top even that with "I love you as big as the universe!"

When most people think about "vision," they think too small. They focus on church-specific or ministry-specific vision. Those are vital areas of focus, and we will learn together how to develop them biblically. But we are going to start bigger than that—much bigger—*universal*. Before you can catch God's vision for your church or ministry area, you have to be caught by God's grand vision for the church. So we will launch part one with the ministry mindset shift that changes everything: *More than Counseling: Catching God's Vision for the Entire Church.*

Then you are ready to do envisioning work, right? Close, but not quite. Before you can catch God's vision for your specific church or specific ministry area, you need to know where you have been and where you are now. Vision points to the future, but to pursue a better future you have to know your history and your current culture. So the second chapter of part one focuses on *Examining Heart Health: Diagnosing Congregational and Community Fitness.*

Once you have caught God's vision for the church and examined the past and current state of your church and community, then you are ready to catch God's vision for your specific congregation. Thus, chapter three explores *Dreaming God's Dream: Becoming an MVP-C Congregation.* Here you learn *what* and *why*: what a *M*ission, *V*ision, *P*assion, and *C*ommission Statement (MVP-C) is, and why—biblically—it is so vital to develop one.

Biblical principles must lead to practical plans that work in the real world of church life. This is why chapter four guides you step-by-step through the how-to of *Living God's Calling: Jointly Crafting Your Biblical Counseling MVP-C Statement.*

I am a coach and teacher at heart. Coaches and teachers love concrete, measurable objectives. In the classroom, I call them SOLOs: Student-Oriented Learning Objectives. For this book I label them ROLOs: Reader-Oriented Learning Objectives. Through your active reading and application of the four chapters in this section, you will be equipped to:

- Be a catalyst for a congregation-saturated shift to the ministry mindset that changes everything—every member a disciple-maker (chapter one).
- Be a spiritual cardiologist who diagnoses the heart health of your congregation and community, to establish a baseline for envisioning God's future dream (chapter two).
- Champion the biblical meaning of and necessity for jointly crafting congregation-wide and ministry-specific MVP-C Statements (chapter three).

- Guide your biblical counseling ministry team in jointly crafting a ministry-specific MVP-C Statement (chapter four).

How big does God love you in Christ? Bigger than the universe! Because He does, He has given you His Word so you can be captivated by His universal vision for His church. Join me in chapter one as we learn about Christ's grand vision for His Bride.

1

More than Counseling

Catching God's Vision for the Entire Church

With our regular attendance of 275 people, ours was an average-size church, at least in the megachurch culture of the day. But because our church served an infinite God and tenaciously pursued a giant vision for every-member ministry, we were significant in God's eyes. Perhaps that's why, in His affectionate sovereignty, He called us to face a significant situation.

At first glance, Steve and Alexis were the all-American couple living the American dream. Married over two decades, three teen children who would make any parent proud, great jobs, beautiful home, active in their previous church . . .

But look beneath the surface and you would see another story, as I did the day that their oldest son, Eric, knocked on my office door. Hesitantly, he unfolded a family narrative that shared how their American dream had become a family nightmare. One child had been physically abused. Another child depressed. The mom was fearful and in denial. The dad was angry and controlling. Infidelity had previously rocked the family.

A church our size should refer them to a counselor, right? As an average-size congregation, surely we did not have the resources to meet such an immense and complicated crisis, right?

There was nothing small or average about this problem. If most churches and Christians are honest, there is nothing that unusual about the problem either. Filled with sin and suffering, yes; out-of-the-norm, no. By God's grace, there was nothing small or average about our response because there had been nothing small or average about our *proactive, congregation-wide preparation* for such messy, real-life issues.

From the day I first candidated to be senior pastor, I asked God to help us change the ministry mindset from small-church, pastor-centered (the Milton Berle church) to big-God, equipping-focused (the Ed Sullivan church). To communicate this shift in perspective, I declined the title "senior pastor," choosing instead the clunky but precise title "congregational discipleship pastor." That didn't mean that I would disciple everyone. It did mean that my main calling was to oversee that *we* discipled every member.

This was the reason that two short but intense and active years later, an entire congregation was prepared to unite as a team, as a family, and as the body of Christ to minister to this young man, his parents, and his siblings. Even before Eric walked out of my office, biblical, relational, relevant plans were in place to begin addressing not only the immediate crisis, but also the ongoing heart issues. Our "average" church had learned the awesome lesson about how to change lives with Christ's changeless truth. Together, we caught and cast the vision of the priesthood of every believer—not as some academic idea, but as our biblical calling.

We understood that "pastoral care" is not just what the pastor does, but what every member is equipped to offer. With my education—master of theology in biblical counseling and doctor of philosophy in counselor education—I could have (unwisely) tried to handle this on my own. Instead, we responded as a united family to minister Christ-centered help to this family.

Steve met with me for formal biblical counseling (while a trainee participated in our sessions). Steve and Alexis met for formal biblical counseling with one of our trained biblical counselors. One of our elders began an informal but intensive mentoring relationship with Eric. One of our deacons began the same with Eric's younger brother. One female biblical counselor met with Eric's younger sister in a mentoring relationship, and another met for formal biblical counseling with Alexis.

We understood that "biblical counseling" is not simply a ministry of a few in one corner of the church, but a mindset of an entire congregation that the Bible is sufficient for every life issue. With our active LEAD (Life Encouragers And Disciplers) group of trained biblical counselors, we could have (unwisely) tried to handle this within the confines of the biblical counseling ministry. Instead, we responded as an equipped congregation to minister to this family.

Because there was evidence of physical abuse, we worked through the proper channels and worked out a plan for the daughter to stay for a period of time in the home of a family in our church—a family equipped to minister biblically and lovingly. Our Iron Sharpeners men's ministry provided Steve with love—tough love. Our women's ministry became a haven, but not an escape, for Alexis.

It took a congregation. It took both formal biblical counseling and informal one-another ministry. Both emphasized the personal ministry of the Word where members spoke and lived God's truth into the lives of this family. We understood that "one-another ministry" is not just shallow chitchat reserved for the "easy stuff," but a biblical vision for the entire church for all of life. With our connections with licensed Christian counselors in the community, we could have referred this family to outside professionals and assumed that our only roles were to pray and hug (both essential callings). Instead, we ministered comprehensively to this family as the unified body of Christ. (Of course, we communicated with outside authorities about abuse, and we consulted with medical personnel about depression.)

The ongoing, intensive, intimate, biblical response of our church exemplifies the purpose of this book. I want to help your church become a place not simply *with* a biblical counseling ministry, but *of* biblical counseling. You don't need another program. You want a congregation saturated by the vision of every-member ministry and equipped to offer one-another ministry. Even more, you want a congregation where *every member is a disciple-maker.*

Every Member a Disciple-Maker

It's *in* to talk about every member being a minister. I agree. However, I don't think the language of "every member a minister" goes far enough. My passion and, most importantly, God's passion focuses on every member becoming a disciple-maker. That ministry mindset shift changes everything.

"Every member a disciple-maker" explains the title of this chapter: *More than Counseling.* Biblical counseling is vital—it is my life calling. Launching biblical counseling ministries is important—you will learn how to do that in this book. You won't learn less than that, however; you will learn more than that—much more.

The 4E Ministry Training Strategy is nothing less than an application of the apostle Paul's admonition in 2 Timothy 2:2 to pass the baton of ministry. "And the things you have heard me say in the presence of many witnesses entrust to reliable men who will also be qualified to teach others." It's the Ed Sullivan church.

"Teach" is the same Greek word Jesus chose in the Great Commission in Matthew 28:20. The word implies much more than academic knowledge. Instead, it embodies the "4Cs" of disciple-making that we will learn throughout this book:

- Biblical *C*ontent/*C*onviction
- *C*hristlike *C*haracter
- *C*ounseling *C*ompetence
- *C*hristian *C*ommunity

In order to help Steve, Alexis, and their family—especially to help them not only in a reactive crisis mode but also in a proactive discipleship mode, our congregation needed 4E equipping for 4C ministry. That's exactly what you are about to learn in this book—how to *make disciple-makers*. This chapter equips you to become a catalyst who spurs your congregation to catch God's vision for every-member disciple-making.

The Big Picture: The End Goal—Transformed People

The end goal of this book and of all church ministry is not simply to launch a biblical counseling ministry. The end goal is transformed people—people transformed into the image of Christ. Remember this core theme:

- A relationship with *the* transforming Person (Christ)
- Produces transforming leaders (you and your team)
- Who relationally lead a transforming process (the 4Es)
- That the Spirit uses in transforming your church (the body of Christ)
- So others (the congregation and community) are also transformed into disciple-makers.

My vision is to equip you to build an equipping culture. God's fundamental vision for body growth focuses on every member speaking the truth in love to one another in every situation. That's it. Get that and you get this chapter—you get God's purpose for His body today.

It's everywhere. It's in Matthew 22:34–40 with Matthew 28:16–20; Romans 15:14; Ephesians 4:11–16; Ephesians 5:19; Philippians 1:9–11; Colossians 3:16; 1 Thessalonians 2:8; 2 Timothy 2:2; Hebrews 3:12–13; Hebrews 10:24–25. God's end goal is for every member to be a disciple-maker who speaks and lives gospel truth in love to help every member grow in content, character, competence, and community.

We have wrongly defined biblical counseling so that it is about solving problems. We've made it a subset of discipleship focused on reactive work with persons struggling with sin. Instead, we should think of biblical counseling as synonomous with comprehensive personal discipleship. Biblical counseling is focused one-another ministry designed to fulfill the Great Commandment and the Great Commission.

35

We don't want to create the ministry mindset where the only way people can relate to one another is by discussing their problems. The goal is to move people forward in Christlikeness whether or not they are facing specific crisis problems. We need a definition of biblical counseling that encompasses all of life.

Christ-centered, church-based, comprehensive, compassionate, and culturally informed biblical counseling depends upon the Holy Spirit to relate God's Word to suffering and sin by speaking and living God's truth in love to equip people to love God and one another (Matt. 22:35–40). It cultivates conformity to Christ and communion with Christ and the body of Christ, leading to a community of one-another disciple-makers (Matt. 28:18–20).

I love biblical counseling, but we can't see it as a ministry of a few people to a few "unhealthy" people. Biblical counseling is the calling of all of God's people all of the time because we are all striving to grow in Christ all the time.

Does that mean we shouldn't launch local church counseling ministries? Not at all. There is nothing unbiblical about people with a special gifting and a special passion wanting to focus their ministry energy on biblical counseling. Just like there is nothing unbiblical about some folks in a church taking extensive training in evangelism. Does that mean that only the "evangelism folks" are called to share their faith? Of course not. We want a church *of* evangelists where everyone is passionate about and equipped to share their faith, even if we have members who focus more time on evangelism. In the same way, we want a church *of* biblical counseling where everyone is passionate about and equipped to speak the truth in love, even if we have some within the church who focus more time on biblical counseling. This book helps you with *both* goals.

In my ministry as a pastor in three churches and in my consulting ministry, I use simple language to identify this "both/and" idea of equipping every member for one-another disciple-making *and* equipping some members for biblical counseling. I call every-member ministry the *Informal Model.* Throughout this chapter and book, you will gain practical insight into how to saturate your congregation with passion for and equipping in every-member disciple-making through the *Informal Model.* You will also be trained to envision, enlist, equip, and empower biblical counselors—the *Formal Model.*

The Big Question: The End Game—Disciple-Makers

When we understand the big picture, then we are prepared to ask the big questions—the right questions. Questions like:

- How do we make disciple-makers?
- How do we leave a legacy of loving leaders?
- How do we encourage our congregation to be caught by God's vision for "every member a disciple-maker"?

It is when we ask and answer these big-picture questions that we are best prepared to ask the more specific questions related to equipping biblical counselors for one-another ministry. Questions like:

- How do we effectively disciple the body of Christ for one-another ministry in the church and community?
- How do we prepare people for the personal ministry of the Word?
- What is God's strategy for preparing a congregation to speak the truth in love to one another?

I asked you the biggest of big questions in the Introduction: "Want to change lives?" There is nothing more life-changing than discipling disciple-makers, passing the baton of ministry, and leaving a legacy of loving leaders.

This was our goal in ministering to Steve and Alexis. Not only is their marriage united and glorifying Christ, not only is their parenting (of their now young adult children) vibrant, they are discipling other disciple-makers. They not only made it through their family crisis, but became disciple-makers as a result of moving through their crisis with Christ and the body of Christ.

The Personal Ministry of the Word: Seven Church "Styles"

Sometimes when I train pastors, especially in seminary settings, I get a push back about "counseling." It typically sounds something like this: "I do my counseling from the pulpit. People don't need anything but the preached Word."

Having been a senior pastor, and rarely having given up the pulpit, I don't take issue with any pastor who is passionate about the pulpit ministry of the Word. I do take issue with anyone who pits the pulpit ministry of the Word against the personal ministry of the Word.

All biblical ministry should involve speaking the truth in love. That should be done from the pulpit to the crowd through an equipped person fully focused and prepared to relate God's truth to people's lives—*the pulpit ministry of the Word*. Speaking the truth in love should also be done one-to-one and in small groups, both formally and informally, as members of the body of Christ change lives with Christ's changeless truth—*the personal ministry of the Word*. If we want a church *of* biblical counseling where everything is saturated with the conviction that God's Word is sufficient for all of life, then pulpit ministry and personal ministry must remain in harmony.

Disciple-Making Champions

As part of my best-practice research, I surveyed two dozen cutting-edge churches that equip their people to speak the truth in love. Throughout each chapter we will hear from these Disciple-Making Champions.[1]

---

1. See Appendix 1.1 for a listing of the twenty-four best-practice churches and para-church agencies.

Steve Viars, Senior Pastor, and Rob Green, Counseling Pastor, Faith Baptist Church

Steve Viars and Rob Green are just two of many leaders of the biblical counseling ministry at Faith Baptist Church in Lafayette, Indiana. At Faith, you find no discrepancy between what happens in the pulpit, what occurs in formal biblical counseling sessions, and what transpires in informal spiritual conversations.

> Our goal is to be a church of biblical counseling—we want these truths to permeate everything we do. . . . Call it counseling; call it specialized discipleship. It doesn't matter. We want to be a progressive sanctification machine, a discipleship factory. We want people growing and changing where God's Word and Spirit make each of us more like Jesus Christ through careful attention to the inner person. That is what brings honor to God. . . . The goal of our biblical counseling training just like the goal of all our ministries is to glorify God by winning people to Jesus Christ (for unsaved counselees) and equipping them to be more faithful disciples (for saved counselees).

Pastor Bill Goode, the senior pastor who preceded Pastor Viars and who launched Faith's biblical counseling ministry, clung to the same vision.

> The local church *is* a counseling ministry. The question is not, "Should Christians counsel each other?" because they already are. Most Christians are ministering to one another on a personal basis. So the question is, "What *kind* of counseling is offered? How *effective* is the ministry? Do people have *confidence* that the Word of God has answers to everyday life problems?"

Pastor Mike Wilkerson, Pastor of Biblical Living, Mars Hill Church

Mike Wilkerson's title screams Ephesians 4 vision: *Pastor of Biblical Living*. Mike pastors at Mars Hill Church in Seattle, Washington. He makes plain their biblical philosophy. "When I say we envision being a church *of* biblical counseling, that's just to say that one-anothering is normative in our church life."

Pastor Wilkerson uses several terms to show the synergy between the pulpit ministry of the Word and the personal ministry of the Word. He describes the pulpit ministry of the Word as the "air war" in which sermons soften and prepare hearts for the personal ministry of the Word. He calls the personal ministry of the Word the "ground war" in which biblical counseling, small-group ministry, and one-anothering help each member of the body to be adisciple-maker.

> When we re-launched the ministry, since our teaching pastor, Mark Driscoll, initiated the process, and he desired unity, we all agreed on the biblical direction. So we had the air war covered—the biblical philosophy of ministry embedded in the preaching. The ground war is an equal priority. We're committed to building it well—theologically and relationally—and having it unified with the air war (the pulpit).

When it comes to the personal ministry of the Word, not every church is like Faith Baptist and Mars Hill. Churches have various styles of doing relational ministry. Knowing how personal needs are met in typical churches helps us to compare and contrast these models with God's vision for His church.

The Staff Model

When a church member has a "problem," many churches respond to that person through the *staff model*, where the main caregiver is one of the pastors. This approach uses the classic pastoral-care model where the pastor marries and buries, ministering from cradle to casket, in the home and in the hospital. The pastor typically focuses in a reactive way on crisis needs.

A potential strength of this model is that theoretically you have well-trained caregivers. Unfortunately, very few pastors believe they have received effective training in the personal ministry of the Word. There are major weaknesses in this approach, including pastoral burnout and the pastor monopolizing the ministry (the Milton Berle church). Also, the majority of members are not ministered to because the focus is on the unhealthy person in crisis. People learn that if they want the pastor's attention, they had better have a problem. As a church grows, there is no way for one person (or even a staff of people) to minister to the entire congregation.

The Shepherding Model

Because the staff model can't work as churches grow, other churches implement the *shepherding model*. In this approach the primary caregivers are deacons, deaconesses, elders, ministry of mercy team members, shut-in teams, and visitation teams. The methods vary, sometimes using tele-care, other times systematic home visitation, crisis response teams, or groups with someone designated to oversee care for members. Typically the ministry occurs on a regular but infrequent basis as the focus is on "touching base" so no one "falls through the cracks."

Strengths of this method include many members having a ministry, every member having a minister, and no one being isolated. Weaknesses include resistance to being assigned to a group, since this model is often based on geography rather than natural relationships. Additionally, the team members may burn out, drop out, or drop the ball. At times training is inadequate and sometimes non-existent.

The Small-Group Model

Since intimacy and frequency is often missing in the shepherding model, many churches use the *small-group model* as their primary vehicle for meeting personal needs. Here the caregiver is the small-group leader and hopefully each small-group member. Methods vary, since small-group ministries have a myriad of philosophies. The frequency of care typically involves weekly to monthly connection on an ongoing basis, sometimes being time-limited.

There are numerous strengths to this model when it is run well. Many members are ministered to, and many members can have a ministry. Close relationships can develop, and spontaneous need-meeting often occurs. There are, however, weaknesses in this model. Those not in small groups (in many churches at least 50 percent of the congregation) fall through the cracks. Unfortunately, many churches provide little equipping in small-group leadership—especially in the personal ministry of the Word of speaking the truth in love.

The Sunday School Model

Larger churches often institute adult Sunday school classes frequently known as Adult Bible Fellowships (ABFs). These ABFs become mini-congregations within the congregation. The caregiver in this *Sunday school model* is the ABF teacher, or the ABF care group leader. Methods include meeting needs through care groups, tele-care, and spontaneous need-meeting. The focus is on crisis need-meeting, plus semi-regular touching base, as well as periodic social/fellowship gatherings.

There are several strengths in this approach. Many members have a ministry and many are ministered to. No one in the ABFs falls through the cracks. Weaknesses include the tendency of those *not* in ABFs to fall through the cracks, along with the possibility of untrained care-givers, few counseling needs' being met, and ministers burning out and dropping out.

The Specialist Model

Some churches, especially with "tough cases," select the *specialist model*. In this method the caregiver, if inside the church, is the pastoral counselor or lay counselor. If outside the church, the caregiver is the licensed counselor, social worker, or psychologist. The focus is on crisis need-meeting and ongoing counseling with scheduled appointments for primary care.

Theoretically the strengths include well-trained caregivers offering intensive help for intense life issues. If inside the church, weaknesses include a professionalized and specialized model of ministry, counselors who are not fully equipped, and few members ministering. If referred out, weaknesses include potentially secular care, or Christian care that is not biblically based. Also, the role of the church as a discipling community is minimized. At best, this model results in a church *with* biblical counseling, but it is not a church *of* biblical counseling.

The Spontaneous Model

In reaction to the professionalized approach, many churches follow the *spontaneous model*. In this method, theoretically every member cares intimately for a few other members. The methods include an Acts 2 spontaneous combustion model aided by a passion for connection built into the preaching, the vision statement, and the hearts of members. The focus is on the holistic care of members as found in Acts 2:42–47. Ideally, the frequency is daily as needs are perceived and shared.

The strengths are obvious: the model is biblically based and involves Holy-Spirit-empowered reciprocal one-another ministry of every member. However, in actuality, often only the deeply connected are cared for. Additionally, this model often minimizes training because it lacks a focus on "organizing the organism." At best, this model results in a church *of* one-another ministry, but it is not always a church *with* biblical enlisting, equipping, and empowering.

The Scripture and Sacraments Model

Other churches react against a therapeutic, seeker-sensitive culture and decide to follow a *Scripture and Sacraments model*. Picture this as the pulpit ministry of the Word minus the personal ministry of the Word. The method involves little structured means for care-giving and need-meeting, with the assumption that the truth preached from the pulpit provides all the biblical counseling necessary, and motivates the body equipped by the pulpit to minister to one another. The focus typically is upon doctrinal correctness and depth.

There are obvious strengths to this model. Truth is preached. Doctrine is learned. People can be inspired to live an Acts 2:42–47 body life. There are also weaknesses. The personal ministry of the Word is de-emphasized, and if it happens at all, the caregivers are often ill-equipped to translate truth to life. They know truth, but they don't know how to bridge the truth-life gap. At times the staunch preaching of doctrine can lead to a mood of truth trumping love, of head over heart.

The Biblical Plumb Line

As you reflect on these seven styles of meeting congregational needs, which do you value? As you ponder your church, which methods does it blend together? How well do they function?

My objective in presenting this overview is not to dissuade you from implementing any of these models. Many have real value. My purpose is to encourage you to evaluate each model using Ephesians 4:11–16 as your biblical plumb line.

My goal is to urge you to use a 4E strategy when you implement any of these models. In my ministry experience, research, and consulting, very few of these models apply a comprehensive *envisioning, enlisting, equipping, and empowering* philosophy to ensure that the model is biblically sound and practically effective.

My aim is to highlight how most of these ministry models fail the "both/and test." They rarely include both the pulpit ministry of the Word and the personal ministry of the Word; both truth and love; both the formal and informal modes of speaking the truth in love; both pastors-teachers equipping the body and the body doing works of service; and they rarely include the vision of a church *of* and a church *with*. They lack a comprehensive approach to training God's people.

Most importantly, none of these models highlight or effectively result in making disciple-makers. Most focus on meeting personal needs—not a bad aim, but not God's ultimate vision. Others focus on caregiving and some on every member a minister—but not on *every member a disciple-maker*. Even the Scripture and Sacraments model, which seeks to prioritize making deep disciples, follows a model that will not result in equipped disciple-makers. Telling truth does not produce 4C disciple-makers. Part three on equipping describes the type of training that best produces disciple-makers who are complete in knowledge (content/conviction), full of goodness (character), and competent to counsel (competence) one another (community).

God's Grand Vision for His Church: Ephesians 4:11–16

In Ephesians 4:11–16, the apostle Paul highlights the Bible's most powerful, focused vision statement for the church. This passage offers God's ministry description for church leaders and for every member. By distilling the essence of God's call, His vision captures our imagination and motivates the shift in ministry mindset that changes everything.

The Résumé of Pastors

Most pastoral search committees would be thrilled to read a candidate's résumé that demonstrated the ability to preach, counsel, and administrate. Most seminaries would be delighted if graduate exit interviews indicated that pastoral ministry students perceived their seminary training as having equipped them for preaching, counseling, and administrating. Being equipped to *do* the work of the ministry seems to be everyone's ideal goal for church leaders.

Everyone but Christ. His pastoral ministry description demands the ability to *equip* others to do the work of the ministry. If seminaries followed Christ's vision for pastoral ministry, they would focus on *training trainers*. If pastoral search committees desired in a pastor what Christ desires, they would throw out every résumé that failed to emphasize experience in and passion for equipping the saints.

You would think we would listen to the Head of the church. Paul spends the chapters and verses leading up to Ephesians 4:11–16 showing why Christ has the right to write the pastor-teacher's ministry description.

- He is our Redeemer in whom our full salvation is complete (1:1–14). We should surrender to His will for His redeemed people.
- He is seated at God's right hand ruling over everything with all authority, appointed the Head over everything for the church, which is His body (1:15–23). We should follow His directives for the church.
- We are His workmanship, created in Christ to do the beautiful work prepared for us from all eternity (2:1–10). We should want to know what He prepared pastors and people for.
- He is the chief cornerstone upon whom the whole building (the church) is being built (2:11–22). We should follow His architectural drawings for the church.
- He is the revelation of God's grace toward which all time and eternity have been moving (3:1–14). We should yield to His infinite wisdom for His people.

45

- His love for us surpasses all knowledge (3:15–21). We should submit to His calling on our lives.
- He ascended higher than all the heavens in order to fill the whole universe (4:1–10). We should listen to the Creator, Sustainer, and Ruler of the universe.

The Pastoral Ministry Mindset Shift That Changes Everything: Every Pastor an Equipper of Equippers

Instead, we listen to modern church culture that screams, "The pastor is the preacher, caregiver, and CEO!" It's time to listen to the Head of the church. "It was he who gave some to be . . . pastors and teachers, to prepare God's people for works of service" (Eph. 4:11–12). *Christ's grand plan for His church is for pastors-teachers to focus on equipping every member to do the work of the ministry.*

Under the Spirit's inspiration, Paul launches verse 12 with a tiny Greek word (*pros*) translated by an even smaller English word ("to") with giant meaning: "with the conscious purpose of, in order for, for the sake of, with a view to." The word indicates the future aim and ultimate goal of a current action. That is, by definition, a vision statement—Christ's grand vision statement for every pastor-teacher.

What is the future view, the future vision for which Christ sovereignly gave His church pastors and teachers? Paul says it succinctly: "*To prepare God's people for works of service*." These eight words must be every church leader's reason for existence.

One central word—"prepare"—must capture every leader's passion for ministry. "Prepare" comes from the word for "artist" or "craftsman." Local church leader, your special craft, your opus, is people, equipped people, disciple-makers. Your spiritual craft or gift is to help others scout out their spiritual gift, identify that area of ministry, and empower them to use that gift.

In Paul's day people commonly used "prepare" in the context of conditioning an athlete. Local church leader, you are a spiritual conditioning coach. Your job is not to play all the positions on the team, but to coach all the players on the team, to strengthen their spiritual

46

condition so they are able to do works of service. This fits perfectly with how Paul uses the word "prepare"—to train others so they are fully fit and mature enough to complete their calling. *The leader's calling is to help God's people fulfill their calling.*

These weren't just words for Paul. He made making disciple-makers his personal ministry description—Colossians 1:28–29. He made equipping equippers his personal ministry practice—Acts 20:13–38. Christ's grand vision so captured Paul's ministry mindset that at the end of his life he passed on to Timothy the vision of equipping equippers of equippers—2 Timothy 2:2. The baton of equipping passed from Christ's hands, to Paul's hands, to Timothy's hands, to the hands of reliable disciple-makers who passed it on yet again.

Let's not drop the baton. Let's keep Christ's grand vision alive and moving into the future.

Yes, But

Some may ask, "Are you saying that pastors should not preach the Word, counsel, and administrate?" Not at all. Christ, the Head of the church, has written the primary ministry description for all pastors. Pastors should equip equippers for the work of the ministry. Within this overriding calling, pastors can preach, counsel, and administrate.

When I was senior pastor, every time I preached I asked myself, "How does this message further my calling to be a catalyst for equipping the saints for the work of ministry?" As a player-coach, when I counseled I had trainees in the room with me. When I visited the hospital, I took apprentices with me. My goal wasn't to be the church's primary caregiver, but to equip a church of caregivers. In my administrative role, I sought to oversee the equipping of every member. Yes, I preached, counseled, and administrated—always within the context of Christ's grand vision for the church, which is the pastor as the equipper of equippers.

Others may be thinking, "I'm with you 100 percent. I'm not an ordained pastor, although I am a recognized, active ministry leader in my church. How should I apply these truths?" Ephesians 4:11–12 provides the ministry description for all those raised up for church leadership.

If you are the small-group director, ask, "How can I orchestrate all our small-group leaders and members to be discipled to speak the truth in love?" If you are the women's ministry director, ask, "How can I fulfill Christ's call for me to equip women to equip others?"

The Résumé of the People of God

Sadly, in far too many churches, the people of God are second-class citizens when it comes to the work of ministry. If a "layperson" makes a hospital visit, that's okay, but we want to know, "Where's my pastor?" Christ's vision is so different. *Pastors and teachers serve the people so God's people can serve the congregation and community.* Far too many "laypeople" are recruited to fill a position and to fill a need—make the coffee, cover the nursery during the service—but not to fulfill a calling.

Paul's phrase "works of service" elevates the ministry of God's people. "Works" has a sense of divine calling and meaningful purpose. We could translate it as "vocation" and "mission." The Bible uses it to describe God's creative work. God the Creator commissions us for creative, zealous, purposeful work—work that glorifies Him as we serve one another.

Paul's word for "service" highlights personal service rather than serving for wages, serving as a slave, and serving publicly. It involves love in action through sacrificial ministry modeled after Christ's sacrifice. Christ calls His people to creative, purposeful, meaningful, sacrificial, personal ministry to one another in His name. In the context of Ephesians 4:11–16, that work is nothing less than making disciple-makers through the personal ministry of the Word.

The Member Ministry Mindset Shift That Changes Everything: Every Member a Disciple-Maker

When leaders and members fulfill their purposes together, the body of Christ builds itself up in two specific, cohesive ways: doctrinal unity and spiritual maturity (Eph. 4:12–13). When a congregation knows the truth not just academically, but personally, their love abounds in knowledge and depth of insight (Phil. 1:9–11).

We often miss the vital real-life, how-to application of every-member disciple-making that Paul embeds in this text. How does the church come to unity and maturity? Exactly what are pastors equipping people to do? Specifically how do members do the work of the ministry?

Paul answers: by "speaking the truth in love" we grow up in Christ (Eph. 4:15). Every word in this passage funnels toward this remarkable phrase "speaking the truth in love." *Christ's grand plan for His church is for every member to be a disciple-maker by speaking and living gospel truth to one another in love.*

Paul selects an unusual Greek word that we often translate as "speaking the truth." Actually, we should translate it both as "speaking" and as "living the truth." We might even coin the phrase "truthing." Paul likely had in mind Psalm 15, where the psalmist asks, "Who may dwell in your sanctuary?" He answers: "He whose walk is blameless and who does what is righteous, *who speaks the truth from his heart*" (Ps. 15:2). Who can serve in God's sanctuary, the church? The one who embodies truth in relationships.

The word for "truthing" that Paul uses indicates being transparent, truthfulness, genuine, authentic, reliable, sincere. It describes the person who ministers from a heart of integrity and Christlike, grace-oriented love. It pictures the person whose relational style is transparent and trustworthy. The tense and context indicate that the body of Christ should continually, actively, and collectively embody truth in love as it walks together in intimate, vulnerable connection. In one word, Paul combines content, character, and competence shared in community!

While the word means more than speaking, it does not mean *less* than speaking. While it means more than sheer factual content, it does not mean *less* than the gospel fully applied. Paul uses the identical word in Galatians 4:16. There he is clearly speaking of preaching, teaching, and communicating the truth of the gospel of Christ's grace (salvation) applied to daily growth in Christ (progressive sanctification).

Combine Galatians 4:16 with Ephesians 4:16, both in context, and we find an amazing description of gospel-centered biblical counseling—of the personal ministry of the Word. Speaking the truth involves:

Communicating gospel truth about grace-focused sanctification in word, thought, and action through one-another relationships that have integrity, genuineness, authenticity, transparency, and reliability, done in love to promote the unity and maturity of the body of Christ for the ultimate purpose of displaying the glory of Christ's grace.

The normal agenda and priority of every Christian is to make disciple-makers. Christ's training strategy for disciple-making is pastors and teachers equipping every member to embody the truth in love through the personal ministry of the Word—biblical counseling.

What happens when leaders focus on equipping God's people to make disciple-makers through the personal ministry of the Word by speaking and living the truth in love? Paul shows us in Ephesians 4:16. The body in robust health grows and builds itself up in love as each part does its work.

Disciple-Making Champion:
Pastor Robert Cheong, Pastor of Care and Counseling, Sojourn Community Church

Dr. Robert Cheong, pastor of care and counseling for Sojourn Community Church in Louisville, Kentucky, is passionate about equipping God's people for gospel-centered counseling. His definition of church-based counseling harmonizes beautifully with Paul's Ephesians 4:11–16 vision.

> Gospel counseling is a way of loving one another by understanding the struggles of unbelief and lies in the midst of sin and suffering through listening to and exploring the heart, while proclaiming how Christ and His gospel truths apply in deeply personal and particular ways, so that we can live out and grow in the gospel by faith in community, enabled by the grace and power of the Holy Spirit.

Pastor Cheong unites counseling and the personal ministry of the Word.

Gospel counseling is an aspect of gospel ministry that represents the relational ministry of the Word in which every Christian is called to participate. In less "technical" terms, the essence of counseling is helping one another to understand and apply the gospel to the details of life so that we can live the gospel by faith in community.

Pastor Cheong's connection between the church and counseling is an apt exclamation point on Christ's grand vision.

Counseling that flows from the gospel reflects the essence of gospel ministry and must be done by the church—the people of God. God calls every member of His church to the relational ministry of the Word where people labor with their entire lives to help those in the church family to grow in maturity in Christ (cf. Col. 1:28–29) and to help those outside the church family to see their need for Christ as Savior and Redeemer. Helping others to live out the gospel and to submit to the gospel is what it means to "be the church." Therefore, the renewal of counseling is not to have such a ministry done *in* the church but *by* the church, so the church can *be* the church.

Commencement: It Takes a Congregation

Most books end each chapter with a conclusion. I don't like that label any more than I like it when counselors call their final session the "termination session." I call my final biblical counseling meeting "commencement" because I want to communicate positive progress on an ongoing journey with Christ. For the same reason, I'm calling the end of each chapter the commencement. Let's commence.

When I started my ministry as congregational discipleship pastor, I didn't begin by launching a biblical counseling program. That never would have been sufficient to minister effectively to Steve, Alexis, Eric, and the others in their family. Instead, I invited our congregation to join me on a journey of catching God's vision for every-member disciple-making. Because of that focus, this family received both formal biblical counseling and informal one-another ministry.

As our congregation engaged in the vision-catching process, we joined together to assess and diagnose the heart health of our congregation and community. We knew that we couldn't understand where to go until

51

we knew where we had been and where we currently were. Join me in chapter two as we learn about that process: *Examining Heart Health: Diagnosing Congregational and Community Fitness.*

Growing Together: Questions for Reflection, Discussion, and Application

1. If the all-American couple entered your congregation, how prepared would your church be to minister to them in their current crisis and in their ongoing Christian lives? What do you think your congregation might need to do in order to be better prepared?
2. Would you say your church is a church with biblical counseling or a church of biblical counseling (a congregation saturated with equipped one-another ministers)? Why?
3. In your life and in your church, how much of a transition would it be to shift from doing the work of the ministry to making disciple-makers? What might that shift look like and involve?
4. Of the seven styles of churches, which do you value? Which methods does your church use? How well do the styles function in your church?
5. Reflect on the résumé and the ministry description of the biblical pastor, teacher, leader.
   a. Who has equipped you to equip others? How did they do it?
   b. Whom have you equipped to equip others? How did you do it?
6. Ponder the definition of "speaking the truth in love":

Communicating gospel truth about grace-focused sanctification in word, thought, and action through one-another relationships that have integrity, genuineness, authenticity, transparency, and reliability, done in love to promote the unity and maturity of the body of Christ for the ultimate purpose of displaying the glory of Christ's grace.

   a. How would you evaluate your personal ministry of the Word based on this definition?
   b. How would you assess your congregation's personal ministry of the Word based on this definition?

2

Examining Heart Health

Diagnosing Congregational and Community Fitness

In my first church, I served as counseling and discipleship pastor at an urban-suburban, white-collar church with three thousand members. The church had a long history of extensive equipping ministries. In my second church, I served as congregational discipleship pastor (senior pastor) at a rural, blue-collar church of one hundred (which God grew to three hundred). As I noted in chapter one, this church had a long history of a pastor-centered mindset. Looking back, I should have realized how different these two churches were.

It took me just two days to learn. A senior saint and longtime member asked to speak with me about a counseling issue. After an initial response of empathy and listening, I instinctively reached into my files for a four-page Personal Information Form for her to complete.

To me, it was natural and caring—it would help me to understand better her current issues, past history, and future goals. For her, it was unusual and uncaring. Thankfully, she told me so in no uncertain terms. "I'm here to talk to my pastor, not to fill out paperwork. I don't know how they did things where you came from, but we're not like that around here."

Although I graduated from a fine Bible college and an excellent seminary, not a single professor ever told me that two churches, especially with predominantly the same ethnicity, could be so drastically different. I was never taught to understand the culture of my church and community—the way things are done, the way people think, the expectations people have, a congregation's history, and a community's values. I was culturally ignorant, culturally tone-deaf.

If not for this encounter, I would have launched the biblical counseling ministry in my new church in the same way I had successfully done it in my first church. Since my former church already had a vision for disciple-making, I started with a formal two-year training program complete with extensive interviews, selection of a limited number of trainees, homework assignments, and supervision.

As I began to understand how vastly different my new church was, I decided to spend my first six months getting to know my congregation and community. As a result, I started my training there with an informal spiritual friendship model of one-another ministry—helping the entire congregation to grow in their ability to speak the truth in love. I waited until my second year before I launched a more formal biblical counseling training ministry.

A Church Cardiologist

Much of what I teach arises from the mistakes I made and from my desire to save you from making those same mistakes. No one taught me how to become a spiritual cardiologist. That's what you are going to learn in this chapter: *how to diagnose the heart health of your congregation and community to establish a present baseline for envisioning God's future dream.*

From Ephesians 4 we know the *eternal baseline* for a robustly healthy church. Christ's grand plan for His church is for church leaders to equip every member to make disciple-makers by speaking and living God's truth to one another in love. Before launching Ephesians 4 ministry, we need to learn *how to diagnose and assess our congregation's and community's current readiness, health, and fitness compared to Christ's vision for His church.*

The church is the body of Christ, and each individual congregation, like each individual human body, has a body type. Christ makes this plain in His unique interactions with the seven churches of Revelation 2–3. Christ has a distinctive purpose, calling, gift-mix, and method of ministry for every local congregation in its specific community.

Biblical counselors are soul physicians who understand people, diagnose problems, and prescribe solutions—biblically. We also need to be church cardiologists who understand our church and community, diagnose the heart condition of the culture where we minister, and prescribe God's cures—biblically. Church cardiology equips us to understand how to move wisely from Christ's universal calling to unique congregation- and community-specific applications.

Don't Just Do It; Do It Relationally

My basic personality is like *Nike*—"Just do it!" I don't like to waste time. Many church leaders think similarly. "Let's just get on with it—launch this ministry already. Enough preparation!" I empathize. However, we must balance the extreme of planning so long that nothing ever happens against the extreme of moving so quickly that we endure a haphazard launch that alienates people and ministers ineffectively.

The wisest way to avoid these two ditches is to follow an unhurried but steady pace, focused on *organizing the organism.* We have to *be* a community before we can *reach* our community. We have to minister to one another *during* the launch process if we want to create a culture of one-another ministry *after* the launch. In ministry, speed kills. Shortcuts are often dead ends. This is especially true when *organizing* is emphasized above the *organism.*

Our starting point is listening to Christ—His vision for His church. Then we listen carefully to one another. Assessment is a personal discovery process involving intentional one-another spiritual conversations that emphasize other-centered listening and understanding. Assessment isn't marketing. People want to be cared for in community, not targeted as customers.

The relational launch process fans into flame the individual and congregational passion that carries forward the entire ministry. Remember our end goal: a relationship with *the* transforming Person (Christ) leads to transforming leaders (you and your team) relationally leading a transforming process (*The 4E Ministry Training Strategy*) that the Spirit uses to transform your church (the body of Christ) so others (the congregation and community) are also transformed into disciple-makers.

Jesus and Paul: Spiritual Cardiologists

That dear saint walked out of my office after an hour of spiritual conversation during which I never lifted another finger to touch another counseling form! Then I prayed. "Lord, what have I gotten myself into? Why did You send me *here*?" After praying, I took the next logical step: I began a biblical study that, twenty years later, became this chapter. I examined how Jesus and Paul wisely moved into new cultures, into new ministry terrain. Through that study I came to the conviction that *before we catch God's future vision, we must first diagnose the past history and current condition of our congregation and community.*

Jesus: Culturally Informed Ministry—John 2:23–4:42

Jesus' interaction with Nicodemus in John 3 is one of the most familiar stories in the Bible. His spiritual conversation with the woman at the well in John 4 is another well-known biblical narrative. Unfortunately, many people fail to connect these two passages because they fail to detect the textual marker John provides. John informs us that Jesus is the ultimate Soul Physician who "knew all men. He did not need man's testimony about man, for he knew what was in a man" (John 2:24–25).

John's introduction is like a flashing neon light screaming, "Pay attention to what lies ahead! I'm going to demonstrate to you how Jesus understands people, diagnoses problems, and prescribes solutions through knowing the human heart universally, internally, and culturally."

Could any two people be more different than Nicodemus and the Samaritan woman? Nicodemus is a well-known Jewish male Pharisee—a hyper-moral religious leader. The woman at the well is a nameless Samaritan female—an immoral, irreligious follower.

Even though they are from vastly different cultures, Jesus understands them both personally. He diagnoses that each has the same "problem" (sin) and prescribes the same "solution"—a personal relationship with God through personal faith in Christ. Yet He gets there in markedly different ways. Nicodemus came purposefully to Jesus at night. Jesus came purposefully to the Samaritan woman in broad daylight. Jesus replies to Nicodemus's overture with a direct declaration of the truth—that you must be born again. Jesus initiates a conversation with the Samaritan woman about His own physical thirst. He illustrates spiritual truth with Nicodemus by focusing on the wind, Spirit, flesh, and birth. He illustrates spiritual truth with the Samaritan woman by focusing on thirst, drinking, and water.

Neither individual got it at first, each thinking too much about physical reality and missing Jesus' spiritual meaning. To penetrate Nicodemus's dense spiritual blindness, Jesus turns His attention to Moses' lifting up a snake in the desert and then declares that God so loved the world that He gave His only Son. To penetrate the Samaritan woman's dense spiritual blindness, Jesus turns her attention to her immorality and to worshiping in spirit and truth. To Nicodemus, He starts as a rabbi, becomes Israel's teacher, and ends as the Son of God. To the Samaritan woman, He starts as a thirsty traveler, becomes a prophet, and ends as the Messiah.

Christ's understanding, diagnosis, and prescription are the same. The people He engages, however, are incredibly different. This is why Jesus' interactions—His personal ministry of the Word, His way of speaking and living gospel truth in love—are unique to each. He models for us that the *message* is the same, but the *methods and means of communication* vary because of the personal and cultural differences of the specific audience.

Paul: Study Scripture/Study Society—Acts 17

Jesus didn't need to do "cultural assessment" because He is the God-man. Paul, and you and I, must do cultural assessment—congregational and community diagnosis.

As Paul arrives in Thessalonica, he enters the synagogue three consecutive Sabbath days to reason from the Scriptures, explaining and proving who Christ is. Chased out of town, Paul follows a similar ministry strategy in Berea. Agitators arrive again, so Paul heads for Athens.

While in Athens, Paul is "greatly distressed to see that the city was full of idols" (Acts 17:16). Paul allows himself to feel and to see—to experience and to understand—the new cultural context in which he is ministering.

After he opens his heart and his eyes, he opens his mouth and the Word. He reasons with them where they are—in the marketplace and in the Areopagus. He feels compassion for their lost culture, understands their unique culture, but doesn't give in to their culture. He offers their culture a biblical message in a culture-specific manner.

Paul interacts with the Epicurean and Stoic philosophers, sharing Christ's truth in language they can understand. He starts where they are. "Men of Athens! I *see* that in every way you are very religious. For . . . I *walked around* and *looked carefully* at your objects of worship" (Acts 17:22–23a).

Do we feel? See? Do we walk among and look carefully at the people in our congregation and community? We fear doing this because we fear capitulating to the culture and becoming need-focused and humanity-centered, instead of remaining God-focused and gospel-centered.

Instead, we need to follow Paul's model. *He is not culturally influenced; he is culturally informed so he can be a culture influencer for Christ.* He preaches the good news about Christ's resurrection in a way that connects eternal truth to their temporal situation. "Now what you worship as something unknown I am going to proclaim to you" (Acts 17:23b). He opens his eyes, and then he opens his mouth to open Scripture in a culturally understandable manner. Paul quotes one of their poets, but he doesn't integrate their philosophy into his theology. He *builds bridges between the two worlds* of God's truth and their lives, boldly and lovingly calling for repentance before the risen Christ.

God calls us, like Paul, to speak the truth in love in a Christ-centered, culturally informed manner.

- We open our hearts to experience the pain of the hopelessness of our society.
- We open our eyes to know our society, listening to their earthly story.
- We open our mouths to share Christ as society's only hope.
- We open the Word to explain Scripture, sharing God's eternal story.

Through diagnosing the spiritual condition of our congregation and community, we learn to communicate Christ's changeless truth to our changing times.

Church Cardiology: Diagnosing Congregational Readiness for Making Disciple-Makers

I am thankful that my three pastoral ministries were in dissimilar churches: an urban mega-church, a suburban church with five hundred members, and a rural church with one to three hundred members. Otherwise, I might advocate a prescriptive strategy that communicates "Do X and then Y will happen." Ministry with real people doesn't work like that. Churches, even with seemingly similar demographics, are each one of a kind.

So consider the following how-to section on diagnosing your church not as a straitjacket, but as a GPS: *God's Positioning Strategy*. The approach I am suggesting is grounded in biblical principles and presented as a guide with directional markers that you can alter and apply to fit your ministry setting. No how-to is one-size-fits-all because we are not franchising a McDonald's restaurant; we are ministering to people.

In teaching about examining spiritual heart health, I am not supporting a pragmatic strategy that says, "It works; do it." Rather, I am saying, "Jesus and Paul practiced culturally informed ministry, and we should follow their lead." The Bible teaches that we are responsible to apply Christ's universal calling in culturally informed ways in our particular ministry context.

Disciple-Making Champion:
Dr. Kevin Carson, Pastor, Sonrise Baptist Church

Dr. Kevin Carson, pastor at Sonrise Baptist Church in Ozark, Missouri, supplies a church-planting perspective on biblical counseling in the local church. Pastor Carson balances the absolute necessity of a biblical theology of ministry with the practical reality of an effective ministry development process built upon that theological foundation.

> As part of the church-plant *philosophy* and subsequent *methodology*, biblical counseling ministry (one-another ministry built upon a biblical theology of sovereignty, sufficiency, sin, suffering, Savior, salvation, and sanctification) was fundamental to the church-plant foundation. The church through *various means* exists together in authentic life to become more like Jesus Christ practicing the one-anothers as part of life lived.

Pastor Carson's ministry includes equipping members to understand people in their context. Pastor Carson believes that "out-of-context ministry" is a frequent problem.

> The tendency is for new churches to copy what is heard in a conference or read in a book. The methods of ministry the church planter is copying were all developed inside a local context. That context includes a regionally based people. . . . To take, for example, the purpose-driven model and try to remake Saddleback Church in Ozark, Missouri would be unwise.

Not only must structure be contextually applied, even more importantly, it must be scripturally derived. Building upon his exegesis of Ephesians 4:11–16, Pastor Carson explains:

> The church's structure must consistently and emphatically engender the work of progressive sanctification in the life of believers,

60

recognizing the importance of ministry that is vertically integrated [Christ-centered] and horizontally mutual [speaking the truth in love].

Scripture provides the structure that we sagely develop in our specific situation.

The Scripture pushes the faithful pastor-teacher to equip every believer in the church, ensuring the congregation's ability to engage in the process of change by speaking the truth in love to each other. To facilitate each member's personal ministry to the body, the church planter must anticipate *forms and structure* necessary to complement the process.

Self-Cardiology: Watch Your Life and Doctrine Closely

Applying biblical principles in congregation-specific ways takes more than IQ. It takes SQ—a high spirituality quotient. In the midst of Paul's instructions to Timothy about "how people ought to conduct themselves in God's household, which is the church of the living God" (1 Tim. 3:15), Paul exhorts Timothy to "watch your life and doctrine closely" (1 Tim. 4:16).

Life and doctrine are the same themes Paul highlighted in Ephesians: unity in the faith (doctrinal intelligence, biblical wisdom) and maturity in Christ (relational intelligence, Christlike character). We can't attempt to examine the heart health of others if we are not turning first to the ultimate Soul Physician (Christ) and to mutual spiritual friends (the body of Christ) to examine our own heart condition. Self-cardiology is the prerequisite for doing the work of a church cardiologist.

As you read this chapter, ask yourself, "How ready and fit am I to live out Ephesians 4 ministry? What is the spiritual condition of my heart? What prescriptions does God's Word recommend for my heart condition?"

The Geography of the Heart: Diagnosis, Not Demographics

Most churches, if they perform cultural analysis of their congregation and community, tend only to collect biographical (age, gender, marital status, education, socio-economic status) and geographical information. In diagnosing congregational fitness, you want to examine the *geography of the heart.* If you are going to assess how ready your church is for the relational ministry of speaking the truth in love, then your mindset must be *relational connection, not data collection.*

As the Bible does, think of your congregation as one body, as one corporate personality. Assess your congregation's readiness for one-another disciple-making by examining the current spiritual fitness of your church according to the Ephesians 4 ministry model. (Throughout this chapter I use "Ephesians 4 ministry" as shorthand for the robustly healthy church we examined in chapter one.)

A survey that is received out of the blue results in out-of-context responses and low return rates. Before you use a survey, precede it with sermons, lessons, and congregational gatherings to explain the Ephesians 4 ministry focus and the purpose of the survey. Use pulpit and bulletin announcements, newsletters, e-blasts, your website, social media pages, and personal contact to encourage participation by a scheduled date.

It is wise to avoid anonymous surveys. If we are going to relate maturely in Christ, then we should be able to put our names behind our loving feedback.

Your launch team should ask at least 10 percent of those who complete the survey if they would agree to a follow-up face-to-face interview. Select people who are representative of the congregation. For effective interviews, use the material from this chapter and from Appendix 2.1 to guide your team in creating congregational and community surveys. In this way, your launch team owns the questions and understands them. Train your team in basic listening skills so they can use the survey questions as a springboard for relational interviewing. Train your team to draw people out by using follow-up questions to probe deeper.

Use the survey interview method in conjunction with other means for becoming culturally informed about your congregation's heart health. Conduct congregational input nights to provide opportunities for members to communicate their sense of where they have been, who they are, and where they are headed. Host leadership community nights with a similar purpose but a more focused audience—those active in church ministry leadership. Participate with your leadership team (pastoral staff, elders, deacons) in similar conversations. Read your church constitution, mission statement, doctrinal statements, and written historical documents. With every method, your goal is to define the gap between God's grand vision for a healthy church, where you are as a congregation, and where you see God calling your church.

Some leaders are nervous about the survey interview process, fearing "the pooling of ignorance." However, since you have crafted your survey based upon the Ephesians 4 ministry model, the process is not pooling of ignorance but pulling out of insight. Using your trained interviewers who lead spiritual conversations about heart health means that conversations are facilitated. Once you've collated the results, your equipped launch team directs the diagnosis of the congregation's spiritual condition and leads the process of prescribing God's spiritual cure.

Designing Congregation-Specific Diagnostic Tools: The Congregational SWORD Heart Exam

If I provide you with only sample survey questions and conversation starters, then you will have a fish, but you won't know how to fish. And your fish will fit my ministry setting, but not yours. Instead, you *first* need transferable principles for creating your own congregation-specific diagnostic tools. I provide those principles for you in the SWORD Heart Exam. With those principles in hand, *then* you can effectively use the sample questions provided later in this chapter and the sample Congregational SWORD Heart Exam contained in Appendix 2.1.

Many people use a SWOT Analysis (Strengths, Weaknesses, Opportunities, Threats) as their diagnostic grid. I use a SWORD Heart Exam (Strengths, Weaknesses, Opportunities, Risks, Diagnosis) because God's Word is sharper than any two-edged sword, able to discern the thoughts and intents of the heart (Heb. 4:12–13). The SWORD examination focuses your attention on responding proactively as you grow in understanding your congregation's past, present, and future heart fitness for Ephesians 4 ministry.

- **S: Strengths**—Identifying strengths: What have we done and are we doing well in Ephesians 4 ministry?
- **W: Weaknesses**—Recognizing weaknesses: Where and why do we need to improve in Ephesians 4 ministry?
- **O: Opportunities**—Picturing opportunities: How can we move toward robust Ephesians 4 ministry?
- **R: Risks**—Evaluating risks: What obstacles stand in the way of healthy Ephesians 4 ministry?
- **D: Diagnosis**—Diagnosing heart fitness: What prescriptions does God's Word suggest, given the state of our congregation's Ephesians 4 heart health?

Identifying Strengths: What Have We Done and Are We Doing Well in Ephesians 4 Ministry?

Identifying strengths is biblical. When Jesus addressed the seven churches in Revelation 2–3, in most cases He began with a positive presentation of their present spiritual strengths. The Spirit promises to sovereignly assemble spiritually gifted believers to form a unified, empowered, one-another body (1 Cor. 12). Starting your SWORD exam by assessing past and present health builds on the positive work God has done and is doing among your congregation.

This is particularly important if you are new to your church. Your perception may be "I have to fix this place." The people's perception may be "Why does it have to be his way or the highway? Is everything going to have to change? Haven't we been doing anything right in God's eyes?" We should appreciate what has gone before rather than arrogantly assume that we are the answer person who knows exactly what the church needs. We create trust by communicating that some things should not change, but rather be valued, maximized, and amplified.

As a spiritual conditioning coach, do what many sports trainers do—view videos of success. Don't observe only times when your congregation struck out. Spot times when they hit a home run. Applaud them. Cheer them on. Affirm the good work God has accomplished and is accomplishing in them. Ponder together how to keep it going and growing.

Recognizing Weaknesses: Where and Why Do We Need to Improve in Ephesians 4 Ministry?

Engaging in spiritual conversations about spiritual weakness is never easy. However, it is necessary. When Jesus addressed the seven churches of Asia Minor, he pulled no punches in exposing their sin.

The objective is to isolate specific samples from the past and present where the congregation lacks Ephesians 4 heart health. Seek to discern heart motivations by looking for long-standing, underlying patterns. What in the corporate system—the congregation's mindset about ministry—is causing heart blockage?

How do you respond to what you see? First, realize that in the assessment process you don't have to solve everything. You are learning the heart of your people. Second, the eventual response may be similar to what Jesus called for in Revelation 2–3—individual and corporate repentance. There are spiritual reasons for unhealthy churches that we must address by speaking the truth in love. Third, chapter five addresses further responses under the headings of relational change management and biblical conflict resolution.

Picturing Opportunities: How Can We Move toward Robust Ephesians 4 Ministry?

Here you look forward to an even brighter future. You prime the congregational pump so members begin envisioning future opportunities. As you talk to people who are excited about this future vision, recruit these change agents as part of your pilot team.

Even in negatives, emphasize positive possibilities. Ask: "What dormant gifts for Ephesians 4 ministry can we fan into flame? What will it look like when we turn this around? What resources are going untapped? Why? How can we tap into them?"

Evaluate linkage. Ask: "Where is Ephesians 4 ministry taking place, but in disjointed ways? How can we organize the organism so these natural, informal gatherings become a supernatural, normal part of our congregational life?"

Seek to determine priorities moving forward. You can't do it all at once, so ask: "Where do we move from here in the Ephesians 4 ministry process? How? Why? Where should we start? What's our next step?"

Evaluating Risks: What Obstacles Stand in the Way of Healthy Ephesians 4 Ministry?

Now you look toward the future, but not with naive eyes. You survey the current landscape and scout the potential roadblocks in the congregation's path toward church health.

Jesus teaches how foolish it is to attempt to build something new without first counting the costs (Luke 14:28–33). The context for that passage is discipleship. In explaining how costly it is to commit to making disciple-makers, Jesus is encouraging disciples to gain a realistic perspective on potential hindrances to ministry. Who and what may stand against us? What apple carts might we upset? What cherished, long-standing ministries may need to die an honorable death because they no longer serve a disciple-making purpose?

We know we are called to Ephesians 4 ministry, but how committed are we? Are we committed enough to work through the change-management process? To wade into conflict-resolution situations? To reach into our pockets, purses, and bank accounts to provide the necessary resources? To give sacrificially of our time and talent?

Diagnosing Heart Fitness: What Prescriptions Does God's Word Suggest, Given the State of Our Congregation's Ephesians 4 Heart Health?

We should not expend our time or ask for others to give their time in the assessment process unless we have a plan for how we will use the insights we glean. Congregations are tired of surveys and questionnaires that go nowhere and accomplish nothing. Diagnosing your congregational heart fitness communicates that you value your people, what they are doing, and the wisdom they have shared with you.

Practically speaking, this begins with the tedious task of collating the responses—written responses, responses from the in-person interviews, and responses from various congregational gatherings. After someone has typed and organized that collation, your team's primary task is to assess the assessment by *identifying themes.* What comes up repeatedly? What messages are you hearing?

As you identify themes, keep your goal in view. Use God's eternal vision for His church as a spiritual EKG to diagnose the heart health of your congregation in order to establish a present baseline for envisioning God's future dream. Pray for a big-picture understanding of who you are as a church family. Ask: What are the past and present strengths and weaknesses, as measured by the Ephesians 4 portrait of God's healthy family? What future opportunities and risks do we face as we move toward growth as Christ's healthy body?

Ask your team, "If Christ were speaking to us as He spoke to the seven churches in Revelation 2–3, what would He say?" Lead your team in using the results of the SWORD Heart Exam to write an extensive paraphrase of Revelation 2–3 as if it were addressed to your church. The letters to the seven churches lend themselves very well to this. In each letter we read Christ's *understanding* of the congregation, His *diagnoses* of their spiritual strengths and sins, His *prescription* of spiritual remedies, and His *prognosis* depending upon their responsiveness.

Report your summary to the church leadership and work with them to craft your next steps. Your final task is to communicate back to your congregation. Again, working with your church leadership, determine what to say in which settings. Your people will be greatly encouraged when they realize that what they shared has played a significant role in shaping your decisions about your ministry launch.

Congregational Survey Samplers

You can find a sample Congregational SWORD Heart Exam in Appendix 2.1. You will note that the questions on the following pages are worded for *your team*—these are the types of issues that you want to raise. You will then note that the questions in Appendix 2.1 are worded for *a specific congregation.*

The following sample questions are intended to spark your imagination so you can create your own congregation-specific interactions—using wording that your congregation will understand and that fits for your ministry focus.

Identifying Past and Present Strengths: Informal Congregational One-Anothering

- What powerful stories does our church tell about amazing times of being together?
- Who are people you point to and say, "That's an encourager! That's a spiritual leader!" What stands out about those people?
- Share examples of ways our church (past/present) has provided equipping for mutual encouragement and one-another care. What methods were used? How long did the training last?
- How confident are you in your ability to provide biblical encouragement to a friend who is suffering or struggling with a sin issue?

Identifying Past and Present Strengths: Formal Biblical Counseling Equipping

- What compelling stories does our church tell about times when lives have been changed through biblical counseling?
- Share examples of ways our church (past/present) has provided equipping for formal biblical counseling and disciple-making. What methods were used? How long did the training last?
- As you look around our congregation, which people are discipling others? Whom would you go to for discipleship?
- How confident are you in your ability to disciple disciple-makers? To counsel biblically?

Recognizing Past and Present Weaknesses: Informal Congregational One-Anothering

- What patterns or mindsets might make it difficult for our church to become a place where we speak the truth in love to one another?
- What training ministries for one-another care have we launched that "fell flat"? Why do you think this happened?

- Have you or someone you know ever needed care from our congregation but been unable to receive it? What happened?
- What are specific ways our church could improve the provision of one-another care?

Recognizing Past and Present Weaknesses: Formal Biblical Counseling Equipping

- When biblical counseling is needed, how long does it take to receive it? Have you or someone you know ever requested biblical counseling but been unable to receive it?
- What are weaknesses of our discipleship ministry that you would like to see us address? How?
- Compared to Ephesians 4:11–16, what priority does our congregation give to discipling disciple-makers? How could we become more effective?
- How would you assess our congregation's ability to provide biblical pre-marital counseling? Marital counseling? Family/parental counseling? Individual counseling? How could we improve?

Picturing Future Opportunities: Informal Congregational One-Anothering

- What would a mission/vision statement look like that helps our church meet the challenge of one-another ministry?
- How can we move forward toward a more robust Ephesians 4 one-another ministry of speaking the truth in love?
- What dormant gifts for Ephesians 4 ministry can we fan into flame?
- What level of interest would you have in being further trained as a spiritual friend who could help others in an informal, friend-to-friend manner through speaking the truth in love?

Picturing Future Opportunities: Formal Biblical Counseling Equipping

- What would a mission/vision statement look like that helps our church meet the challenge of equipping one another to make disciple-makers?

- Who is God calling us to be as a unique disciple-making church within the larger body of Christ in our particular community?
- Where is Ephesians 4 ministry taking place, but in disjointed ways? How can we organize the organism so these natural, informal gatherings become a supernatural, normal part of our congregational life?
- What level of interest would you have in being further trained as a biblical counselor who formally relates Christ's truth to people's lives?

Evaluating Future Risks: Informal Congregational One-Anothering

- In the past, how has our church responded to change and to the launch of new ministries? How might similar responses hinder a renewed focus on every-member disciple-making?
- What obstacles might stand in the way of healthy one-another ministry in our church?
- Where do we need to grow or change if we are to move forward as a church where every member speaks the truth in love?
- What potential hindrances and limitations might we face as we move toward Ephesians 4 ministry?

Evaluating Future Risks: Formal Biblical Counseling Equipping

- Rate how large the gap is between where we are now and where you think we need to be in order to build a healthy equipping church.
- If we launched a biblical counseling training ministry, who and what might stand in the way? What apple carts might we upset? What objections might people raise?
- What would you add, subtract, or reprioritize in our church for us to become a more effective disciple-making church?
- What people, time, and financial limitations might we face as we move toward launching a biblical counseling training ministry?

Community Cardiology: Diagnosing Community Readiness for Gospel-Centered Ministry

God calls us to be a church *of* biblical counseling *to* the community *for* His glory. Paul's request should be our prayer. "Pray also for me, that whenever I open my mouth, words may be given me so that I will fearlessly make known the mystery of the gospel" (Eph. 6:19).

Community cardiology follows the gospel-centered biblical counseling passion of equipping every member to speak and live gospel truth in love to fulfill the Great Commission of going and making disciples. The *4E Ministry Training Strategy* prepares God's people for ministry not only *in* the body but also *to* the community. Community cardiology asks, "Who is God calling us to be as a unique church within the larger body of Christ in our particular community?" It seeks to understand how to build gospel-centered bridges of connection between the congregation and community to relate Christ's changeless truth to our changing times. In a culturally informed manner we influence our culture for Christ.

Disciple-Making Champions:
Steve Viars, Senior Pastor, and Rob Green,
Counseling Pastor, Faith Baptist Church

We met Pastors Viars and Green of Faith Baptist in chapter one. A church *of* biblical counseling, Faith has a counseling ministry that is not only *within* their congregation, but also *to* their community. Every week over one hundred community members receive free biblical counseling.

Their vision moves beyond the traditional way we envision counseling—office, chairs, appointments. Their mission explains why. "Faith Baptist Church is a family of followers of Jesus Christ who desire to honor God by applying His sufficient Word *to all areas of life and ministry.*" They are reclaiming biblical counseling for the community.

To fulfill their vision, they built a community center, not for the congregation, but for the community. The list of community ministries includes Big Brothers/Big Sisters, community blood drives, community foster care, Habitat for Humanity, Red Cross disaster shelter, and Court Appointed Special Advocates, among others.

71

Faith also built a state-of-the-art outdoor skateboard park. Many skaters end up in church every Sunday with their skateboards, torn jeans, body piercings, and tattoos to hear the pulpit ministry of the Word. Equipped members hang out at the skate park to engage skaters through the personal ministry of the Word.

Faith's Vision of Hope residential treatment center offers biblical counseling for girls ages 14 to 28 who are struggling with unplanned pregnancy, alcohol or drug abuse, eating disorders, or self-harm. State agencies and the court system regularly refer girls to Vision of Hope with the full knowledge that the program is based upon biblical counseling.

Reclaiming Biblical Counseling for the Community: Diagnosing Your Community's Heart

Consider three primary ways to understand the heartbeat of your unique community:

- Be in your community to understand your community.
- Ask your congregation about your community.
- Ask your community about your church.

Be in Your Community to Understand Your Community: Incarnational Cultural Awareness

Like Paul, we have to be in our community to understand our community. For the past quarter-century I have coached youth and high school wrestling in public schools. I have learned a great deal about how people in my community think, what their passions are, where they struggle, and what they think of Christ and the church.

Take advantage of natural connections—yours and those of your members. Discover who is already serving in non-church volunteer agencies and learn about your community from them. Actively teach your people to view their lives beyond the walls of the church as places that hold opportunities for the personal ministry of the Word. Affirm and celebrate the ministries of your people in your community. Establish relationships with non-profit organizations, local agencies, and the school system.

Ask Your Congregation about Your Community: Intentional Cultural Awareness

In the Congregational SWORD Heart Exam in Appendix 2.1, you will find questions for your congregation about your community. Here are some sample probes that you can word to match your congregation and change to fit your ministry context.

- How can we support you in your connections with our community?
- What community activities/agencies are you involved in, and what are you learning about the people of our community?
- Tell me about the history of our community.
- List five words that come to mind when you think of the folks in our community.
- What are some unique characteristics of the residents of our community?
- What are people in our community passionate about?
- How do the people of our community spend their time?
- What are the five greatest concerns of the residents of our community? Five greatest struggles? Five greatest counseling needs? How could we address these issues biblically?
- What is the typical resident of our community looking for in a church home?
- What type of person is attracted to our church? Who feels at home in our church? Why?
- What would the average community member consider to be the five greatest strengths of our church? The five greatest weaknesses?
- How would community members describe our church in one sentence or word?
- How can we minister biblically to our community?
- What impact might a more intentional, structured approach to biblical counseling have on our community?
- How responsive do you think our community would be if we offered biblical counseling?

- Who is God calling us to be as a unique disciple-making church within the larger body of Christ in our community?
- Ephesians 3:20 says that God will do more than we could ever think or imagine in our church for His glory. What do you think God wants to do through our church in this community?

Ask Your Community about Your Church: Invitational Cultural Awareness

Only the brave ask their community about their church. Be brave and train your pilot team to enter into probing conversations with community members, asking questions such as:

- What first comes to mind when you think about our church?
- How would people you know describe our church in one sentence or one word? How would you? What impressions do you have about our church?
- How can our church make a positive contribution to this community?
- What are the five greatest concerns of the residents of our community? Five greatest struggles? Five greatest needs? How well or poorly has our church been addressing these issues? What more could we do moving forward?
- What would you consider the five greatest strengths of our church? The five greatest weaknesses?
- What is the typical resident of our community looking for in a church home? What would you look for?
- Who do you think would feel at home in our church? Why?
- What questions do you have about our church?
- What counseling needs do people in our community have?
- Would the people of our community be open to receiving biblical counseling from our church?
- Could I share with you the mission, vision, and passion of our church?

Commencement: Gospel Truth Fitly Spoken

"I don't know how they did things where you came from, but we're not like that around here." Those blunt words aptly encapsulate why we must diagnose our congregation's and community's readiness, health, and fitness compared to Christ's vision for His church. If we don't, then our application of God's truth will sound more like us than like Christ communicating His timeless truth through us. There's nothing Christ-centered about communicating truth with a my-way-or-the-highway mentality.

We need to follow Paul's specific application of speaking the truth in love. He insists that our conversations must be "helpful for building others up according to their needs, that it may benefit those who listen. And do not grieve the Holy Spirit" (Eph. 4:29–30a). We grieve the Holy Spirit when we stubbornly refuse to be culturally informed spiritual cardiologists. Grace-oriented gospel conversations build up others when our personal ministry of the Word suits the present time and the present person in their present context.

As we begin to understand Christ's eternal vision for His church in the context of our current congregation and community, then we have a present baseline for envisioning God's future dream for our church. It is to that dream that we next turn our attention as we learn how to lead God's people in jointly crafting a congregation-wide MVP-C Statement (Mission, Vision, Passion, Commission). Be prepared to be captured by what captures the heart of God—bringing Christ glory in the church by showing His people His vision for them, which is immeasurably more than all we could ask or imagine (Eph. 3:20–21).

Growing Together: Questions for Reflection, Discussion, and Application

1. Reflecting on Jesus and Paul:
   a. What can you apply to your ministry from Jesus' culturally informed ministry?
   b. What can you apply to your ministry from Paul's focus on studying Scripture and studying society?

2. What self-cardiology processes are you regularly involved in? How often do you turn to Christ your Soul Physician for a spiritual heart exam? What spiritual friends help you watch your life and doctrine?

3. Even beyond the purposes of this chapter, how could you use the Congregational SWORD Heart Exam as a model for evaluating various ministries?

4. How could you take the Congregational SWORD Heart Exam sampler questions and make them congregation-specific for your ministry?

5. How could you take the questions that ask your church about your community and make them specific for your ministry in your particular community?

6. How could you take the questions that ask your community about your church and make them specific for your community?

3

Dreaming God's Dream

Becoming an MVP-C Congregation

I vividly recall the responses I received when I introduced the idea of "vision casting" to my church. Naively, I was excited. Just looking at the body language of my elders, I quickly discerned that they failed to share my enthusiasm.

Their skepticism about vision follows similar doubts that others—perhaps you—share. One elder explained, "Pastor Bob, we tried this before you came and it seemed like a major waste of time—lots of work and little lasting benefit."

Another elder stated, "I work in industry and we do 'vision stuff' all the time. So what makes this anything more than 'secular' marketing strategies?"

A third elder added, "Well, when we did this in another church, it felt like it came down from Moses on high. It was more 'dictatorial' than congregation-based."

Still a fourth elder countered, "My experience was the opposite. I've been involved in the process twice. Once it felt like 'pooling ignorance' because it was so 'democratic.' The other time it seemed 'seeker-sensitive' and 'man-centered' and little about God."

Men Wanted for a Hazardous Journey

Not one to be easily deterred, I responded to their less-than-enthusiastic reactions by telling them the story of Sir Ernest Shackleton (1874–1922). The British Antarctic explorer placed the following advertisement in London newspapers in preparation for the National Antarctic Expedition—which subsequently failed to reach the South Pole.

> "MEN WANTED FOR HAZARDOUS JOURNEY. Small wages, bitter cold, long months of complete darkness, safe return doubtful. Honor and recognition in case of success."
>
> —Ernest Shackleton

Shackleton later said of his call for volunteers, "It seemed as though all the men in Great Britain were determined to accompany me, the response was so overwhelming."[1]

I then told my elders, "I'm convinced that we ask too little of God's people. Gone are the days when, without apology, we summoned God's people to an arduous journey like Ernest Shackleton. *The ways we typically invite people to do church and be the church are not compelling enough. We cater to consumers with eye-candy instead of challenging Christians to live courageously for Christ.*"

I continued, "What if, together as a congregation, we searched God's Word for His compelling mission, vision, passion, and commission (MVP-C) for our church in our community? What if we did it in a Christ-focused, other-centered, biblically based manner that rallied people like Shackleton did?" I then wondered if such a calling might sound like this.

> "GOD'S PEOPLE WANTED FOR ARDUOUS JOURNEY. No human wages, but the internal reward of joy and the eternal reward of hearing, 'Well done!' Bitter cold and long months of complete darkness because servanthood is lonely. Safe return of your spirit guaranteed. Complete safety doubtful because in this world we will

1. Roland Huntford, *Shackleton* (London: Hodder & Stoughton, 1985), 362, 365.

have tribulation, and all who attempt to lead a godly life will be persecuted. Honor and recognition guaranteed from God. Henceforth there is laid up for you the crown of righteousness."

—Your Elders

Not Your Father's Vision Casting

When these godly elders glimpsed a vision of vision catching and casting, they became as excited as I was. We became champions for the MVP-C (Mission, Vision, Passion, Commission) process. Together, we helped our congregation see what envisioning was and was not about.

- Vision catching and casting is *not* about catering to consumers; rather, it challenges committed Christians to follow Christ for God's glory. Envisioning involves a biblically based, Christ-centered, God-focused process of determining God's will for our congregation in our community.

- Vision catching and casting is *not* dictatorial Moses-like vision handed down from on high; it is *not* so democratic that it becomes a pooling of ignorance; rather, it requires humble leaders facilitating a congregation-wide dialogue. Envisioning involves leaders and members together searching God's Word for His wisdom for their ministry.

- Vision catching and casting is *not* secular marketing strategies or worldly business principles; rather, it follows a biblical theology and methodology of discerning God's will congregationally. Envisioning involves searching the Scriptures to become captivated by God's specific calling for our church in our community for God's glory.

- Vision catching and casting is *not* a waste of time; rather, the envisioning process produces further unity and maturity as the body grows together into Christ the Head. Envisioning results in an increasingly clear picture of God's mission, vision, passion, and commission for our church in our community.

I don't know your past experiences related to the envisioning process. Nor can I guess your visceral, "gut" reaction to "vision talk." I do know that I have experienced the joy of an entire congregation, like the men of Great Britain, determined to accompany their leaders in an overwhelming response to catching God's vision. This is why I long to see you equipped to lead God's people in jointly crafting a compelling MVP-C Statement.

Now that you have caught God's vision for the entire church (chapter one), and examined the current state of your church and community (chapter two), you are ready to catch and cast God's dream for your specific church in your unique community. To accomplish that, we need to understand *what* an MVP-C Statement is and *why* it is so vital (chapter three). Then we need to learn *how to* jointly craft a biblical counseling ministry MVP-C Statement (chapter four).

Capturing Your Biblical Calling

Church ministry can be filled with activities that seem disjointed and disconnected. We sometimes wonder, "What's the big picture? Where are we headed? What's our biblical purpose?" The MVP-C process addresses this confusion by bringing focus to our ministries.

People who write and speak on envisioning use different terms in various ways. I'll be the first to acknowledge that MVP-C is *not* inspired. What follows is one way to organize and communicate a practical theology that assists God's people to catch and cast God's plan for ministry.

Through the congregational process of envisioning God's ministry, we discover why we do what we do. Envisioning involves:

- Determining our biblical reason for existence (*Mission*).
- Detecting our unique future focus (*Vision*).
- Depicting the essence of who God calls us to be (*Passion*).
- Mapping out how to move from here to there (*Commission*).

Congregational and community diagnosis shows us where we are today.

- *M*ission tells us where we should be according to God's Word.
- *V*ision pictures where God is leading us.
- *P*assion tells us who we are on our journey.
- *C*ommission provides the road map to travel from the present to the future.

Mission: Your Universal God-Given Calling and Purpose— God's Compass

One of the legitimate concerns that some Christians express about the envisioning process is that there is typically little or no Bible or theology involved. To counter that problem, before we launch any ministry, we should examine a biblical theology of that ministry. That is true whether we are planting a church or launching a biblical counseling ministry.

The mission statement process examines what God calls *every* biblical counseling ministry to be. It clarifies God's timeless purpose. Picture how this revolutionizes the mission process. You invite everyone who is interested in your biblical counseling ministry to explore together what the Bible says about biblical counseling in the local church.

A pastor I was consulting with described the benefit. "It's a no-brainer. How can it be a bad thing to bring your team together to study the Scriptures!" He reported later, "Even if we had never launched a biblical counseling ministry, just our time of joint exploration of God's Word would have made the whole process worthwhile. We *became* a team, a family, a group *of* biblical counselors as we studied what the Word says *about* biblical counseling!"

Mission is a Word-saturated, Bible-focused process of answering these questions: "Why do we exist? What is our purpose? What does the Bible say about how we should minister in this area?" Mission answers are *universal*, timeless, and clearly revealed in God's Word—they are always true for everyone.

A biblical mission provides the theological foundation for ministry. It is God's compass pointing true north. To use God's compass, mission statements seek to finish the sentence: "According to the Bible, we exist to . . ." or "According to the Bible, the mission of our church is to . . ."

To help you to understand the MVP-C process, I will provide two sample MVP-C Statements from my pastoral ministry.[2] One is a church-wide statement and the other is a biblical counseling ministry-specific statement. These are simply illustrative, not statements you must use for *your* church.

After several months of congregational interaction about God's Word, our congregation united around the following church-wide mission.

Our Uniontown Bible Church Mission Statement

According to the Bible, the mission of Uniontown Bible Church is to make disciples who love Christ, love the body of Christ, and love the world on behalf of Christ. Therefore, the fivefold purpose of our church is to fulfill the Great Commandment and the Great Commission through:

Discipleship: Equipping God's People
Worship: Exalting and Enjoying God
Fellowship: Encouraging God's People
Stewardship: Empowering God's People
Ambassadorship: Evangelizing the Unsaved

Building upon the congregation-wide mission statement, two years later we developed a biblical counseling mission statement. We called our ministry LEAD (Life Encouragers And Disciplers).

Our LEAD Biblical Counseling Ministry Mission Statement

According to the Bible, LEAD exists to equip encouragers and disciplers who lovingly, wisely, and powerfully relate God's truth to human relationships. We will apply Christ's grace to the evils we have suffered and to the sins we have committed. Through the personal ministry of the Word, we will empower one another to grasp the truth that:

2. To view the complete MVP-C Statements, see Appendices 3.1 and 3.2.

It's normal to hurt (Rom. 12:15; 2 Cor. 1:3–9);
It's possible to hope (Rom. 8:28; 2 Cor. 1:8–11);
It's horrible to sin, but wonderful to be forgiven (Rom. 1–6);
It's supernatural to mature (Rom. 7–15).

Vision: Your Unique Ministry Dream and DNA— Your Fingerprint

In the envisioning process, you travel from the present (mission) to the future (vision). You move from the universal and biblical (mission) to the unique and contextual (vision). Your mission focuses on the purpose of your church or ministry, while your vision focuses on the projected future state of your church or ministry. You ask, "How do we move forward as we advance His mission? How has God shaped us to complete His mission?"

It is helpful to picture vision as a future dream that seeks to glimpse a better future. When Disney opened the Epcot Center in Florida, someone leaned over to Mike Vance, creative director of Disney Studios, and whispered, "It's really too bad that Walt didn't live to see this." To which Vance replied, "He did see it. That's why it's here." To focus on this better future, vision statements seek to finish the sentence: *It is our dream to . . .*

It also helps to see vision as a church's DNA or fingerprint. No two are alike. That is why in the vision process we ask, "How does our unique congregation use its distinctive gift-mix to fulfill our special calling in our specific community?" It is also why I have launched three very different biblical counseling ministries in three very different congregations.

Vision answers are idiosyncratic—they apply uniquely to your congregational ministry team in your setting. Vision orients your congregation to your sovereign gifting and to the profound thirst of your community. You determine your ministry vision by prayerfully and jointly pondering your congregational SWORD Heart Exam, your community diagnosis, and your biblical mission. At Uniontown Bible Church, as we walked through this process, we co-created a vision statement that united our congregation around the following jointly pursued future dream.

Our Uniontown Bible Church Vision Statement

It is our DREAM to be a dynamic family, creatively and relevantly sharing Christ's grace with our neighbors in Carroll County and beyond. We will skillfully equip one another through small-group and one-another discipleship ministries that empower us to build loving relationships that last through all the storms of life.

Our biblical counseling vision statement built upon our congregational vision.

Our LEAD Biblical Counseling Ministry Vision Statement

It is our DREAM to be a dynamic family of soul caregivers and spiritual directors who encourage one another through the personal ministry of the Word to turn upward in worship of our Father to find grace to help in our suffering and sin, and to turn outward in fellowship with our brothers and sisters to give and receive Christ's grace.

Passion: Your Captivating Ministry Identity and Imprint— Your Heartbeat

Mission is our universal calling—where God wants us. Vision is our unique future—where God is leading us. Passion is our captivating identity—*who* we are as we serve Christ together. We can picture passion as a pithy phrase capturing and communicating the essence of who we are as we fulfill God's calling and our ministry dream.

Passion communicates what we will die for and therefore what we will live for. Passion is our ultimate purpose statement. For my ministry, RPM Ministries, I have captured it as *Changing Lives with Christ's Changeless Truth*. For my life, I have pictured it with one word: *Coach*. I am writing this book because the passion of my life is to coach people to coach others.

Passion statements answer the question, "How do we convey our mission and vision in a compelling way?" Passion answers are creative, imaginative, and memorable. Passion statements typically develop out of prayerful, joint pondering where someone has something of an "Aha!" experience.

For our church, after three months of studying our biblical mission and catching God's vision, one of our deacons had just such an experience. He reported, "We've been praying about this and thinking about this. Last night on the way home, it hit me. What do you think of this? *A Loving Place to Grow in Grace.*" We didn't have to think much more. That caught the essence of who we wanted to be as we moved into the future for God's glory. As one of our elders said, "That's it! That's us!"

Our Uniontown Bible Church Passion Statement

A Loving Place to Grow in Grace

In a similar way, our LEAD biblical counseling ministry united around the following passion statement.

Our LEAD Biblical Counseling Ministry Passion Statement

Sharing Christ's Grace Face-to-Face

Commission: Your Strategic Ministry Action Plan— Your MAP

In my consulting ministry, I have found that few people start with a mission process focused on biblical theology. I have also discovered that most churches end the process before the commission statement. The lack of a biblical foundation is a major reason some churches hesitate to start an envisioning process. The lack of a strategic plan (commission statement) causes some churches to believe that the envisioning process was wasted time.

The commission statement addresses how, *in practice*, you fulfill the mission, vision, and passion. That explains why I place the hyphen after the MVP and before the C. A well-crafted commission statement maps out how we become an MVP ministry.

A commission statement provides the strategy for getting from here to there, how you will "pull it off" and keep your ministry going and growing. Picture the commission statement as a signpost, directional markers, or a GPS. It is your MAP—*Ministry Action Plan*.

I find it instructive that Jesus provided exactly such a map for His disciples. Jesus fulfilled His mission by preaching and teaching the good news (Matt. 9:35). He pursued His vision as He saw the crowds and had compassion on them because they were like sheep without a shepherd (Matt. 9:36). He followed His passion of being the Chief Shepherd by calling His disciples to become under-shepherds (Matt. 9:37–38).

Then Jesus did something that we sometimes miss. "These twelve Jesus sent out with the following instructions" (Matt. 10:5a). For the next thirty-seven verses Jesus drew His disciples a map—a ministry action plan. He organized the organism. He ad-ministrated the ministry. To His relational and spontaneous compassion, Jesus added a relational and specific commission.

Our commission, like His, should answer questions such as: "What is our strategy? What is our action plan? How will we work cooperatively to fulfill God's call?" Commission answers are practical while including the big picture. They don't describe every step (that's more tactical than strategic). Instead, they outline the journey by providing signposts. To convey this practical-yet-broad perspective, commission statements strive to complete the sentence *We will seek to fulfill our mission, vision, and passion through* . . .

Our Uniontown Bible Church Commission Statement

We will seek to fulfill our MVP through mutually overseeing the equipping of God's family as servant leaders, modeling maturity, mentoring disciple-makers, managing ministers and ministries, and mending the flock.

We will mutually equip one another to lovingly evangelize the community for Christ, we will encourage the congregation toward vital connection with Christ and the body of Christ, and we will empower one another to become makers of disciple-makers.

Two years later we stated our LEAD Biblical Counseling Ministry commission as follows:

Our LEAD Biblical Counseling Ministry Commission Statement

We will seek to fulfill our LEAD MVP through the 4Es of envisioning, enlisting, equipping, and empowering a congregation of spiritual friends, biblical counselors, and small-group ministers.

We will comprehensively equip soul caregivers and spiritual directors in the 4Cs of biblical *content*, Christlike *character*, counseling *competence*, and Christian *community* so they can sustain, heal, reconcile, and guide individuals, couples, and families in our congregation and community to know Christ, grow in Christ, and become Christlike disciple-makers.

Each of the components of our commission statement contained operational definitions that we then used to chart our journey forward. For example, envisioning, enlisting, equipping, and empowering suggested for us the tactical plans you are learning in this book. They became our map throughout each step of our journey to help us plan and assess our progress.

Disciple-Making Champions:
Pastor Greg Cook, Soul Care Pastor, and Leigh Ann Stull,
Soul Care Minister, Christ Chapel Bible Church

Pastor Greg Cook and Leigh Ann Stull oversee the Soul Care training ministry at Christ Chapel Bible Church in Fort Worth, Texas. In his doctorate dissertation, Pastor Cook assessed how his congregation, in particular staff leaders, viewed the Soul Care ministry and perceived the need(s) for biblical counseling. Their Soul Care team used that information, their biblical studies, and their joint reflection to develop their purpose statements.

Their mission statement affirms:

> Soul Care exists to glorify God by caring for sufferers, restoring sinners, and equipping the saints.

They explain, "Our fundamental purpose is to create disciples. We exist to equip the body of Christ to care for others within the church and in the community so that they will in turn take the comfort they have received from Christ and help and train others how to do the same."

Their vision is:

> To stretch *every* involved person from the threshold of their spiritual pilgrimage toward becoming a fully developing follower of Christ.

In describing to their church leaders the outworking of their vision, they note, "Clearly there are quite a few for whom no readily available ministry exists that could 'stretch' them. We seek to heal and restore the lost and wounded of our flock so that they may become active contributors to the ministry. This ministry seeks to go after the one that has wandered away from the 99."

Though they do not list a passion statement per se, they clearly have a passion. When asked to describe their biblical counseling training ministry in one brief phrase, they choose one word. When asked to define biblical counseling, they choose the same word:

Discipleship.

Their version of a commission statement revolves around a sequence of caring, restoring, and equipping. The following figure shows how they picture the sequence.

In their words, "We make sure that people are initially cared for, work toward having them restored to God and to others, and then train them so that they can in turn care for others. Our ultimate goal in the supervision of our lay counselors is that we have experienced lay counselors leading the supervision groups and then the staff oversees those key leaders." They map out their ministry training commission in detail. They include five core components (training of soul care ministers, ministry and staff support, personal ministry, specialized small groups, and marriage mentoring), each with underlying stages and process plans.

Thinking Biblically about Ministry

It is not enough to know what M, V, P, and C mean. More importantly, we need a biblical answer to the question, "Why is an MVP-C Statement so vital?"

Everyone Has an MVP-C; Some Let the Bible Shape It

We commit the time and energy to develop an MVP-C Statement because something always guides our choices about how we do church and ministry. Some develop their MVP-C purposefully and biblically; others don't realize or understand what guides them. In my consulting, I have detected at least seven factors that influence church decision-making, either on their own or combined: tradition, the world, negative people, the neighboring church, finances, consensus, and the pastor's opinion.

Some churches allow tradition to lead them, rather than letting the Bible shape their direction. Ben Franklin astutely noted, "The past is quite valuable as a guide, but dangerous as a hitching post." We have all heard the seven last words of the church: "We've never done it that way before." When assessing a congregation-wide or ministry-specific direction, we would be wise to ask: "How did that tradition develop? Is it biblical? Is what we are doing and where we are heading what God wants for us?"

Some churches allow the world to guide them, rather than letting the Bible shape their purpose. This can be fad-oriented: what's the latest fad, trend, or bandwagon we can jump on? Others are felt-need-oriented: what do people want that we can give them? Still others are relevance-oriented: what's relevant to our culture? I have already indicated that we need to be good students of our congregation, community, and culture. However, like Jesus and Paul, the Bible must direct how we communicate God's changeless message to our changing times.

Some churches seem to run more on the fuel of negative people than on guidance learned from God's Word. The "squeaky wheel gets the grease." Anyone who has been a church leader has faced the temptation to say, "We can't upset _____." Will we make church decisions in reaction to negativity, or will we determine direction based upon wisdom from the Word? This doesn't imply that we should become defensive about criticism or close our ears to negative feedback. It simply means that we must develop our ministry focus through what we learn from God in His Word and not based upon what we hear from the vocal minority.

Others model their church off the church down the street. We can become shaped by the big-name organization or the big-church orientation. We are tempted to think, "We have to do it the way the best-selling Christian author does it." Or we think, "That church is growing. Let's do church the way they're doing church." While there is nothing wrong with learning from others, there's plenty wrong with plopping someone else's MVP-C focus on your church without doing your own biblical work.

Still others decide how to do church based upon finances. The mentality can become "We do this because it's all we can afford." A past orientation can develop: "Last year's income becomes this year's budget, which becomes this year's vision." Even worse, we can become fear-oriented: "There are giants in the land! We can't do *that*!" Obviously, any MVP-C must be realistic. It must set priorities. However, tight times provide more reason to be sure that every penny spent is directed toward God-shaped ministry.

Some let consensus or "secular democracy" shape the church's envisioning process. Majority rules. I understand congregational government—I was saved and discipled in a Baptist church. I am not disputing that style of church decision-making. Rather, I am raising the issues of pooled ignorance and of decisions guided by human opinions instead of God's Word. Even in churches governed by congregational rule, God still calls spiritual leaders to guide people to use biblical principles to make wise church decisions.

The opposite of consensus is the pastor's opinion or "secular dictatorship." This method reflects a problem that many people have with the way vision casting has frequently been practiced. It is top down, Moses-like. The pastor sees himself as uniquely and directly receiving God's vision for the entire church. Although some popular Christian authors and church leaders teach and practice this method of vision catching and casting, that is not the model I will present. The authority does not lie in a person; the authority lies in God and His Word. The model we will follow suggests facilitative leadership in which mature, equipped, and called church leaders guide the congregation through the process of *jointly* catching and casting God's vision.

But Is It Biblical?

After I shared with my elders these seven factors that influence church direction, they all wholeheartedly agreed that the Bible must shape our purposes. However, some still wondered whether these mission, vision, passion, and commission ideas were biblical. I explained that while we do not find one specific passage that unites these four concepts, we do find systematic biblical support for the envisioning process. Because we were committed to building our ministry on the sufficiency of Scripture, we explored the following biblical theology of envisioning.

Facilitative Envisioning Leadership

First we studied what the Bible teaches about how God makes His people aware of His purposes. Does He give His will directly to one visionary leader or does He call leaders to facilitate an envisioning process? While this wasn't a "hill we would die on," it did have practical ramifications.

Our understanding of mission focused on a biblical theology of God's calling. We believed in the equipping of the saints (Eph. 4:11–16), we believed in a team of equipped equippers (2 Tim. 2:2), and we believed in the priesthood of all believers (1 Tim. 2:5; 1 Peter 2:5), so one elder spoke for us all: "God works through His Word to His people, not just through one individual, no matter how godly or learned."

With Bibles opened, another elder quickly thumbed to Proverbs 15:22. "Plans fail for lack of counsel, but with many advisers they succeed," he read for us all. "We need the combined wisdom of God's people to discern jointly His will for our church," he summarized.

Another elder read portions of the vital decision made by the church in Acts 15, including 15:22. "Then the apostles and elders, with the whole church, decided to choose some of their own men and send them to Antioch." "Clearly," this elder stated, "the leaders facilitated a process that actively engaged the people of God."

Yet another elder said, in his typical to-the-point style, "We don't get to make this stuff up. God's Word tells us how to function as a church." He then read 1 Timothy 3:14–15. "I am writing you these instructions so that, if I am delayed, you will know how people ought to conduct themselves in God's household, which is the church of the living God." Our ever-frank elder continued, "Since the Bible is our authority, no one person can hoard the process of setting our ministry direction as a congregation."

Based upon these principles and others, we determined together that we would engage in facilitative envisioning leadership. We would not abdicate our role of shepherding (1 Peter 5:1–5), guiding (1 Tim. 3:5; 1 Tim. 5:17), protecting (Acts 20:13–38), and equipping the flock (Eph. 4:11–16), but neither would we rob from our flock the privilege of studying with us God's mission, vision, passion, and commission for our church.

God's Planning and Ours

Next we probed what the Bible says about planning and purposing. One elder read Jeremiah 29:11. "'For I know the plans I have for you,' declares the LORD, 'plans to prosper you and not to harm you, plans to give you hope and a future.'" Pastor Steve Viars, whom I introduced you to as one of our Disciple-Making Champions, derives the following principle from this passage. He says, "We all know that God has a plan—a strategic plan that will be carried out to perfection and on time. God is the ultimate planner. His Word gives us the instruction, motivation, cautions, and consequences (both good and bad) for planning. In many places, His Word models strategic planning and accomplishing a God-given goal."

Our elder board also examined in some detail the meaning of Proverbs 29:18. "Where there is no revelation, the people cast off restraint; but blessed is he who keeps the law." In the context of wisdom literature, we interpreted that verse to mean that we have two choices when it comes to planning: to do what is right in God's eyes as revealed in His Word, or to do what is right in our own eyes.

We applied that truth in conjunction with Proverbs 19:21. "Many are the plans in a man's heart, but it is the LORD's purpose that prevails." God wants us to plan—according to His plans. And, as we saw in 1 Timothy 3:14–15, we have God's plan for His people outlined in His Word. One elder recapped our thoughts: "A church without a theology of ministry is like a ship without a rudder or a hiker without a compass. Our mission, vision, passion, and commission study will provide the spiritual glasses so we do what is right in God's sight."

God's Word and the Mission of the Church

Building upon our first two studies, it was easy for our elder ministry team to see that God wanted every church and every ministry team to understand its God-given mission. We quickly isolated several church-wide mission statements such as Matthew 22:34–40; Matthew 28:16–20; Acts 2:42–47; Ephesians 4:11–16; and the Pastoral Epistles. These became the foundation for leading our church in a joint development of our congregational mission statement.

Later, motivated by our study, we joined together to do a thorough examination of God's mission, vision, passion, and commission for our elder ministry team. We studied specific passages related to elders, pastors, and shepherds to develop the following Elder Ministry Team Mission Statement.[3]

Our Elder Ministry Team Mission Statement

According to God's Word, our elder ministry team exists to disciple one another as servant leaders who oversee, empower, and equip our Father's family to reproduce in themselves and others Christlike love for Christ, Christians, and those who do not yet know Christ.

3. To view the complete MVP-C Statement, see Appendix 3.3.

God's Word and the Vision of the Church

Exploring mission was easy. However, we started off with a little more debate regarding whether the Bible teaches that every person, every church, and every ministry team has a unique purpose, fingerprint, and DNA. Then, even without looking at the verses, one elder paraphrased Psalm 139:13–14, Jeremiah 1:4–10, and Ephesians 2:10. "We're each fearfully and wonderfully made. God told Jeremiah that He uniquely formed him in the womb for a specific purpose that God clearly laid out from all eternity. And we know that we are each God's workmanship—His poem—designed for a special purpose no one else can fill."

We then looked at the seven churches in Revelation 2–3 (as chapter two noted). We observed how each of the seven churches had unique ministry emphases, strengths, and weaknesses.

One of our elders then mentioned how the Bible teaches that the Spirit sovereignly assembles the exact gift-mix of every congregation (1 Cor. 12:1–31). Another chimed in with the message of 1 Peter 4:10. "Each one should use whatever gift he has received to serve others, faithfully administering God's grace in its various forms."

Another elder highlighted the apostle Paul's principles and practice. "Paul said that he became all things to all people so that by all means some might be saved," he said, paraphrasing 1 Cor. 9:19–23. Then we traced Paul's very different ministry methods throughout Acts—all based upon Paul's awareness of the uniqueness of the culture in each city he entered. Paul's practice concurred with his specific calling, which Paul described as "the field God has assigned to us" (2 Cor. 10:13).

Convinced of the biblical wisdom behind the vision process, we later jointly developed our distinctive elder ministry team vision statement.

Our Elder Ministry Team Vision Statement

It is God's plan for us to be a team of humble, caring, loving leaders united in Christ and committed to prayerfully discerning our Father's will for His family. We will mentor faithful disciple-makers, coach committed ministers, and shepherd God's flock.

God's Word and the Passion of the Church

We were a bunch of skeptical elders, so it was easy to wonder out loud, "Passion statement? Where do we see anything like that in the Scriptures?" Then we started to brainstorm passages where the Bible captures the essences of individuals, churches, or ministries in succinct, captivating wording. We thought of Joshua 1:9. "Be strong and courageous." That passionate theme encapsulates Joshua's entire life.

We meditated upon Philippians 1:21. "For to me, to live is Christ and to die is gain." That scarlet thread runs throughout Paul's whole ministry. Paul develops his passion further in Philippians 3:13–14. He specifically communicates the "one thing" he lives for, the one purpose he is willing to die for: pressing for the prize of the high calling of God in Christ Jesus. Paul succinctly expressed to the Ephesian elders the one race he wanted to finish: "testifying to the gospel of God's grace" (Acts 20:24). Paul's passion was laser-focused: "the apostle to the Gentiles" (Rom. 11:13).

Paul could abridge the passion of the saints at Thessalonica with the phrase: "your work produced by faith, your labor prompted by love, and your endurance inspired by hope" (1 Thess. 1:3). Jesus shared His eternal passion: "the Son of Man did not come to be served, but to serve, and to give His life as a ransom for many" (Matt. 20:28).

These biblical insights and many more led our elder team to craft a statement of our succinct passion.

Our Elder Ministry Team *Passion* Statement

Servant Leaders Serving Our Leader

God's Word and the Commission of the Church

We explored a number of commission statements, including the Great Commission (Matt. 28:16–20). We detected not only the calling or mission, but the commission, the *how-to and the follow-through*: going, making disciples, baptizing, and teaching.

95

We noticed the same detail in what Paul described as "the commission God gave me" (Col. 1:25). God called Paul to present to the Colossians "the Word of God in its fullness" *through* making known the glorious riches of Christ, proclaiming Christ, admonishing and teaching everyone with all wisdom, presenting everyone mature in Christ, and laboring and struggling with all of Christ's energy (Col. 1:25–29).

It was these and other scriptural statements of commission that we thought of a year later when we summarized our ministry team commission.

Our Elder Ministry Team Commission Statement

God is calling and equipping us to fulfill our Elder Ministry Team MVP *through* ad-ministrating the ministry, organizing the organism, and overseeing the equipping of our church family by modeling maturity, mentoring disciple-makers, and mending the flock.

Our biblical study led to a systematic theology of mission, vision, passion, and commission. We weren't tied to "MVP-C" as an inspired outline, but we were convinced that it condensed a powerful way to summarize a consistent concept woven throughout the Bible. We were now a united team equipped and motivated to champion the MVP-C process.

Disciple-Making Champions
Pastor Deepak Reju, Pastor of Biblical Counseling,
Capitol Hill Baptist Church

Pastor Deepak Reju equips biblical counselors in America's capital at Capitol Hill Baptist Church (CHBC). A true pastor-theologian, Pastor Reju has a *Vision for Biblical Counseling at Capitol Hill Baptist Church* that develops nine scriptural pillars "meant to be building blocks that uphold and sustain a counseling ministry over the long haul." These pillars "paint a picture—a vision for what biblical counseling could look like" at CHBC.

These nine pillars combine to present a biblical mission and a congregation-specific vision for biblical counseling. The biblical counseling ministry at CHBC will be: (1) God-glorifying; (2) Word-founded and -grounded; (3) Christ-centered and -honoring; (4) serious about sin; (5) serious about suffering; (6) church-based; (7) discipleship-focused; (8) change-oriented; and (9) lovingly partnering with other equipping resources.

At CHBC their passion is a culture of discipleship—to embed counseling into the mainstream of discipleship. Biblical counseling "is a particular form of discipleship, where Christians pull off the river for a period of time to focus on the 'problems' that are slowing their movement down the river. It's a time to stop and ask, 'What slows us down from growing closer to our Savior?'"

As a theologian-practitioner, Pastor Reju transitions seamlessly between biblical theology categories and practical theology realities. To his nine pillars he adds four strategies (his version of a commission statement). Together, they provide "a feel for what a Christ-centered vision for biblical counseling could look like in our church, and also answer some of those pesky questions" about how that counseling ministry functions.

While readily confessing that there are many ways to approach counseling in a local church, for his particular congregation and community he suggests four strategy components. CHBC seeks to fulfill its mission, vision, and passion for biblical counseling through the following: (1) one-on-one counseling ministry conducted by the pastoral staff and trained counselors designed to move people back into the broader discipleship mode; (2) small-group ministry focused on aspects of the gospel that encourage members who are struggling; (3) lay members who are trained in ongoing, informal, one-another ministry; and (4) lay counselors who are trained for formal, structured biblical counseling. To each of these broad commission strategies, Pastor Reju adds several specific tactics and process steps that flesh out the how-to of their commission.

Commencement: God's Plumb Line

What does it mean to be a person or a church after God's own heart? David was such a man. Reflecting on David's life and death, Luke recorded, "For when David had served God's purpose in his own generation, he fell asleep" (Acts 13:36a). What a fascinating, crisp portrait of mission and vision. How reminiscent of 1 Chronicles 12:32, and the men of Issachar "who understood the times and knew what Israel should do." God calls each of us to find and fulfill His explicit purpose (mission) in our distinctive time and setting (vision).

For such a time as this, in such a manner as this, God has called every congregation and every ministry team. In the fullness of time, our time-God orchestrates the mission, vision, passion, and commission of every biblical counseling ministry team. Our first role is to trust that God desires us to know His universal calling and our unique exercise of that calling. God reveals His plans to His people (Amos 3:7) as a plumb line (Amos 7:7–8). God insists that we build our ministries true to plumb by developing a biblical theology for our specific ministry—what we are calling an MVP-C Statement.

You will recall that one of my elders initially sensed that the MVP-C process might smack of being "seeker-sensitive" and "man-centered." That same elder, after working through our biblical study and working on an elder MVP-C, a congregational MVP-C, and a LEAD biblical counseling MVP-C, had a very different take. "This biblical process has pointed us true north. Never again will I launch any ministry without first going to the Word as my compass. This has been the most Bible-focused and Christ-centered time I've ever spent as a church leader."

The starting point for the MVP-C process involves knowing what mission, vision, passion, and commission are all about. Becoming a champion for the process requires learning the practical and biblical value of developing an MVP-C Statement.

Something imperative remains: the how-to. In chapter four we learn how to facilitate and lead a biblical counseling ministry team through the steps of jointly catching and casting God's mission, vision, passion, and commission.

Growing Together: Questions for Reflection, Discussion, and Application

1. Think about the envisioning process:
   a. Before this chapter, what was your "gut reaction" to words like "mission" and "vision statements"?

b. Now that you have read this theological introduction to "vision work," in what ways is your mindset about the envisioning process changing and growing?

2. Think about mission:
   a. Which of the various descriptions and samples of mission embedded in this chapter most resonate with you? How? Why?
   b. In an introductory way, how would you finish the following statement: *According to the Bible, my life and ministry mission is to . . .*

3. Think about vision:
   a. Which of the various descriptions and samples of vision embedded in this chapter most resonate with you? Since vision is unique, what parts do not resonate with you?
   b. In an introductory way, how would you finish the following statement: *In serving Christ and others, I see my life and ministry dream as being to . . .*

4. Think about passion:
   a. Which of the various descriptions and samples of passion embedded in this chapter most resonate with you? How? Why?
   b. In an introductory way, what one phrase captures your life and ministry calling?

5. Think about commission:
   a. Which of the various descriptions and samples of commission embedded in this chapter most resonate with you? How? Why?
   b. In an introductory way, how would you finish the following statement: *I will seek to fulfill my life and ministry mission, vision, and passion through . . .*

4

Living God's Calling

JOINTLY CRAFTING YOUR BIBLICAL COUNSELING MVP-C STATEMENT

For over a dozen years I have had the privilege of serving as the chairman of the Christian Counseling and Discipleship department at Capital Bible Seminary, where students bring to the classroom tremendous wisdom for ministry. Many have entered seminary later in life as career-changers or as seasoned pastors seeking further theological education and ministry training.

Their life experience and ministry involvement make my job much easier. Occasionally one of my younger students with little ministry background will say, "Dr. Kellemen, why do we need to put time into the envisioning process? Can't we move right into recruiting folks, training them, and overseeing them?" I rarely have to answer that question. My established, ministry-savvy students speak up.

I love the response one mature pastor shared as he addressed a student's questions about envisioning. "You're probably too young to remember the moonwalk." This pastor then stood up and demonstrated the moonwalk—the backsliding dance step that presents the illusion of being pulled backward while attempting to move forward.

Sitting down, he explained, "In ministry you can take the time up front to do the hard and wise work of preparation—of getting it right the first time. Or you can take twice as much time later doing the ministry moonwalk—being pulled backward while you spend all your time cleaning up the mess you made." Envisioning minimizes the need for the ministry moonwalk.

As I have noted, the first church I ministered in was an urban-suburban, white-collar church of three thousand. The second church I served was a rural, blue-collar church of one hundred that God grew to three hundred. The third church I pastored was a suburban, white-collar/blue-collar church of five hundred.

The envisioning processes in these three churches led to three quite distinct biblical counseling ministries. The first included a two-year training program leading to a full-blown individual and group counseling ministry where scores of people were counseled every week in formal sessions and group meetings. The second resulted in time-limited equipping leading to informal but focused spiritual friendships occurring throughout the church and community. The third gave rise to a network of equipped believers who used their training in semi-formal settings such as spiritual friends, small-group leaders, and ministers of mercy (hospital visitation, tele-care).

Your church setting is different from any of the churches I have served, different from any of the thousands of churches where my students have ministered, and different from the hundreds of churches where I have consulted. This chapter teaches you how to launch a biblical counseling ministry that fits your particular church. You will learn to translate the biblical principles of mission, vision, passion, and commission into a practical, step-by-step process that equips you to lead a team to catch and cast a biblical counseling ministry MVP-C.

Sadly, many try to launch biblical counseling ministries without a biblical purpose, a clear future focus, a well-defined sense of identity, or a workable plan of action. You are about to learn how to lead a team to discover:

- What makes biblical counseling truly biblical? (Mission)
- What is our unique biblical counseling calling in our church and community? (Vision)
- Who are we as we provide biblical counseling? (Passion)
- What is our MAP (Ministry Action Plan) as we move forward as biblical counselors? (Commission)

Forming Your Biblical Counseling Envisioning Team

I love God's sovereignty. As I finalized the outline for this chapter, I received an e-mail from two people (we'll call them Brock and Michelle) in the early stages of launching a biblical counseling ministry. Their questions aligned perfectly with my planned outline.

"Bob," they e-mailed, "we have four questions we're trying to sort through. First, we already have a congregation-wide mission/vision statement, so what's the relationship between that and how we develop our ministry-specific MVP-C? Second, how do we enlist a team to a mission and vision when we want them to help us to craft that mission and vision? Third, who should be involved in the process of developing the biblical counseling MVP-C Statement? Should it be the pastors, elders, deacons, the whole congregation? Fourth, how long should we allot for the envisioning process, including assessment?"

Brock and Michelle's four questions correspond to the four actions you need to take to form and facilitate a biblical counseling envisioning team:

- Building the foundation for your envisioning team
- Enlisting your envisioning team
- Organizing your envisioning team
- Structuring your envisioning team

Building the Foundation for Your Envisioning Team

When Brock and Michelle told me that their church already had a congregation-wide mission and vision statement that people rallied around, I told them to count themselves blessed. Ideally, a biblical coun-

102

seling ministry MVP-C should build upon any church-wide statements of purpose, mission, vision, and values. Specific ministries should never reinvent the wheel.

In chapter three you saw a clear relationship in mindset and wording between the church-wide MVP-C and the two ministry-specific MVP-C Statements (LEAD biblical counseling ministry and elder ministry team). That is no accident. Throughout the process we asked ourselves how our specific ministry could come under, support, and advance the mission, vision, passion, and commission of our church.

The envisioning process works best when leaders develop three types of MVP-C Statements:

- A Personal Ministry MVP-C Statement
- A Congregation-Wide MVP-C Statement
- Ministry-Specific MVP-C Statements

Every pastor, elder, deacon, and ministry director should craft a personal ministry MVP-C Statement. I still remember what motivated me to craft mine. I was in my first pastoral ministry (yes, it would have been better to have one *before* then) and I had just finished counseling a couple. I looked at my to-do list, pondered all the spinning plates, and asked myself, "What am I supposed to focus on in ministry?" I wasn't asking, "What activity do I do next?" Instead, I was asking, "What calling drives how I decide where to concentrate my energies as a pastor?"

Over the next several months, I stumbled and bumbled through what became the MVP-C process. I crafted a statement of personal ministry mission that helped me identify what the Bible says God calls every pastor to be and do. I developed a personal ministry vision that helped me clarify how I could use my specific gifts in my unique setting to fulfill God's calling. I prayerfully created a personal ministry passion statement: *speaking the truth in love*. Over the years that has matured into my passion to be a *coach who equips others to speak the truth in love*. I created a personal ministry commission—a detailed map of how I would accomplish my mission, vision, and passion.[1] It was *after* that process that I led my team to create a biblical counseling MVP-C Statement.

A team of church leaders each with a personal ministry MVP-C Statement is well prepared to lead a church in developing a congregation-wide MVP-C Statement. And a church with a congregation-wide MVP-C Statement is the best context in which to build a ministry-specific MVP-C Statement.

A logical and practical question arises: what does a biblical counseling ministry do if the church does not have a clear statement of mission and vision? First, avoid becoming too attached to the lingo in this book. Remember that MVP-C is simply one way of summarizing a common process. Don't panic if your church doesn't use my language. Second, most churches have at least some documents related to mission. You should be able to identify some statements of purpose.

A more specific question may surface: what if our church does not consciously follow a biblically developed mission and vision? If you are *the* pastor, *a* pastor, an elder, a deacon, or a ministry leader, then humbly suggest that the church either revisit the existing statements or jointly develop a fresh, biblical statement of purpose.

In the absence of any clearly followed biblical statements of purpose, as the leader of the biblical counseling ministry team, share with the church leadership your desire to develop a ministry-specific MVP-C Statement. Invite them to participate. I have often seen this create a pocket of excellence that motivated a church to develop a congregation-wide MVP-C Statement.

Enlisting Your Envisioning Team

I recommend avoiding the tired method of recruiting people to fill an opening. Instead, recruit people to a compelling mission and vision. This relates to Brock and Michelle's second question: "how do we enlist a team to a mission and vision when we want them to help us craft that mission and vision?"

---

1. See Appendix 4.1 for my Pastoral Ministry MVP-C Statement from my ministry at Uniontown Bible Church as congregational discipleship pastor ("senior pastor").

Start by clearly stating the function of this team—it is an *envisioning* team and not an *equipping* team. This group may not provide the training when you get to that stage. And not everyone in this group may decide to receive the biblical counseling training. Members of the envisioning team are working with you to think through what a biblical counseling ministry could look like in your church and community. To communicate the specific purpose and function of this team, you may want to call it the Envisioning Team, the Launch Team, or what we called it: *SALT*—*S*trategic *A*ssessment and *L*eadership *T*eam.

As you enlist team members, have just enough of a plan to give everyone some direction, but not so much that anyone is left out. This is the essence of facilitative leadership in the envisioning process. You are calling people to a big-picture idea. You are inviting people to join you in honing a somewhat general dream of every member a disciple-maker and of equipped members providing one-another biblical counseling for your congregation and community.

Encourage each team member to treat the team as a small group. This shifts the mindset from a work team oriented only toward getting a task done to a ministry group oriented toward experiencing one-another ministry as you plan for your church's one-another ministry.

Organizing Your Envisioning Team

This leads to Brock and Michelle's third question regarding who should be involved. Should it be the pastors, elders, deacons, some members, or the whole congregation? The answer will be different for every church. To sort through the answers for your church, consider three concentric circles.

- Circle One: Church Leadership—Pastor(s), elders, deacons, ministry directors
- Circle Two: Biblical Counseling Ministry Team—People passionate about one-another ministry and disciple-making
- Circle Three: The Congregation—People who might become involved in the ministry and who might receive help from the ministry

105

You may find yourself in all three circles, or at the very least the second two. If you are not a part of the first circle—church leadership—then from the start be sure to take your biblical counseling dreams to your church leadership. A biblical counseling ministry will not thrive in a church if the church leadership, especially the senior pastor, is not actively engaged. I feel so strongly about this that I will not sign a consulting contract unless the senior pastor and other church leaders agree to be involved in the consultation.

If you are the senior pastor, be sure to engage your church leadership team from the ground floor. Disaster is lurking anytime a biblical counseling ministry remains the passion of only one point person. A passionate point person is needed, but that person, regardless of title, needs the support of the rest of the church leadership, and that person needs a team.

The biblical counseling ministry point person must ask several questions regarding this first circle: "How can I obtain the passionate support of the church leadership? Who among the church leadership team should be invited to be part of the biblical counseling envisioning team? What role on the envisioning team should each person play?"

With circle one in place, focus on building the remainder of your biblical counseling ministry team. If you do not have a team, then stop. Pray for a team of like-minded people passionate about one-another ministry—disciple-making, comforting the hurting, and care-fronting those struggling against besetting sins. Identify people in your congregation who already provide spiritual friendship, offer encouragement, visit the sick, and take an active lead in "recovery" group ministries. Personally invite them to join your core envisioning team.

With the third circle, the congregation at large, you have several options. Option one is to send a congregation-wide invitation to join the envisioning team. Decide whether everyone who desires to join the team is automatically in or whether there is a size limit. If you limit the size, then first-come, first-in is the best selection screening method.

Option two is to host biblical counseling envisioning meetings open to anyone in the church. I have facilitated meetings with more than one hundred people where we have worked on MVP-C Statements.

Option three is for your envisioning team to interact with, engage, and interview select members of the congregation to seek their input and insight. Design these as follow-up meetings to the SWORD Heart Exam, where you now ask specific questions related to biblical counseling mission, vision, passion, and commission.

Structuring Your Envisioning Team

As navigator of a crew, you now have your sailing orders. Here is your structured goal as you form your biblical counseling envisioning team: *facilitate the development of a biblical counseling ministry MVP-C Statement that is in sync with your church-wide MVP-C and that is crafted by some combination of church leaders, people passionate about biblical counseling, and members of the congregation.*

Anytime you ask people to join you on a voyage, it is only fair to estimate the length of your trip. Brock and Michelle wisely asked how long they should allot for the envisioning process. When you include the congregational and community assessment, plus each step in catching and casting the MVP-C, you can anticipate six to nine months for the start-up phase. When you also factor in the change-management process (chapter five) and the development of your enlisting/recruiting philosophy, policies, and procedures (chapter six), you add an additional three months. Overall you can anticipate a yearlong launch process. While that may seem like a long time, it is much healthier than a two-year moonwalk.

Remember a simple principle for making consistent progress: a team that does not meet is not a team. Your initial pilot envisioning team needs to schedule regular meetings. I recommend at least two meetings each month.

Catching Your Biblical Counseling Ministry MVP-C

Envisioning is a team process where each team member contributes in different ways at different levels. Each team needs a coach—a facilitative leader, a navigator. The following material equips you as the leader of the biblical counseling envisioning team to navigate the process of jointly discovering God's MVP-C for your biblical counseling ministry.

Facilitating the Joint Development of Your Biblical Counseling Mission Statement

Track with me what has occurred so far. Working within the leadership structure of your church, you have a process in place for communicating the big picture: *more than counseling, a vision for the entire church.* With the enthusiastic blessing and active participation of your church leadership, you have recruited a biblical counseling envisioning team. You have used your SWORD Heart Exam to interview members of your congregation and community. And you have analyzed the results in order to diagnose your congregation and community's heart health, culture, current readiness, and specific issues for which biblical counseling is needed.

Prepare Prayerfully and Wisely

As you convene your envisioning team, begin with a time of focused prayer for wisdom, unity, and maturity. Pray that the process itself will draw each team member closer to one another and closer to Christ. Pray for discernment to understand what God's Word says about biblical counseling in the local church.

If you haven't already, teach your team the specific meaning of mission, vision, passion, and commission. With that understanding in place, study together any documents that communicate the mission/purpose of your church.

Examine the Bible's Teaching on Biblical Counseling

Now you are ready to discover the mission of your biblical counseling ministry by studying what makes biblical counseling truly biblical. What is universally true about all biblical counseling ministries in the local church?

This is an exciting time as your team examines what the Bible says about biblical counseling. You want to discern constant, universal, biblically central beliefs that describe God's purpose for the one-another ministry of the Word. As you study the Bible, keep the end in view. Your goal is to complete one of these sentences: *According to the Bible, our biblical counseling ministry exists to . . .* Or: *According to the Bible, the mission of a biblical counseling ministry is to . . .*

Lead your team in brainstorming and collating passages that relate to biblical counseling. Or, as a facilitative leader, provide a collated list (such as the one that follows) and prepare a study guide/discussion sheet. In Appendix 4.2, you will find a sample discussion guide: Discovering Our Biblical Counseling Mission.

Disciple-Making Champions

Foundational Biblical Counseling Passages

As part of the *4E Ministry Training Strategy Questionnaire*, two dozen best-practice churches answered the question, "What are the Scriptures upon which you founded and base your biblical counseling ministry?" Collated below are the fifty passages listed most often. These are the types of passages that your team can study to develop a biblical counseling mission statement.

> Psalm 1:1–2; Proverbs 15:23; Proverbs 18:13, 21; Proverbs 25:11; Proverbs 27:6; Isaiah 9:6; Isaiah 11:1–4; Isaiah 55:11; Matthew 22:34–40; Matthew 28:16–20; Mark 12:30–31; John 1:1–18; John 6:32–33; John 8:38; John 10:10; John 14:15–31; John 17:1–26; Acts 2:40–47; Acts 20:17–38; Romans 6:1–14; Romans 8:1–39; Romans 12:1–2; Romans 12:15; Romans 15:14; 1 Corinthians 12:12–27; 2 Corinthians 1:3–11; 2 Corinthians 3:16–18 and 4:16–18; Galatians 6:1–5; Ephesians 1–3; Ephesians 4:11–16; Ephesians 4:17–24; Ephesians 4:29; Philippians 1:9–11; Colossians 1:25–29; Colossians 2:1–10; Colossians 3:1–16; Colossians 4:2–6; 1 Thessalonians 2:8; 1 Thessalonians 4:13; 1 Thessalonians 5:14; 2 Timothy 2:2; 2 Timothy 2:24–26; 2 Timothy 3:16–17; Hebrews 3:7–16; Hebrews 4:12–16; Hebrews 10:19–25; James 4:1–4; 1 Peter 2:5–9; 2 Peter 1:3–4; 1 John 4:7–21

Many participants included not only specific verses, but also categories or concepts. Collated below are those categories that were listed the most.

109

- One-another
- Body life
- Comforting the suffering
- Counseling the sinning
- Sufficiency of Scripture
- Sanctification and growth in grace
- Listening
- Seeing God's perspective
- Spiritual formation/spiritual discipline
- Verses using *noutheteo* (Greek for "confronting out of concern for change")
- Verses using *parakaleo* (Greek for "comfort," "encourage," "console")

Brainstorm a "Whiteboard" of Common Themes: Storyboarding

For this stage, you need all your facilitative skills. Reconvene your smaller groups for a time of large-group brainstorming. Have access to a whiteboard, blackboard, or flip chart. If you used a discussion guide and a collated list of passages, be sure to ask if there are other passages to study and other questions to ask.

At this point you are not focusing on "your target audience," "the needs of your community," or "your unique gift-mix." That is vision talk, not mission work. For now you are clarifying God's timeless purpose for every biblical counseling ministry in any local church. Include and listen to everyone. Write summaries on the whiteboard. Highlight and organize recurring themes. Keep the conversation moving. Have fun. Work cooperatively.

The end result of the brainstorming session should be a very messy whiteboard. Take a picture of it or somehow capture the essence. Be sure to assign someone to be the recorder or secretary. Make sure everyone has access to a copy of these brainstormed themes. Give the group time to reflect prayerfully on the themes.

Create a Straw-Man First Draft

Then ask each person to draft a straw-man biblical counseling mission statement. Ask one brave soul to volunteer to have his or her draft edited to death. Jointly shape the wording in first-draft, rough form as everyone shares input. Don't worry about getting it perfect.

At some point you need to decide to close the discussing and tweaking. Agree upon and provide each team member a copy of the first draft. After that, it is often wise to adjourn or at least take a break. Ask everyone to craft a second draft during the intervening time.

Craft a Working Second Draft

When you meet again, jointly craft a second draft. Before you start, remind your team of several important points:

- The biblical counseling mission statement needs to advance the church-wide mission.
- This is still a working draft. You will further tweak it as you develop the vision, passion, and commission.
- The overall church leadership team will weigh in on the final wording.

As you did with draft one, have your whiteboard or flip chart ready. Ask someone to share his or her straw-man second draft. Lead the group in editing this draft into an agreed-upon working second draft. Aim at between fifty and one hundred words. Include supporting verses. Keep it concise, clear, and creative.

Chapter three shared sample mission statements from my second church. Below you will find a sample LEAD (Life Encouragers And Disciplers) Biblical Counseling Mission Statement from my first church.[2]

Our LEAD Biblical Counseling Mission Statement

According to the Bible, the mission of LEAD is to equip biblical counselors and small-group leaders to speak the truth in love to people struggling with suffering and sin, in order to promote Christlike maturity in the body of Christ.

2. See Appendix 4.3 for the LEAD Biblical Counseling MVP-C Statement collated onto two pages.

LEAD exists to assist our church to become an equipping center (Eph. 4:11–14), a fully functioning family (Matt. 22:34–40), a Christ-centered community (Heb. 3:7–16; 10:19–25), a healthy body (Eph. 4:15–16), and a "teaching hospital" for soul physicians healing hurting and hardened hearts (Matt. 23:23–26).

Facilitating the Joint Development of Your Biblical Counseling Vision Statement

With a working second draft of your mission in hand, your biblical counseling envisioning team is now ready to start vision catching. Your goal is to facilitate the process of discovering your team's unique biblical counseling ministry dream. What will your DNA, your fingerprint, be? What sets apart your biblical counseling ministry—not as better than, but as distinctive from any other church anywhere on the planet?

Prepare Prayerfully and Strategically

In discovering your vision, the three key words are not "location, location, location," but "prayer, prayer, prayer." Pray that your team will grasp a unified sense of God's dream. Ask, "Father, what are You calling our biblical counseling ministry to be like in our congregation and community as we move forward together into the future?"

Review with your team the difference between mission and vision. Spend time studying the biblical value of mission and vision and share examples of vision in the Bible (see chapter three). Teach your team that vision derives from a combination of prayer, the results of the congregational SWORD Heart Exam, the community diagnosis, the church-wide mission, the biblical counseling mission, and the church-wide vision. Study and discuss these documents. Summarize what they indicate about your special calling in your specific community.

Take DNA Soul Samples

Guide your group to see themselves as servants of the congregation and community. They are not simply pondering, "What is the DNA, the fingerprint, of *our* group?"; they are seeking to represent accurately the uniqueness of your *entire congregation and community*. Rather than determine the looks of a biblical counseling ministry created in *my* image, the group will ask, "How will a biblical counseling ministry match who God has created *our church* to be in *our community*?" There is a world of difference between those two mindsets, and it takes otherworldly humility to maintain the second mindset.

Your first calling as the group leader is to model that other-centered mindset. As you respond to the whiteboard, the straw man, and the rough-draft work, your team needs to see that it's not about you. You are not manipulating them to write the statement you wanted to write all along. It's all about Him. And it's all about your congregation serving your community in His way.

As you "take DNA soul samples" and as you respond to vision-catching probes (see Appendix 4.4 for sample vision-catching probes) about your past, present, and future, respond representatively. Answer the questions *on behalf of* your congregation and community, as you believe they would. This argues for the wise selection of group members who are representative of the diversity in your congregation and community. It also argues for the wisdom of interviewing and/or surveying your congregation and perhaps your community using probing vision-catching questions.

At the very least, you want your team to take some DNA soul samples. Either as a large group or divided into smaller groups, your team members should record their responses to vision-casting probes such as those provided in Appendix 4.4. If you use a list like this, be sure to craft the wording (biblical counseling, one-another ministry, the personal ministry of the Word) in terms that *your* people will understand.

Whiteboard and Straw-Man Your Vision

Once you reconvene everyone into one larger group, follow the same facilitation principles outlined for the mission work when you brainstormed a whiteboard of common themes and created a straw-man draft. As everyone shares, highlight not only recurring themes but also imaginative, pictorial words. Fill the board with adjectives and adverbs.

After a time of sharing, ask each person to produce his or her own rough-draft vision of twenty-five to seventy-five words beginning, *It is the dream of our biblical counseling ministry to . . .* Have one volunteer share, and then allow everyone to "tinker" with it. Tweak it and edit it, emphasizing richly descriptive words that make you, you. Turn this into a first draft and then let it simmer and percolate.

Craft a Working Second Draft

After allowing your first draft to sit either during a break or between meetings, return to craft a working second draft. After someone shares his or her straw-man second draft, remind your team that you want this draft to advance the church-wide vision and to richly communicate in pictorial words what makes your biblical counseling ministry unique in your church and community. Lead your team in crafting a twenty-five- to seventy-five-word creative second draft that points your ministry to a future possible only by the grace and power of God. Below you will find a sample LEAD Biblical Counseling Vision Statement from my second church.

LEAD Biblical Counseling Vision Statement

It is the DREAM of our LEAD ministry to be a maturing team of loving encouragers and dynamic disciplers equipped to make God's house a home.

We will be empowered toward personal maturity, encouraged by biblical community, and equipped for relational ministry to God's family and our community.

Through spiritual maturity, biblical wisdom, and relational skillfulness, we will speak the truth in love so that we all may mature in Christ.

Facilitating the Joint Development of Your Biblical Counseling Passion Statement

In chapter three, I described "passion catching" as something of an "Aha!" experience. You really can't teach that, though you can provide a relational context for it. That relationship begins with Christ as we relate in the body of Christ. Lead your team in praying that you would grasp together with all the saints God's passion for your biblical counseling ministry. Pray, "Father, help us to trust in You with all our hearts and lean not on our own understanding. Help us in all our ways to acknowledge You, so that You will direct our path."

Explore with your team biblical passion statements like the ones listed in chapter three and others such as Joshua 24:15; Nehemiah 2:12; Esther 4:14; Matthew 9:13; Acts 1:8; Acts 9:15; and 2 Timothy 1:6–7. These verses encapsulate the essence of someone's mission and vision—the heart of a passion statement.

Review your biblical counseling ministry mission and vision statements. Also review your church's passion statement (any brief phrase that summarizes your mission). Create a discussion guide for your team with questions such as the following:

- What phrase captures our biblical mission and unique vision?
- Which of the biblical passion statements most resonate with us?
- If we had one phrase to portray who we are to a stranger, what would it be?
- How can we communicate in a memorable way the essence of our calling?
- How can our biblical counseling ministry passion reflect our congregation-wide passion?

Then brainstorm possibilities, being careful not to reject anything. Often the final passion statement is a combination of several partial statements.

At my first church, we shared various phrases: "speaking Christ's truth in love to love like Christ," "encourage one another daily," "relational ministry promoting relational maturity," "equipping every member to minister maturely," "changing lives," "a teaching hospital training soul physicians," "equipping for relational maturity leading to mutual ministry," "making God's house our home," "and relating God's truth to human relationships."

The process was exciting because our summary pictures confirmed that our team understood our mission and vision. Even better, the passion-catching process deepened our understanding of and our commitment to our calling.

We stopped to thank God for His calling and ask Him for further clarity about our passion. Then we left . . . without a final passion phrase . . . for now. When we met next, one of our members shared the passion statement that we all agreed captured us.

LEAD Biblical Counseling *Passion* Statement

Changed People Changing Lives with Christ's Changeless Truth

Disciple-Making Champions

Biblical Counseling Passion Statements

As part of the *4E Ministry Training Strategy Questionnaire*, two dozen best-practice churches answered the question, "If you had to describe your 'biblical counseling' training ministry in one brief phrase, how would you capture the essence?" Collated below are sample passion statements.

- Promoting Heart Change That Brings Life Change
- Returning Biblical Soul Care to the Church
- Transforming Lives by the Word of God, in the Spirit of God, with the Community of God
- Bringing Christlike Comfort to the Hurting and Forgiveness to the Hardened
- Reconnecting the Relationally Disconnected to Christ
- Counseling in Community
- Glorifying God by Caring for Sufferers, Restoring Sinners, and Equipping the Saints
- Training People to Live Life in Biblical Perspective
- PEACE: Pointing People to Christ, Encouraging People to Live Like Christ, Assisting the Hurting, Comforting with the Word, Equipping Disciplers
- Equipping the Church to Make Disciples Using God's Sufficient Word
- Equipping the Saints in Gospel-Centered Counseling Ministry Where They Live

- Equipping the Saints to Live Life with a Healthy Heart
- Equipping Real People to Handle Life Effectively by Handling God's Word Accurately
- Training God's People to Multiply Disciples through Compassionate Biblical Counseling
- Bringing the Hope of Christ to the Hurting
- Connecting the Transforming Power of Christ to Everyday Life
- Personal Change through the Personal Ministry of the Word
- Applying the Gospel to the Deepest Wounds and Breaking the Tightest Bonds of Sin

Facilitating the Joint Development of Your Biblical Counseling Commission Statement

Your Commission Statement is your MAP—*M*inistry *A*ction *P*lan—that guides how you will fulfill your mission, vision, and passion. It summarizes your more detailed ministry training strategy. In your ministry training strategy, you seek to address five components represented by the acronym SMART.

- *S*tructure: What is our overall training strategy?
- *M*inisters/*M*inistries: Who are we training for what ministry?
- *A*bilities/*A*ptitudes: What knowledge, character, skills, and relationships will our trainees need?
- *R*esults: What ministry goals do our ministers focus on?
- *T*arget Participants: Whom do our ministers minister to?

Revisiting the LEAD biblical counseling ministry commission from chapter three shows how we used the SMART MAP.

Our LEAD Biblical Counseling Ministry Commission Statement

We will seek to fulfill our LEAD MVP through the 4Es of envisioning, enlisting, equipping, and empowering a congregation of spiritual friends, biblical counselors, and small-group ministers.

We will comprehensively equip soul caregivers and spiritual directors in the 4Cs of biblical content, Christlike character, counseling competence, and Christian community so they can sustain, heal, reconcile, and guide individuals, couples, and families in our congregation and community to know Christ, grow in Christ, and care like Christ.

- The 4Es of envisioning, enlisting, equipping, and empowering described how we *structured* our LEAD ministry—the big picture we used to launch and lead our ministry.
- We were training people we identified as soul caregivers and spiritual directors (*ministers*) whom we envisioned ministering as spiritual friends, biblical counselors, and small-group leaders (*ministries*).
- We used the 4Cs of content, character, competence, and community to identify four main *abilities* our equipping sought to impart.
- Once trained, we released our ministers for real ministry in the real world where they sustained, healed, reconciled, and guided people to know Christ, grow in Christ, and become Christlike disciple-makers (*results*).
- We wanted them to reach individuals, couples, and families in our congregation and our community (*target participants*).

In working with your team, don't overcomplicate this. If SMART MAP makes your head spin, set it aside; if it helps organize your thinking, wonderful. The main idea is to think through, from the start, concrete, measurable action plans. The failure to outline a workable strategy is the number-one reason MVP Statements fail. Don't waste your work. Plan your work and work your plan.

Structure: Outline Your Overall Training Strategy

With your MVP Statement in hand, guide your team to answer the question, "Specifically, how will we accomplish our mission, vision, and passion?" Use the diagnosis from your assessment process (chapter two) to identify your current strengths, weaknesses, opportunities, and risks. That's where you are now. Your vision is where you want to go. Ask the following questions: "What structures, processes, resources, and plans do we need to develop to get from here to there? What specific steps do we need to take to pull this off successfully for God's glory? How do we outline those steps in measurable ways?" I'm partial to the 4E outline of envisioning, enlisting, equipping, and empowering, but your team can draw any map it desires. Just draw something concrete and practical.

Through my consulting ministry, I have found that in the team/group setting it is wisest to limit your brainstorming to (1) a list of steps, and (2) Commission Statement wording. When your group has accomplished those two goals, then delegate the development of the detailed ministry training strategy. The person who assumes that task could be you as the leader, it could be a smaller group of detailed, process-oriented team members, or it could be an individual team member skilled and experienced in strategic development.

Ministers/Ministries: Identify Whom You Are Training for What Ministry

In my first church, because we had an expansive view of biblical counseling, we envisioned extensive areas of ministry. We wanted every graduate to be a skilled spiritual friend, regardless of his or her specific ministry area as an elder, a worship leader, a husband, a mother, or some other role. We also wanted some of our graduates to serve as biblical counselors, providing individual, marital, or parental counseling. Additionally, we envisioned our graduates launching new small groups, especially recovery groups, and leading existing groups. Regardless of the area of ministry, we wanted all of our graduates to see themselves as soul caregivers (people who could help the suffering) and as spiritual directors (people who could help others struggling with sins).

Lead your team to brainstorm about current and future ministries that your graduates might launch or join. Discuss what ministry identity a graduate would have. Envisioning the successful graduate empowers you to launch with the end in view.

Abilities: Envision the Mature Graduate

In addition to knowing where your graduates might serve and in what roles, it is vital that your team members envision what the mature graduate looks like. For our LEAD ministry, we identified biblical content (head), Christlike character (heart), counseling competence (hands), and Christian community (home) as our four marks of a successful graduate. That guided everything we did in our selection, training, and supervising of our trainees.

Develop a succinct, but concrete list of measurable objectives. These will communicate the essence of your ministry focus. Done well, they will also become the best recruiting tool you can fashion. People will clamor for your training because they want changed lives and they want to be able to change lives.

Results: Describe the Point of Your Ministry

What's the point? That's the question your envisioning team needs to ponder. Why are we doing this? Once our trainees graduate, once they are counseling someone or leading a group, so what? What are we equipping them to equip others to do and be?

For our LEAD ministry, the end game was changed people changing lives with Christ's changeless truth. People with changed lives know Christ, grow in Christ, and become Christlike disciple-makers. Changed lives occur as we apply Christ's changeless truth to help suffering people know that it's normal to hurt (sustaining) and possible to hope (healing), and as we help sinning people know that it's horrible to sin but wonderful to be forgiven (reconciling), and supernatural to mature (guiding).

Target Participants: Determine Who Your Ministers Minister To

Some biblical counseling ministries focus within the church. Others focus almost exclusively outside the church—as a means of outreach. Some focus only on certain types of issues and choose to refer other issues, and some offer only individual counseling, not marital or family counseling. Our statement focused on individuals, couples, and families in our congregation and community.

120

Your team should determine from the outset your target participants—the people who will be ministered to by the people you train. I prefer the word "participants" to "audience" because it speaks to the active role that a counselee or small-group member must take if he or she is to grow.

Casting Your Biblical Counseling Ministry MVP-C

Though I am using the standard language of "casting your vision," a better analogy is "planting your vision" (MVP-C). Vision is a seed best planted in fertile soil. When you catch the biblical counseling ministry MVP-C in community, you win over a team of committed people passionate about planting the MVP-C seed. When you involve the church leadership in catching your MVP-C, you gain influence from those who can spread the seed most broadly. When you build your ministry-specific MVP-C upon the congregation-wide MVP-C, you can plant your MVP-C seed deep in native soil. When your vision for counseling is a vision for the entire church, your MVP-C seed spreads not to a few, but to all. When you base your MVP-C upon a biblical mission, a unique vision, a compelling passion, and a strategic commission, your seed is robust, healthy, and sure to grow. The most important principle of fruitful vision casting is fruitful vision catching.

To continue the analogy, you know that the seed of vision is bearing fruit when people own the vision by living the vision. This is imperative to remember because too many people who talk about vision casting seem more concerned about whether someone can quote the vision than whether everyone is embodying the vision. People also mistakenly focus on the external growth of the vision—how many people can say it. When we view vision as a seed, then we primarily focus on the internal growth of the vision—how deeply the seed is planted in each person's soul as evidenced by how much each person is growing and maturing in Christ.

When you grasp these vision principles, then the vision practices flow naturally. Those practices include real-world matters, such as when you cast the vision, who casts it, to whom you cast it, and how you cast it.

121

When Do You Cast the Vision?

Since biblical counseling is a vision for the entire church, ideally people are always casting the vision for one-another ministry. Hopefully, long before you ever formulated the biblical counseling envisioning team, people were planting the seed of one-another ministry and discipleship. You start to cast your specific ministry vision as soon as you start forming a team, sending out surveys, interviewing church and community members, and holding church-wide envisioning meetings. This is why vision catching should never be done by a few behind closed doors.

Once the church leadership has officially and enthusiastically endorsed your ministry MVP-C, spread the vision seed everywhere. Announce the launch, the birth, of your new biblical counseling ministry. When you start the enlisting process, spread the vision. During your equipping training, spread the vision. When you start employing/deploying trained spiritual friends, spread the vision.

Who Casts the Vision?

Since you created the vision in community, cast the vision through community. The senior pastor and senior leadership should join in the task of planting the vision. Your entire envisioning team will plant the vision.

Once you begin equipping trainees, their changed lives will enflame the vision. Once your equipped ministers start counseling and discipling, the changed lives of the people they minister to will advance the vision.

To Whom Do You Cast the Vision?

Cast the vision as wide as the vision. If your commission statement identifies the target participants as your congregation and community, then you need to spread the seed far beyond the church property. All vision casters always need to ask the following questions: "Whom do we want to minister to? How do we reach them with the word of the great work God is doing?"

How Do You Cast the Vision?

So far it's easy: everyone always casts the vision everywhere. Though easy, a few how-to's can help.

Name your biblical counseling ministry. This is a basic idea that many ministries neglect. It helps if you have a catchy, memorable name. This is why we used an acrostic that fit our MVP-C: LEAD—Life Encouragers And Disciplers. Along with a name, create a ministry logo that captures the passion of your ministry. Spread your name, logo, and passion statement everywhere with business cards, a website, a letterhead, and training materials. Print and post your complete MVP-C Statement on your website, in the foyer, everywhere.

Preach it and teach it. Since your ministry is not just about biblical counseling, but about every-member ministry, pastors and teachers can embed the vision in every message. Since you have based your ministry upon foundational principles like the sufficiency of Scripture, progressive sanctification, the priesthood of all believers, and gospel conversations, your vision should naturally flow from the pulpit and the lectern, in small groups and in private conversations.

Share stories and testimonials. Start with your envisioning team sharing stories about how powerful it has been for them to study what the Bible says about biblical counseling. Your trainees can share private and public testimonies about how they are growing in the 4Cs. Once your biblical counselors start counseling, one of the most powerful ways to spread the word about your ministry is through testimonies from counselees. Many will fearlessly share, "I don't mind admitting it. I needed counseling, and God used my LEAD encourager to change my life."

If you want your biblical counseling ministry to reach the community, the best "marketing" is word-of-mouth testimonials from the changed lives of other community members. Of course, you have to "break into that market" somehow. Offer free seminars to the community on topics such as overcoming anxiety, parenting adolescents, and defeating depression. Promote these through public-service radio announcements, newspaper announcements, fliers, and, most importantly, personal invitations from members. Also offer free community-based ministries (see samples from Faith Baptist Church in chapter two).

Use social media. Create a section on your church's website with information about your ministry, stories, free resources, and your MVP-C

Statement. Start a blog with daily posts about biblical counseling topics. Create a Twitter account, launch a Facebook ministry page, and start a YouTube page with videos on counseling-related topics.

More than anything else—live the vision. Embody your MVP-C in how you live, relate, and do ministry.

Commencement: Launch the Ship and Start the Voyage

The six-to-twelve-month envisioning launch is an arduous voyage. It is well worth it. You have been a community in order to launch a community that reaches your congregation and community. Plus, it sure beats the other option—the two-year grueling moonwalk!

Still, the launch isn't the voyage. You have envisioned where you are, where God wants you, where God is taking you, who you are, and how you will get there. Soon it will be time to enlist the crew members who will voyage with you in the equipping and empowering process.

You might assume that your next step is to enlist trainees. However, there is another vital phase as you start leading the revolution. You need to foster a climate for ongoing ownership.

One of the great failures of the "vision-casting movement" has been the lack of teaching about people's resistance to change. Chapter five explains why people resist change, how to prepare for change, how to manage change, and how to deal with conflict biblically. Many a ministry launch has been sidetracked by unresolved conflict. Chapter five teaches a proactive approach to preparing the congregation for change through strategic change management and biblical conflict resolution.

Growing Together: Questions for Reflection, Discussion, and Application

1. In forming your envisioning team, what specific steps do you need to take to:
   a. Build the foundation for your envisioning team?
   b. Enlist your envisioning team?

    c. Organize your envisioning team?

    d. Structure your envisioning team?

2. As you think about developing your Biblical Counseling Mission Statement:

    a. What verses and categories would you add to those listed by the Disciple-Making Champions?

    b. If you were creating a discussion guide, what questions would you use, add, subtract, or edit from Appendix 4.2: Discovering Our Biblical Counseling Mission?

3. As you think about developing your Biblical Counseling Vision Statement:

    a. What questions would you use, add, subtract, or edit from Appendix 4.4: Vision-Catching Probes?

    b. Select five questions from the Vision-Catching Probes to answer now.

4. As you think about developing your Biblical Counseling Passion Statement, answer the five bulleted passion questions from this chapter.

5. As you think about developing your Biblical Counseling Commission Statement, how would your ministry answer the five SMART MAP questions?

6. Which of the vision-casting (planting) principles and practices seem most important to you? Why? How could you implement them in your church?

PART 2
Enlisting God's Ministers for Ministry

Decades later, they still refer to it as "the miracle on ice." The 1980 United States Olympic hockey team shocked the world with its epic defeat of the vastly favored Soviet team. The movie *Miracle* tells the story, beginning with head coach Herb Brooks assembling the team of amateur college players who would face the most dominant hockey team in the world.

Molding this ragtag group of individuals into a well-oiled, united team was a daunting task. *Miracle* depicted Brooks asking the players during practice, "Who do you play for?" Each player responded by naming his college team.

It took every ounce of Brooks's coaching genius and personal tenacity to connect these young men. At the end of one particularly brutal practice, they finally yelled out, "I play for the United States of America!" It was a turning point, *the* turning point. They became a team that day.

You might think, and certainly would hope and pray, that the church would not need such an extreme makeover. But we all know the truth—whether it's young college hockey players or seasoned members of our congregations, it's all too easy to say, like the Corinthians, "I am of Paul; I am of Apollos; I am of Cephas." Because that is true, we would be naive to attempt to move directly from envisioning to equipping. Yet many people unwisely try to do just that. The results are traumatic because the stakes are much higher than even an Olympic gold medal.

The apostle Paul knew, which is why in chapter five we will learn from him and from Nehemiah how to shepherd the congregational transformation. We'll learn how to cultivate a climate where the entire congregation owns the MVP-C through:

- Transformed Lives: Changing Ministers before Changing Ministries
- Relational Change Management: Stewarding the Change Process
- Biblical Conflict Resolution: Restoring Relationships

As amazing as that change is, like Brooks, we still realize there is more work to do. As Brooks built his dream team, he looked for players who would be more committed to the name on the front of the jersey (USA) than the name on the back. After he chose his team, some insisted that the best players were missing. *Miracle* depicted his response: "I am not looking for the best players. I am looking for the right players."

The apostle Paul understood that principle, which is why in chapter six we will learn from him and from Jesus how to mobilize ministers. We'll learn how to nurture a family and build a team by:

- Conducting Christ's Opus: Saturating the Congregation with One-Another Ministers
- Calling People to Connection: What People Need to Know about Your Ministry
- Matching the Right People to the Right Ministry: What You Need to Know about Ministers

A coach like Herb Brooks loves measurable objectives. If he were penning this section, his ROLOs (Reader-Oriented Learning Objectives) might sound like this. Through your active reading and application of the two chapters in this part of the book, you will be equipped to:

- Shepherd a congregational transformation that unites your entire congregation around the right Person (Christ) and the right purposes (loving God and others) (chapter five).
- Mobilize ministers so that you are able to match the right people to the right ministry for the right reasons at the right time in the right way—relationally (chapter six).

"Do you believe in miracles? Yes!" Al Michaels yelled those famous words when the United States hockey team upset the Soviets.

Do you believe in miracles? Do you believe that Christ's resurrection power is available to His church so that we can defeat the very gates of hell? If you do, *since* you do, join me as we join Christ in building His church.

5

Shepherding the Transformation

CULTIVATING A CLIMATE FOR ONGOING OWNERSHIP

When I teach the material in this chapter, I start with a change exercise. I ask participants to stand and face each other in pairs, observing each other's appearance. Then I instruct them to turn back to back and make five changes to their appearance. Typically, they roll up a sleeve, take off their glasses, loosen a tie, remove an earring, or make other basic changes.

Next I tell them to face each other and identify the five changes their partner made. They'll laugh, point out changes, and instinctively start to change back. Before they do, I ask them to turn around again and make five additional changes to their appearance. From some people I hear murmuring; from others I observe enthusiastic creativity. Hair braids come off, pant legs are pulled up, jackets are put on backward, pens are placed over an ear, shirttails come out. Once again they face each other and identify these changes.

Then I start to say, "Okay, turn around again . . ." Vocal resistance begins. I respond, "Just kidding. Let's sit down and talk about our CQ—our Change Quotient." We discuss:

- Were you comfortable or uncomfortable with the assignment?
- Were the changes easy or hard for you to make? To identify?
- Were you in a cooperative mode or a mutiny mood?
- At what point, if any, did you experience change overload?
- How quickly did you revert back to your former look?

We then discuss the implications that we can derive for change management. People mention applications such as these: Change takes an initiator. The initiator of change must be trusted. Change requires clear instructions. People can handle only so much change—don't overload. Change takes energy and creativity. Change can be minor yet feel dramatic. Change can cause people to feel uncomfortable and even fearful about losing the old and facing the new. People focus on what they have to sacrifice. People feel isolated when they lose the familiar. People have different levels of readiness for change. Change is not one action but a journey. People often revert back to their old style.

Shifting Teutonic Plates

If a little game like this prompts such turmoil, imagine the angst when we ask a congregation to make a major ministry mindset shift. For many congregations, it is a monumental shift to move from the pastor as the doer of ministry to the pastor as the equipper of equippers. For many church members, it is a massive shift to move from receiving counseling from the pastor to providing counseling to one another.

This is why it is unwise to move directly from envisioning to enlisting. Yet we do it all the time. We get all excited after attending a seminar on gospel-centered preaching, or the purpose-driven church, or the disciple-making pastor, or the equipping-focused church. Then we return home, gather other like-minded people, create a vision statement, tell others about it, and announce a grand new approach to church life. Instead of creating a following, we generate a family feud.

132

Been There, Done That

I know, because I just described my experience. Armed with the best of intentions but not with the greatest wisdom, I tried to shift our congregation from a pastor-centered model to an equipping-centered approach. I made enough mistakes and learned enough from those mistakes to write a book—this book.

My heart was right—I wanted to transform the way our congregation lived the gospel. My initial process was wrong—I expected people to make dramatic changes without preparing my heart and their hearts for change.

That's why I entitled this chapter "Shepherding the Transformation." Before you seek to change church structure, seek to shepherd changed hearts. It's also why I subtitled this chapter "Cultivating a Climate for Ongoing Ownership." Before you enlist individuals to be equipped to counsel, invite a congregation to become stewards of a transformational vision.

You may say, "But haven't we done a lot of that already? We've involved the congregation in the SWORD Heart Exam and in the community assessment. We've welcomed the whole church into the envisioning process. We've cast the vision in community."

Doing all those things places you way ahead on the transitioning curve. However, so far you've only *talked about* the future vision. What happens when Sister Gwen wants to counsel with Pastor Gordon, and instead you invite her to counsel with Sister Kirstin? What happens when Brother Dwayne expects a visit in the hospital from Pastor Varney, but instead receives a visit from Brother Thomas? Change is what has happened, and conflict is what may occur. In response, wise leaders understand that transformed lives, relational change management, and biblical conflict resolution are required.

Don't think of these as stages in a process. Though you are reading this book chapter-by-chapter in a linear way, life and ministry don't work like that. Though chapter five precedes the chapters on enlisting, equipping, and empowering, the need for transformed lives, change management, and conflict resolution doesn't stop somewhere between envisioning and enlisting. This is why the word "ongoing" is central to the title of this chapter.

Cultivating ongoing ownership is always relevant. We are going to learn that it was necessary in Nehemiah's day, it was needed in Paul's day, and it is indispensable in our day. In our changing times, we need timeless truth about change.

Transformed Lives: Changing Ministers before Changing Ministries

The Bible has a theology of change, which we can summarize with one word: "transformation." Transformation starts with hearts—changed leaders change people who change churches who change communities. Before you prepare a change-management plan, prepare people. Before you prepare people, prepare your own heart.

Nehemiah and Paul each led God's people through transformative change. We think of Nehemiah as a wall builder, and we sometimes use the book of Nehemiah to distill organizational leadership principles. However, Nehemiah never prayed to be remembered as a wall builder, but rather as a people builder. In Nehemiah 5:19; 13:14, 22, and 31 he prays that God would remember him for empowering God's people to serve, for leading God's people to worship, and for motivating God's people to live transformed lives. The book of Nehemiah is not about organizational leadership. It *is* about shepherding people whose transformed lives lead to a transformed community.

Likewise, Paul's ministry in 2 Corinthians focuses not simply on conflict resolution, but on personal reconciliation—first with God and then with one another (2 Cor. 5:17–21; 6:11–13). Paul's letter is not about transitioning ministries but about transforming ministers. In the midst of conflict, Paul fixes his eyes on the prize. "Though outwardly we are wasting away, yet inwardly we are being renewed day by day" (2 Cor. 4:16). Paul laser-focuses his goal. "And we, who with unveiled faces all reflect the Lord's glory, are being transformed into his likeness with ever-increasing glory" (2 Cor. 3:18).

Taking up the leadership mantle of Nehemiah and Paul, we must focus on transforming people before we start transitioning ministries. Transformational spiritual leaders emphasize:

- Transforming my heart
- Transforming my attitude toward God's people
- Transforming our worship of God

Transforming My Heart: Taking My Sin and Suffering to Christ

Biblical counselors don't say, "Physician, heal thyself." Instead, we say, "Soul physician, go to *the Soul Physician* for healing before counseling others." When we do, we follow the ancient path of Nehemiah. Before he implemented a single change-management principle, he prayed to the Soul Physician. "I confess the sins we Israelites, *including myself* and my father's house, have committed against you" (Neh. 1:6). To address his sin, Nehemiah turned to God for transformation.

Paul, perhaps the greatest human soul physician, focused first on his own heart. "We were under great pressure, far beyond our ability to endure, so that we despaired even of life. Indeed, in our hearts we felt the sentence of death. But this happened that *we might not rely on ourselves but on God*, who raises the dead" (2 Cor. 1:8–9). To address his suffering, Paul turned to God for transformation.

Transitioning a church is hard work. Leading a congregation through the change process of a pastor-centered church to a church where every minister is a biblical counselor is demanding. It is impossible if the leader or leadership team is not addressing personal sin and suffering. Does your team want to change lives? If so, when you meet, don't just talk about launching a biblical counseling ministry; be biblical counselors for one another.

Transforming My Attitude toward God's People: Seeing People as My Brothers and Sisters in Christ

Let's be honest. When people resist the changes we believe God wants us to implement, it is easy to start seeing them as the enemy. I

135

find it fascinating that before Nehemiah dealt with change management, he *identified with* God's people. I find it instructive that before Paul dealt with conflict resolution, he *identified with* the very people who were criticizing him.

Nehemiah questioned Hanani about the Jewish remnant. Told that they were in great trouble and distress, he tells us that he "sat down and wept. For some days I mourned" (Neh. 1:4). Nehemiah had it made in the shade, living the life of luxury eight hundred miles away from Jerusalem. Yet he cared about his brothers and sisters. The word "questioned" (Neh. 1:2) indicates much more than a passing interest. It means to inquire and express a genuine concern for the welfare of others.

When he heard of their defeat (they were shattered and broken), when he heard of their disgrace (their reproach and shame), he mourned. He was deeply grieved and moved by the plight of God's people—of his people. His heart broke for their suffering and sin.

Paul, even with the Corinthians with whom he experienced excruciating conflict, began his second letter to them by identifying with them. Ten times in five verses he repeated a form of the Greek word for "comfort" (2 Cor. 1:3–7). Think about that. When you are in conflict with people, is your first thought (and your second and tenth thoughts) about helping them connect to Christ's comfort? We can't lead the launch of a biblical counseling ministry, which in part is about comforting one another in Christ, unless we can offer Christ's comfort to our brothers and sisters in Christ.

As leaders, are we making changes that are self-centered or self-focused? Are we leading change because it's all about our leadership image? Or are we shepherding a transformative process out of a heart changed by Christ with a changed attitude toward our brothers and sisters in Christ?

Transforming Our Worship of God: Shepherding People to Christ

Nehemiah begins his ministry with worship. "O LORD, God of heaven, the great and awesome God, who keeps his covenant of love"

(Neh. 1:5). His prayer of confession is a prayer of worship—Nehemiah links each sin to God's people's failure to respond wholeheartedly to God's holy love. Worship is embedded throughout the book, and it provides the bookends that frame the book. Nehemiah's closing prayer of remembrance is a plea that God would remember how Nehemiah purified the priests and Levites for worship.

Worship is the ultimate focus of Paul's introductory vignette concerning his despair over his suffering. Why did he share? So that "many will give thanks" (2 Cor. 1:11). In every description Paul provides of his troubles, and there are many, his purpose is to direct people to God-dependence—to worshiping and trusting Christ alone.

The end goal of biblical counseling is worship—entrusting ourselves to God, exalting God, and enjoying Him (Matt. 22:34–40). The end goal of *the process* of launching a biblical counseling ministry should be the same—to shepherd Christians to a deeper worship of Christ. Launching a biblical counseling ministry isn't a task to accomplish. It is a relationship—with God and others—to nourish and enjoy.

Relational Change Management: Stewarding the Change Process

The most nurturing context for healthy change is a transformed congregation. It is from within that healthy environment that we plant and grow a biblical counseling ministry. Transformation is the seedbed for transition.

Still, change is not easy. Change is like a ship that we simultaneously sail and refit. We don't get to stop the rest of life and ministry while we launch a new ministry. This is why we need wise, practical principles of relational change management.

Translate the Two Languages of Leadership: Purpose and People

Many churches spend far too little time in preparation and move far too quickly into making changes. We need to go slow if we want a biblical counseling ministry to plant deep and stay long. Other churches seem to spend forever talking about transition and never transitioning. The difference can be explained, in part, by understanding leadership styles. Some leaders tend toward a purpose-driven style and others toward a people-focused style.

The Two Languages of Ministry

Purpose-Driven	People-Focused
Task	Relationship
Organization	Organism
Product	Process
Road Maker	Caretaker
Church as an Army	Church as a Body
Ministry	Maturity
Captain	Chaplain
Exhorter	Encourager
Manage (1 Tim. 3:5)	Take Care Of (1 Tim. 3:5)

Guide your leadership team to ponder the impact of their style as they interact with the congregation. Think about the following questions: "Which style are we each prone to? Where did we learn and hone our style? How might a purpose-driven person lead this change in this congregation? How might a people-focused person lead in our setting? What tensions might exist on our team between the two styles? What tensions might each style create for our congregation? How will we resolve tensions biblically? What style is our congregation accustomed to? How could we wisely blend our two leadership styles?"

Participate in Two-Way Conversations: Telling Is Not Communicating

Relational change management is a continuing conversation, not a lecture. Too many churches think that they have communicated when they have posted a notice in the bulletin or made an announcement from the pulpit. Those methods are fine first steps, but they must also include an invitation to a conversation.

As you discuss the launch of your biblical counseling ministry, commit to dialogue rather than monologue. In fact, commit to trial-ogue—in every conversation invite God's perspective through praying, depending upon the Holy Spirit for guidance, and seeking direction from the Word.

Where to Share

In churches where I pastored, we used various venues to start the conversation. We offered Fireside Chats open to the entire congregation. In these informal settings, the leadership of the church and of the biblical counseling team met with the congregation to share the preliminary vision and to invite open sharing of feedback, questions, concerns, and suggestions. Other churches call these Congregational Input Nights. Still other churches choose to use business meetings as a forum for such discussions.

I have also used Leadership Community (LC) as a medium for discussion. Open to everyone in the church, but especially geared to all church ministry leaders, LC meetings typically follow a vision, huddle, strategy format. The biblical counseling team shares their vision. They then huddle with participants in smaller groups to hear their responses. The larger group then reconvenes to discuss implementation strategies.

It is crucial that you work with other ministry leaders because your new ministry will impact their existing ministry. In my first church, two sisters wanted to join our LEAD biblical counseling training. The problem? They were the two primary soloists for the church choir, and choir practice met the same night as our proposed training. The worship leader and I had some planning (relational change management) to do.

Whom to Share With

Your biblical counseling team needs to foster a climate of ongoing support with each group within your church. In *The Purpose Driven Church* Rick Warren outlines five such groups: the community, the crowd, the congregation, the committed, and the core. Your team should ask, "How are we communicating with people in each of these groups?

What are we doing to nurture ownership of this ministry among the members of each group?"

You can connect with the *community* in many ways, including through the community assessment process, seminars, church outreach events, and your personal relationships with community members. The *crowd* includes those who are coming to church but are not yet members. Membership classes are a great place to discuss the vision of one-another ministry and biblical counseling. The *congregation* includes all those who are members and regular attenders. Spiritual-gift classes are one means to engage them in discussions about biblical counseling.

The *committed* are the types of people you invite to Leadership Community. Their ownership of and support for your biblical counseling ministry can make or break your ministry. Churches often overlook this group because they may not be official decision-makers, board members, or staff. However, they are the influencers, the doers, and the givers. And, as noted, they are often the most affected by the launch of any new ministry.

The *core* includes your church leaders, pastors, staff, elders, deacons, and board members. They must own the dual vision of every member doing informal one-another ministry and of equipped members providing formal biblical counseling. This is why you need to involve them in the envisioning process (see chapter four).

It is especially important that you build trusting relationships with the committed and the core. Some people resist this idea because it feels like politics. However, the word "politics" comes from the word *polis*, meaning "people." Communicating with the committed and core is not playing politics; it is respecting people. True leaders want and deserve to be informed and consulted. They want to know if their wisdom counts and whether anyone cares what they think.

Nehemiah built trusting relationships with the committed. In Nehemiah 2:16, we see his connection with the priests, nobles, and officials. He also built trusting relationships with the core. You don't get any more core than King Artaxerxes (Neh. 2:1–9).

Communicate the Desperate Need for the Ministry: Holy Discontent

As you interact in various settings with different groups, discuss why the ministry is necessary. Your congregation will take ownership and invest their time and money in a biblical counseling ministry if they understand the desperate needs it will address. This occurs when people become dissatisfied with the status quo, when they experience holy discontent.

Nehemiah experienced this when he heard that the wall of Jerusalem was broken down and its gates burned (Neh. 1:3). Hearing the report, he sat down, wept, mourned, fasted, and prayed. He had a holy response to the desperate state of Jerusalem and its inhabitants.

Your congregational assessment will raise red flags of discontent. When you ask people where personal needs are not being met, they will tell you. It's easy to respond to their feedback defensively and see it as unhealthy complaining. Instead, view it as an open door, as an enormous opportunity to secure the congregation's passionate support.

Respond as Nehemiah did. After a detailed inspection of Jerusalem (Neh. 2:11–16), he gathered the Jews, the priests, the nobles, the officials, and others who would be doing the work and said to them, "You see the trouble we are in: Jerusalem lies in ruins, and its gates have been burned with fire. Come, let us rebuild the wall of Jerusalem, and we will no longer be in disgrace" (Neh. 2:17). The need exposed, they responded without hesitation. "Let us start rebuilding" (Neh. 2:18b). Instead of attempting to solve the problem himself, Nehemiah used the need as an opportunity to give ownership to the community.

Communicate the Amazing Benefits of the Ministry: Holy Celebration

We learn something further from Nehemiah. "I also told them about the gracious hand of my God upon me and what the king had said to me" (Neh. 2:18a). It wasn't only holy discontent that motivated ownership; it was also Nehemiah's holy celebration.

141

The NIV's translation of their response is somewhat blasé: "So they began this good work" (Neh. 2:18c). We could translate the original language, "They set their hands together bravely" or "They vigorously set their hands to go about building" or "They strengthened their hands together to do God's work." That's ownership!

You might be thinking, "We haven't launched the biblical counseling ministry yet, so we don't know what some of the amazing results might be." This is why it is important to expose your key leaders to model biblical counseling ministries in your area, around the country, and around the world (through personal visits, reading materials, and visiting their websites). Additionally, our Disciple-Making Champions provide the show-and-tell you need.

Disciple-Making Champions

Testimony Time

As part of the *4E Ministry Training Strategy Questionnaire,* two dozen best-practice churches responded to the questions: "Testimony time—what excites you and brings you the most joy about your biblical counseling ministry? How has the ministry impacted your church and community?" Their answers could fill this chapter.

- Leading this ministry has radically changed my life! It's dramatically impacting the hurting souls of men and women.
- I love seeing the dawn of hope in the eyes of people who have been told and believe they are beyond help or hope. I rejoice in being able to *visibly* see the paradigm shift take place on the face of a counselee who "gets it" for the first time. I love showing people that the Word of God truly has all the answers for the problems they face.
- Biblical counseling brings life where once there was not. How exciting to know that what we share as biblical counselors carries the power of the resurrection to enable growth and change. The icing on the cake is that this new growing and changing person then comes alongside another person who needs the same love of Christ lived out and helps another grow and change.
- Seeing men and women understand the gospel in broader, deeper, and richer ways; seeing the Lord "turn the lights on" in the hearts

of His people; helping them connect the dots between His grace and their daily lives; giving people a taste and zeal for gospel ministry in the body of Christ and in reaching an unbelieving world.

- When we have eyes to see, we realize that counseling is really a ministry of spiritual transformation and discipleship. This is not about a ministry on the side. Our entire congregation has been forever changed by our biblical counseling focus.
- It excites me to see people helping others. We're equipping members to care for one another. It has a geometric effect. When you teach a person how to grow and change to be more like Christ, you have equipped him or her to go and help someone else grow and change.
- People share testimonies regularly about the benefits of the training—they are growing spiritually through the equipping, they feast on the depth of the relationships in our training group, and their counselees' lives are being changed forever.
- God has gifted and called many to serve Him, and it brings me joy to see them equipped and released as ambassadors of reconciliation.
- The benefits include maturity in knowing the Lord, obedience to God's Word, people learning to solve problems biblically, stronger marriages and families, and so much more.
- Some people have the idea that counseling kills your evangelism. That is simply not true. Effective biblical counseling enhances your outreach. Scores of people come to Christ every year through our biblical counseling ministry.
- An effective biblical counseling ministry has helped our church become known in our community as a church where people can get answers.

Communicate the Biblical Basis of the Ministry: Practical Theology

We should not expect people to change because we said so, but because God says so. Through sermon series, Sunday school classes, private conversations, fireside chats, and congregational meetings, communicate the vision shared in chapter one. Develop a common commitment that the local church *is* a biblical counseling ministry.

Assist your people to grasp the direct relationship between biblical counseling and all the foundational doctrines and beliefs your church values. Discuss the sufficiency of Scripture. Do we have confidence that the Bible has answers to everyday life problems? Well, biblical counseling is the personal application of God's Word to everyday life situations and relationships.

Discuss progressive sanctification. Do we believe that God wants us to grow more like Christ every day in every way? Well, biblical counseling is a one-to-one means of helping one another to become more conformed to the image of Christ.

Discuss the priesthood of all believers. Do we believe that God calls and equips every Christian for one-another ministry? Well, biblical counseling empowers every Christian to speak the truth in love.

Address Concerns: Communicate Humble Confidence

It would be naive to think that communication alleviates every possible concern. Your people will raise issues—some of which you will have thought of and some of which will be new. If you have thought through the issue previously, share your plan and seek additional feedback. If the issue is new, ask the person for his or her thoughts on how to address it, and commit to doing additional research.

In the Redwood National Park there is a hollowed-out tree that you can drive through. Since you don't do that every day, there's a sign before the entrance to the tree that says, "Others Have. So Can You." That's the attitude you want to convey to your congregation. It's an attitude that says, "We're not the first people to ever launch and lead a church-based biblical counseling ministry. We don't have all the answers, but others at least know the questions. We're doing our homework, and we're willing to do more. We're confident that God who calls us also equips us."

Part four on empowering/employing godly ministers addresses the typical concerns people raise about a biblical counseling ministry. Many of those relate to ethical and legal issues. As I note in more detail in that part, you should develop a written plan that clearly and honestly represents the qualifications of your counselors, the type of counseling offered, the type of issues addressed, and the ethical standards you will follow. Secure an attorney on retainer to counsel you regarding the structure and focus of your ministry and to assist you should any issues arise. I also recommend that churches purchase malpractice insurance for each person counseling in their ministry.

Every organization can and should function in a well-organized, ethical, and legal fashion. However, in our litigious society, no organization can guarantee that it will not be sued. Churches should not let the possibility of a lawsuit discourage them from serving God in their communities.

Prioritize the Implementation of Change: Start Small and Grow Slow

You can teach an old dog new tricks, but you must be very patient with the dog. Much more importantly, we are not dogs. God created us in His image. He knows us, commands us to change, and empowers us to change. Relational change management asks, "How much change can our people appropriately digest? How much change can our people realistically implement?"

If you have just launched several other ministries, it may be wise to delay the formal launch of your biblical counseling ministry. If you have a small team, it may be wise to start small and to grow slow.

I recommend equipping no more than a dozen people in the first round of training. One of my graduates started by training more than 225 women. Because the training emphasized working on your own struggles, she soon had scores of people requesting counseling. Once the training was done, she had over two hundred people to supervise. She now speaks in my class and tells students, "Listen to Dr. Kellemen when he says to start with no more than a dozen trainees!"

Mourn Change: Grieve the Loss of the Old

No matter how well you prepare your people, all change involves some loss. Something new replaces or alters the old, the familiar. People will have to reckon with the fact that their pastor may not be the person who counsels them or visits them in the hospital. Someone who has been serving alongside them in ministry may leave to join the biblical counseling ministry. The church may grow and change as people are won to Christ through biblical counseling.

We would be uncaring biblical counselors if we dismissed such loss as inconsequential. We need to give people permission to grieve, and we need to shepherd the entire congregation through the grief and growth process.[1]

Call for a Vote: A Conclusive Statement of Congregational Ownership

Depending on your church government and how your church has historically launched new ministries, you may call for a formal vote. If so, after you have taken the steps outlined in chapters one through five, your biblical counseling team and church leadership can craft the wording for a congregational vote. It will include the name of your ministry, the mission of the ministry, a summary of financial commitments, and a summary of policy and procedure matters. You can find a sample call for a vote in Appendix 5.1.

Taking a vote can be valuable even if it is not constitutionally required. It communicates the central role that your biblical counseling ministry has in your vision for the entire church. It also provides a specific, tangible way for the entire congregation to express ownership of and support for the ministry.

Biblical Conflict Resolution: Restoring Relationships

In an ideal world, the combination of transformed lives and relational change management would eliminate the need for biblical conflict resolution. Sadly, we no longer live in an ideal world. Even with a congregation that is growing in Christ and with a wise transition process, conflict can arise. When it does, biblical counselors, of all people, should be prepared for biblical conflict resolution.

1. I present a biblical model of grief and growth in *God's Healing for Life's Losses: How to Find Hope When You're Hurting* (Winona Lake, IN: BMH Books, 2010).

146

Be Proactive: Respond Wisely to Potential Sources of Conflict

Nehemiah crossed all his *t*'s and dotted all his *i*'s, yet many people still resisted his ministry. Like him, when we seek to build up God's people, we may expect pockets of envy, dishonesty, apathy, fury, mockery, and hostility.

Prayerfully, you will face few or none of these. Picture the following discussion as the worst-case scenario, the perfect storm. Nehemiah models how to weather the worst storm imaginable.

Anticipate Pockets of Envy: Respond with Unity

When Sanballat and Tobiah heard that the king approved Nehemiah's plan, "they were very much disturbed that someone had come to promote the welfare of the Israelites" (Neh. 2:10b). They questioned Nehemiah's character not because they were concerned, but because they were afraid and envious. The intrusion of this outsider would strip away their power base and influence.

Rather than going toe-to-toe with these men, Nehemiah encouraged God's people to minister shoulder-to-shoulder (Neh. 2:11–20). He invited a trusted circle of colleagues to assess the need, and then, like Shackleton, he called people to unite to conquer the problem. It wasn't avoidance of the enemy, but rather a purposeful focus on God's family.

Anticipate Pockets of Dishonesty: Respond with Humility and Integrity

When Geshem joined Sanballat and Tobiah, between the three of them their nations nearly surrounded Jerusalem. When they saw God's people united in service, they falsely accused them. "Are you rebelling against the king?" (Neh. 2:19). They painted Nehemiah's good as if it were evil because Satan curses whom God blesses.

In response to their dishonesty, Nehemiah spoke the truth in love with humility and integrity. Instead of standing up for himself, he exalted God. "The God of heaven will give us success" (Neh. 2:20). Rather than exalting himself, he saw himself through God's eyes. "We his *servants* will start rebuilding" (Neh. 2:20).

It is not that Nehemiah stubbornly refused to search his heart. Rather, he had already been doing that, as we have seen. The same is true of Paul in 2 Corinthians 1:12. "Our conscience testifies that we have conducted ourselves in the world, and especially in our relations with you, in the holiness and sincerity that are from God. We have done so not according to worldly wisdom but according to God's grace." Biblical self-awareness is God's antidote for false accusation.

Anticipate Pockets of Apathy: Respond with Tenacity

Problems from without are hard enough, but problems from within are even more difficult to endure. Nehemiah launched the work with great enthusiasm, only to face a potential interruption. "But their nobles would not put their shoulders to the work under their supervisors" (Neh. 3:5).

Interestingly, the text offers not a single word in response. The work continues unabated. While welcoming the support of all who offered it, Nehemiah had sufficient inner resources to stand alone if need be. In the tenacious discharge of his responsibilities, he was prepared to have no one but God. His energy was not dictated by others' apathy.

Anticipate Pockets of Fury: Respond with Vulnerability

In Nehemiah 3, thirty-eight diverse work crews labor harmoniously to advance God's kingdom. Then we read, "When Sanballat heard that we were rebuilding the wall, he became angry and was greatly incensed" (Neh. 4:1).

When someone pushes us, our inclination is to push back. When someone gets in our face, we're tempted to get in their face. Nehemiah chose to get face-to-face with God. Vulnerably he prays, "Hear us, O our God, for we are despised" (Neh. 4:4). "Despised" means to view someone as insignificant, useless, worthless. In the Old Testament this frequently results in discouragement. Think of that word: "dis-courage," to have your courage melt away as you curl up in a fetal position feeling overwhelmed and undermanned. Rather than give in to that, Nehemiah gave up to God.

Paul takes it a step further. He vulnerably exposes his discouragement even to his critics. He tells the Corinthians, of all people, that he despaired of life and felt the sentence of death (2 Cor. 1:8–9). We might see that as foolish weakness, until we understand what Paul understands, "For when I am weak, then I am strong" (2 Cor. 12:10b).

Anticipate Pockets of Mockery: Respond with God-Reality

Critics generally run in packs. Sanballat and Tobiah did. In the presence of their associates, Sanballat ridiculed the Jews. "What are those feeble Jews doing? Will they restore their wall? Will they offer sacrifices? Will they finish in a day?" (Neh. 4:2). Tobiah, who was at his side, said, "What they are building—if even a fox climbed up on it, he would break down their wall of stones!" (Neh. 4:3). They pile on top of one another cruel character assaults, relentless mocking, and malicious slicing and dicing.

Drop after drop, drip after drip, it takes its toll. Verse ten records what the people felt. Commentators believe it was actually sung as a funeral dirge. We might translate it as:

> The strength of our burden bearing is drooping,
> The rubbish heap so vast.
> And we ourselves are stooping,
> Unable to fulfill this impossible task.

If ever a people needed perspective—God-reality—it was them and it was now. Nehemiah looked things over, gathered his people, and said, "Don't be afraid of them. Remember the Lord, who is great and awesome" (Neh. 4:14). When life stinks, our perspective shrinks. When our perspective shrinks, we need a full dose of eternal perspective, of God-perspective. We need to remember who God is, who we are in Christ, who is calling us, and what He calls us to do.

Anticipate Pockets of Hostility: Respond with Creativity

When they reached the halfway point, opposition went from bad to worse. "So we rebuilt the wall till all of it reached half its height, for

149

the people worked with all their heart" (Neh. 4:6). When Sanballat and his crew heard about their progress, "they were very angry. They all plotted together to come and fight against Jerusalem and stir up trouble against it" (Neh. 4:7–8). To make matters worse, their own people told them "ten times over, 'Wherever you turn, they will attack us'" (Neh. 4:12).

The halfway point is often the point of greatest opposition and greatest temptation to abandon our post. It's the point at which others begin to take notice of our progress, but when we begin to focus on the huge task still ahead. Great leaders respond to the potential death and destruction of a dream with life and creativity. You can define the greatness of leaders by what it takes to discourage them and by how they encourage everyone around them.

Creative thinking in a crisis often requires both/and thinking, such as prayer and practicality. "But we prayed to our God and posted a guard day and night to meet this threat" (Neh. 4:9). Nehemiah creatively suggests both working and protecting: "From that day on, half of my men did the work, while the other half were equipped with spears, shields, bows and armor" (Neh. 4:16). He creatively emphasizes both individuality and community: "Fight for your brothers, your sons and your daughters, your wives and your homes. . . . We all returned to the wall, each to his own work. . . . Wherever you hear the sound of the trumpet, join us there" (Neh. 4:14, 15, 20).

Be a Peacemaker: Respond Lovingly to Resolve Conflict

A proactive approach to potential conflict prepares us so that we are not shocked if conflict occurs and so that we are able to lead effectively during conflict. However, as biblical counselors, we desire more—we desire reconciliation.

Ken Sande in his excellent book *The Peacemaker* outlines a "4G" process of reconciliation. When I consult with churches ready to launch their biblical counseling ministry, I encourage them to follow Sande's biblical model:

- *Glorify God* (1 Cor. 10:31): "How can I please and honor God in this situation?"
- *Get the Log Out of Your Eye* (Matt. 7:5): "How can I show Jesus' work in me by taking responsibility for my contribution to this conflict?"
- *Gently Restore* (Gal. 6:1): "How can I lovingly serve others by helping them take responsibility for their contribution to this conflict?"
- *Go and Be Reconciled* (Matt. 5:24): "How can I demonstrate the forgiveness of God and encourage a reasonable solution to this conflict?"

Glorify God: Pleasing God as My First Priority

The apostle Paul faced conflict with the Corinthians over several issues, especially their questioning of his integrity and authority. No small matter, Paul repeatedly clarified what motivated his ministry—God's glory. "For we do not preach ourselves, but Jesus Christ as Lord, and ourselves as your servants for Jesus' sake" (2 Cor. 4:5). "So we make it our goal to please him" (2 Cor. 5:9).

Paul teaches us that we must always place our human conflict within the much larger context of God's eternal glory. If conflict arises related to your biblical counseling ministry, strive to help all parties, including yourself, to ask, "How can I please and honor God in this situation?" It's not about "winning" the conflict. It's not even about "win/win" scenarios. It's about joining together to advance God's kingdom. Sometimes that may require that I "lose" in the eyes of the world.

Get the Log Out: Examining My Heart as My First Responsibility

While Paul does not identify any particular sins, it is clear that he continually opened his heart to God's all-knowing eyes. "I call God as my witness that it was in order to spare you that I did not return to Corinth" (2 Cor. 1:23). Paul lived every nanosecond aware that "we must all appear before the judgment seat of Christ" (2 Cor. 5:10).

ENLISTING GOD'S MINISTERS FOR MINISTRY

Paul models for us that when conflict occurs, our first responsibility is to examine our own heart based upon God's Word. If conflict arises related to your biblical counseling ministry, strive to help all parties, including yourself, to ask, "How can I show Jesus' work in me by taking responsibility for my contribution to this conflict?" When we do this, we embody the biblical counseling principles we teach.

Gently Restore: Loving Others as My First Ministry

Paul mastered the art of gentle restoration. "Even if I caused you sorrow by my letter, I do not regret it. Though I did regret it—I see that my letter hurt you, but only for a little while—yet now I am happy, not because you were made sorry, but because your sorrow led you to repentance. For you became sorrowful as God intended and so were not harmed in any way by us" (2 Cor. 7:8–9). You can almost feel the conflict *within* Paul as he reflects on his past loving confrontation of the Corinthians. "I don't regret it. I did regret it. My letter hurt you. My letter did not harm you."

Paul demonstrates that when conflict occurs, my first ministry, even before I launch any other ministry, is to love others with Christlike love. If conflict arises related to your biblical counseling ministry, strive to help all parties, including yourself, to ask, "How can I lovingly serve others by helping them take responsibility for their contribution to this conflict?"

Go and Be Reconciled: Restoring Relationship as My First Necessity

If Paul is the master of gentle restoration, then he is the gold standard of being reconciled. Is there a more tender, yet compelling example than his words in 2 Corinthians 6:11–13? "We have spoken freely to you, Corinthians, and opened wide our hearts to you. We are not withholding our affection from you, but you are withholding yours from us. As a fair exchange—I speak as to my children—open wide your hearts also."

As if that were not enough, he pleads again, "Make room for us in your hearts. We have wronged no one, we have corrupted no one, we have exploited no one. I do not say this to condemn you; I have said before that you have such a place in our hearts that we would live or die with you" (2 Cor. 7:2–3).

Paul not only wanted to demonstrate forgiveness, but also longed to encourage godly restoration. When the Corinthians were unrelenting in their punishment of a sinning brother, Paul taught them what to do instead. "Now instead, you ought to forgive and comfort him, so that he will not be overwhelmed by excessive sorrow. I urge you, therefore, to reaffirm your love for him" (2 Cor. 2:7–8).

Paul demonstrates that when conflict occurs, my first necessity is restoring the relationship, not pushing forward the biblical counseling ministry. If conflict arises related to your biblical counseling ministry, strive to help all parties, including yourself, to ask, "How can I demonstrate the forgiveness of God and encourage a reasonable solution to this conflict?"

Commencement: Sail On

I have mentioned that change is like a ship that we simultaneously sail and refit. Sometimes, in the midst of change and conflict, we just wish someone would stop the boat and let us get off!

Nehemiah and Paul surely felt the same way at times. Ultimately, their eternal goal of glorifying God kept them afloat. Their life purpose of empowering and equipping God's people kept them sailing the seas of ministry. Prayerfully, you are at the same place on your voyage.

If you are, then you are ready to expand your crew by enlisting people to your biblical counseling ministry. Chapter six will turn upside down the typical non-relational recruitment process, which is often driven by the tyranny of the urgent need to find a warm body. So in chapter six we will replace the word "recruitment" with "connection." As a leader, you will learn how to connect to those who may join your ministry team and how to help prospective team members assess how well their gifting and calling connects to your ministry MVP-C.

153

Growing Together: Questions for Reflection, Discussion, and Application

1. Share about a time in your church life when change took place and it was handled well. Or when conflict began, and it was successfully resolved.

2. As you launch and lead your biblical counseling ministry, what are specific actions you can take and attitudes you can develop to apply the principles of:
   a. Transforming my heart: taking my sin and suffering to Christ?
   b. Transforming my attitude toward God's people: seeing people as my brothers and sisters in Christ?
   c. Transforming our worship of God: shepherding people to Christ?

3. As you launch and lead your biblical counseling ministry, what are specific actions you can take and attitudes you can develop to apply the relational change-management principles of:
   a. Translating the two languages of leadership: purpose and people?
   b. Participating in two-way conversations: telling is not communicating?
   c. Communicating the desperate need for the ministry: holy discontent?
   d. Communicating the amazing benefits of the ministry: holy celebration?
   e. Communicating the biblical basis of the ministry: practical theology?
   f. Addressing concerns: communicate humble confidence?
   g. Prioritizing the implementation of change: start small and grow slow?
   h. Mourning change: grieve the loss of the old?
   i. Calling for a vote: a conclusive statement of congregational ownership?

4. Of the six potential sources of conflict and the six positive responses, which ones might you need to apply to your situation?

5. How could you apply each of the 4Gs of biblical conflict resolution to your situation?

6

Mobilizing Ministers

NURTURING A FAMILY AND BUILDING A TEAM

In my consulting ministry, I encourage church leaders to keep their eyes focused on four words that you are becoming very familiar with: "envisioning," "enlisting," "equipping," and "empowering." It helps them to design a simple process of discipling biblical counselors in their church.

I constantly see the need for simplicity even with the first two aspects of the process. Some churches are great at envisioning, but they get so entangled in the details that they drop the ball and never move to enlisting people. Other churches skip the envisioning process, which causes their enlisting to be more about recruiting volunteers than calling disciples.

I want to help you to simplify. *Connect (enlist) people to your purpose (envision).*

We birth a family and build a team not by asking, "How can we recruit more volunteers?" Our question is, "How can we connect committed people with our disciple-making vision?"

To help churches make this shift, I walk with them through the disciple-making ministries of Christ and Paul. The response to this Bible study is always the same. "It's all about connecting. Jesus called people to Himself—to connect with and abide in Him. It's a thoroughly relational process!" We learn together Christ's transformational, relational process: come and see Me, come and follow Me, come and be with Me, come and remain in Me, come and be like Me.

This returns us to the theme we first learned in chapter one. A relationship with *the* transforming Person (Christ) produces transforming leaders (you and your team) who relationally lead a transforming process (the 4Es) that the Spirit uses in transforming your church (the body of Christ) so others (the congregation and community) are transformed also.

People display a similar response to our study of the apostle Paul's equipping ministry. They say, "Enlisting is not about mechanical recruiting; it's about connecting! Paul connected deeply with people and connected people deeply with one another. Then he made sure he connected the right people with the right calling to the right ministry."

Paul worked to ensure that everyone was equipped to do their unique work—the work that was the right fit for how God designed them, for their spiritual shape and personal calling. We see this in his ministry with Timothy, Titus, Silas, Aquila, and Priscilla. We see it in his discussion of spiritual gifts in Romans 12:3–8; 1 Corinthians 12:1–31; and Ephesians 4:1–16. In these passages, Paul teaches that the body of Christ has many members, and though these members are one, they do not all have the same function. There are different kinds of gifts and different kinds of service. Enlisting connects people to God's unique calling.

When church leaders understand this, I hear a universal sigh of relief. They had feared that enlisting people to their biblical counseling ministry might imply "screening people out." They think, "Who am I to tell people they can't get equipped?"

Soon they begin to understand that they want to include *everyone* in various formats that equip the whole congregation for *informal* one-another ministry. They also see that even when they enlist *some* to be equipped for *formal* biblical counseling ministry, the focus is on finding the right ministry match and fit, not on creating barricades to ministry.

As we mobilize ministers, let's keep it simple and relational. You already caught and cast your *core values* in community—*envisioning* your biblical counseling MVP-C. Now connect deeply with people and connect *committed people* to their calling—*enlisting* to your MVP-C.

Nurturing a Family: Conducting Christ's Opus

Christ promises that He will build His church (Matt. 16:18). Graciously, He invites us to join Him as expert builders (1 Cor. 3:10). Notice that we are not expert programmers; we are expert *builders of people* conducting a strategic relational transformation process.

To keep the process clear-cut, remember our simple twofold template from chapter one:

- *The Informal Model:* Equipping *every* member for *informal* one-another disciple-making. You *nurture your church family* through saturating your congregation with passion for and equipping in every-member ministry—speaking and living God's truth in love.
- *The Formal Model:* Equipping *some* members for *formal* biblical counseling. You *build a team* by calling and connecting committed people to comprehensive equipping in in-depth, ongoing ministry as biblical counselors.

Most of this chapter and the bulk of this book focus on the formal model. However, as we saw in chapter one, every church must be a church *of* biblical counseling—the informal model. Ephesians 4:16 points the way. From Christ "the whole body, joined and held together by every supporting ligament, grows and builds itself up in love, as each part does its work." That pictures Christ's opus—His grand creation, His grand design for the church.

Conducting the Orchestra

You've heard it—the cacophony of noises when the orchestra begins to warm up. The disharmony is like screeching fingers on a blackboard.

157

Churches become like that when they are churches *with* a biblical counseling ministry but not *of* biblical counseling. The biblical counseling ministry sets up shop in the corner and competes for attention with the small-group ministry and the women's ministry and the men's ministry and the children's ministry. There's no harmony or synergy. The ministries are always tuning up, but never quite in tune with one another because no one is conducting them so they play the same music.

The solution is not to make the biblical counseling ministry the favored ministry. The answer is to have every ministry saturated with the church-wide commitment explored in chapter one—*every member a disciple-maker*. The women's ministry pursues that goal, the men's ministry follows that goal—everyone and every ministry aligns with that goal.

The first responsibility of pastors, teachers, and church leaders (including the leaders of the biblical counseling ministry) is to create a synchronized passion for speaking and living God's truth in love. We have seen that process in many places in chapters one through five. We will learn how to equip and empower the biblical counseling team throughout chapters six through twelve. What is missing is how to oversee that the entire church is being trained to speak the truth in love.

Training the Musicians

Even if you wanted them to, not everyone in your church would participate in your six-month, one-year, or two-year training in biblical counseling. If the whole congregation is excited about one-another ministry, but only some are able to join your extensive training, now what?

Our disciple-making champions (see below) offer a host of practical suggestions. I have used many of these in order to:

- Saturate the whole congregation with the mindset of one-another ministry through speaking the truth in love.
- Equip the whole congregation in basic principles of one-another ministry and biblical counseling, which they can use as spiritual friends in real-life settings.

- Whet people's appetite for more. Churches have me present a one-day *How to Care like Christ* seminar. They use this to say, "Since you benefited so much from one day, just imagine what could happen if you took our one-year training!"

Disciple-Making Champions

Saturating the Congregation

As part of the *4E Ministry Training Strategy Questionnaire*, two dozen best-practice churches responded to the question, "How do you ensure that the entire congregation remains excited about and becomes equipped for one-another ministry?" Here's a sampling of their strategies.

- Preaching on topics such as one-another ministry, the sufficiency of Scripture, body life, the priesthood of all believers, disciple-making.
- Modeling how to apply truth to life through preaching and teaching.
- Hosting one-day seminars by nationally known leaders in the field.
- Hosting our own seminars and in-services on one-another topics.
- Encouraging our members to attend regional and national biblical counseling conferences.
- Using Adult Bible Fellowships (Sunday school), Leadership Community, and our small-group ministry to train people in one-another ministry.
- Taking our people through DVD series on soul care, spiritual friendship, and disciple-making.
- Purchasing one-another and biblical counseling resources (books, videos, pamphlets) for our church library/resource room.
- Having individuals give testimonies regularly about how they are growing spiritually through one-another ministry and biblical counseling.
- Providing bulletin inserts with basic training in one-another ministry.
- Counseling—people who receive counseling become our most passionate proponents of one-another ministry and biblical counseling.
- Using our Wednesday night Lay Institute For Equipping (LIFE) for a thirteen-week series on disciple-making and one-another ministry.
- Teaching our leaders how to implement biblical counseling principles in our deacon groups, elder groups, everywhere!

- Offering free resources and blogs on our website on one-another ministry principles.
- Using our church quarterly e-zine, newsletter, and weekly e-blasts to teach disciple-making.
- Having a special "Soul Care Sunday" focused on one-anothering.
- Starting from the ground up by talking about one-another ministry in our membership class.
- Letting counseling principles inform everything we do—they are part of the typical ebb and flow of our life together.

If you are to unleash the whole congregation, then you must orchestrate a synergy between these equipping opportunities and your envisioning process. Help people to make practical connections in the real world. Tell them, "The vision we've been talking about, and the training you've just received—use that in your everyday life. With your family members. With your neighbors over the backyard fence. At McDonald's and Starbucks. Be sensitive to opportunities to turn mundane conversations at work into spiritual conversations. In your small groups, enter deeply into each other's lives as you apply the Word together."

Communicate to your people that one-another ministry is just as vital as preaching from the pulpit or offering formal biblical counseling. Structure your church so that doing life together and speaking the truth in love *is* church.

Building a Team: Assembling Your Dream Team

Picture where you are in the process so far. Your whole church has a growing vision for disciple-making ministry. Your biblical counseling envisioning team has diagnosed the readiness of your congregation and community. You have jointly crafted your ministry MVP-C Statement—catching and casting it in community. You are working through the relational change-management process and employing biblical conflict-resolution principles. Through an ongoing strategic process, you are equipping the whole congregation to speak and live God's truth in love.

Some individuals in the church deeply resonate with everything they are hearing. They don't know all the details yet, but the big picture draws them to want to know more. Now they hear that you are about ready to start building a biblical counseling ministry team.

Picture Myron. Part of him feels like a kid in Little League. "Pick me! Pick me!" Another part of him feels a tad reluctant: "I'd better count the cost before I make any major commitment."

Part of you feels extremely excited. "I can't wait to build a team!" Another part of you thinks more strategically: "I want to be sure we match the right people to the right ministry for the right reasons at the right time." To address these dual and dueling thoughts and feelings, use the following team-building rubrics:

- Calling people to connection: what people need to know about your ministry
- Matching the right people to the right ministry: what you need to know about ministers

These two categories should work together because, whenever possible, the decision whether someone becomes a part of the biblical counseling ministry should be mutual. With Myron, ideally it would be a combination of his deciding whether he thinks he is a good match and your leadership team's determining whether they think Myron is a good fit. You might even picture it as "dating" or "courtship."

Calling People to Connection: What People Need to Know about Your Ministry

I love the joy and freedom leaders experience when they see team building as calling people to connection. They no longer rely upon non-relational, panicked recruiting of warm bodies to fill a program void. Now they focus on relationally enlisting committed people to a captivating vision.

I love the joy and freedom God's people experience when they realize that you are inviting them to consider a call to a dream team.

They appreciate that you are calling them not out of desperation or as a last resort. They respect that you are asking them to consider seriously a calling to connect to a:

- People: you, your leadership team, and their fellow team members
- Purpose: your biblical counseling ministry MVP-C Statement
- Philosophy: your biblical approach to biblical counseling
- Profile: your portrait of a mature trainee and a nurtured graduate
- Process: your specific plan for training and for ministry after training
- Promise: your covenant to fulfill your mutual commitment

If people are to make intelligent, Spirit-led decisions about whether they want to join your biblical counseling ministry, then they need clear and specific information. These six categories provide what they need to make an informed decision.

Calling to Connect to a People

Jesus always called people to Himself—to be with Him to become like Him. While that may seem like a daunting task to us mere humans, Paul sent the same invitation. "Follow my example, as I follow the example of Christ" (1 Cor. 11:1). Nothing is more intimidating to me as an equipper than the realization that my first responsibility is to be like Christ.

This is why the decision-making process needs to be relational. It is why I believe team leaders should be church members for at least two years and potential team members for at least one year. Your equipping team needs to be able to say, "You've watched our lives for some time now. We're going to be like family. You need to decide whether our lives warrant your trust and whether you want to join our ministry family."

It is also why I believe people need to be aware of who else is considering and being considered for team/family membership. Plan to have at least one in-person meeting with all prospective trainees. Tell them, "Look around the room. Here are the other folks who could potentially join our biblical counseling family. We're going to get real and raw, close and involved. Is this the group you want to call home?"

Calling to Connect to a Purpose

After you call people to yourself and your team, call them to your MVP-C. Include your biblical counseling ministry MVP-C Statement in the packet of information that every prospective trainee receives (see Appendix 6.1 for a sample Information and Application Packet). In your written and oral interview process, assess each person's understanding of and commitment to the MVP-C—does he or she own it?

Your MVP-C Statement should become the arbiter when any issues arise about the focus of your ministry. It takes personalities and power struggles out of the equation. It becomes your blueprint for how you will do ministry, and all must agree to abide by this standard.

Calling to Connect to a Philosophy

The various approaches to biblical/Christian counseling are numerous and diverse. In your packet include a document that spells out your philosophy of counseling. Present a clear definition and a detailed description of your convictions about what makes biblical counseling truly biblical (see Appendix 6.1 for one example).

The idea is not to force everyone to walk lockstep with everything you teach. I tell potential team members, "We desire you to be Bereans (Acts 17:11), not Corinthians (1 Cor. 1:10–17). Based upon your understanding of God's Word, test what we teach. As a Berean, we expect that you'll display a critical mind minus a critical spirit. Our team can't function biblically if any member has a Corinthian attitude of negativity, biting criticism, and againstness. If your philosophy and theology of counseling differs noticeably from what you've read about ours, then we won't be a good ministry training match."

Calling to Connect to a Profile

People deserve to know what you hope they will gain from their training. What are your anticipated goals and results? We communicate this through including in our packet and our interview process "A Profile of a Nurtured LEAD Graduate" (see Appendix 6.1).

This includes the heart desires that we are looking for in our trainees at entry. We are looking for answers to questions such as the following: "Do you dream of being a spiritual friend who can deeply weep with those who weep? Do you desire to be a soul physician who can listen well and then wisely guide others through their problems to the Father's heart?" For some people these descriptions deeply resonate. They are praying, "Please, Father, lead the team to invite me to be equipped." Others realize this is not exactly what they were looking for, and they self-select out of the process.

The profile also outlines the qualities that we anticipate developing in each trainee's life as a result of our equipping and empowering ministry. We briefly describe the 4Cs of biblical content/conviction, Christlike character, relational competence, and Christian community. Again, these either attract people in with enthusiasm or lead people to opt out politely.

The third aspect of the profile sketches the types of ministries that your successful graduates could become involved in after their training. Your training may not be only for counselors. At my first church, of the twelve people we trained during our first two-year training, two launched and led a small group focused on sexual abuse recovery, two launched and led a small group focused on parenting adolescents, and two led a small group focused on victory over addictive behaviors. The other six graduates provided individual, marital, or parental/family counseling.

Calling to Connect to a Process

People also deserve to know what they are getting themselves into. This is part of wisely counting the cost. In our packet we provide specific information about time and energy expectations while in training as well as our expectations after training (see Appendix 6.1).

The in-training components include how many hours each week or month the trainee would commit to lecture/lab training, meeting with an encouragement partner, meeting with a supervisor, meeting with a counselee, and outside reading. We are also very clear about the nature of the training. "We're going to be real and raw, and mess with your life. Our training is not simply about academic head knowledge. We're going to speak the truth in love to one another—we're going to experience biblical counseling and discipleship. It's going to be intense and intimate."

We also expect people to commit to ministry after they complete their training. While people can plan only "as the Lord wills," we ask that trainees commit to a year of ministry after training for every year they were in training. This includes the time they would give to counseling others or to leading small-group ministries and their preparation time for those ministries. It also includes ongoing education such as individual supervision, group supervision, and other advanced training.

Calling to Connect to a Promise

You can imagine why a good number of people self-select out of the training. They count the cost and, at least for the present training period, they opt out. You can also imagine that those who join are red-hot in their commitment to be equipped to counsel and disciple.

We think it is important to get that commitment in writing. So we created the LEAD Personal Commitment Form (see Appendix 6.1).

Your Calling Cards: How You Invite People to Connection

Use all the typical church communication means for getting the word out about your training: pulpit and bulletin announcements, individual e-mail, group e-blast, snail mail, church newsletter or e-zine, church website, and blog. Word-of-mouth and personal contact remain the most productive means of communication—especially if your goal is connection.

Since our packet is pretty hefty, we don't distribute it to everyone. Our initial communications, which build upon the buzz created by the envisioning process, make people aware of how to obtain the information packet (see Appendix 6.1 for a sample cover letter). They can download it from our website, pick it up in the church office, receive it as an e-mail attachment, or even receive it via old-fashioned snail mail. We also include information on next steps if they resonate with our biblical counseling training process.

Matching the Right People to the Right Ministry: What You Need to Know about Ministers

In the first phase of the enlisting process, you provide people with what they need to know to make an informed decision about your ministry. After processing all your materials, some will still say, "I'm interested in being considered." That leads to the second phase where they provide you with what you need to know to make an informed decision about their fit and readiness for your biblical counseling equipping.

During the selection phase, seek to avoid ditches or extremes on either side of the enlisting process. One ditch to avoid is accepting anybody and everybody into your training. Given the commitment your equipping team is making and the expectations you have for your trainees, you need to be sure that you accept the people who best fit your ministry. Additionally, if your training emphasizes a lab/small-group component and a supervisory aspect, then realistically you can't accept more than twelve people per trainer.

The other extreme to avoid is accepting only those people who are 100 percent ready. There's no such person—including you and me. Think about the imperfections of each of the twelve disciples Jesus called. The enlisting process is about selecting people with a maturing level of commitment to Christ, commitment to the body of Christ, and growth in Christ and then scouting out whether their heart passion matches the passion of your ministry.

Addressing a Common Concern

Before we move too far in describing this process, I need to address a common concern that I briefly broached earlier. You may wonder, "So what do I do if at the end of the mutual process some people want into my training, but I don't have room for everyone, or I don't think someone is a good match? How can I tell a member of my church that I won't train them?"

First, as noted, a number of people are going to opt out due to the commitment level—they simply can't commit the time and energy at this point in their life. Second, if you implement the whole-congregation training discussed earlier, then every person still has numerous opportunities for training in one-another ministry. You are not saying, "You can't be trained at all." You are saying something like, "At this point in time, I think it would be good if you took our thirteen-week encouragement class; then let's consider the LEAD biblical counseling training the next time we offer it."

Third, there are also many other ministries in your church where this person might be a better fit. So you are saying, "Based upon your spiritual gift analysis, the assessment you completed, and our interview, I think a better fit for you in ministry at our church could be _____."

Fourth, you could be saying, "I think you're a great fit. Unfortunately, we have resources to train only a dozen people, yet we have two dozen folks we could select. We'd like to ask you if it would be okay to put you at the head of the list for our next round of training."

Fifth, in some cases, your assessment process will raise some red flags. Some folks, *at this point in their lives*, would be better served by *receiving* biblical counseling instead of being trained to *be* biblical counselors. Speak the truth in love to them: "Myron, we really appreciate your candor in responding to our written and oral questions. You've mentioned a couple of specific struggles in your life that we think would best be addressed by some biblical counseling and small-group discipleship. If history is any indication, as you work through these issues, when our next round of training starts you'll be an excellent candidate."

In more than a quarter-century of training counselors, I have never ended the mutual process with an open conflict. Sure, a few times people were disappointed. But each time they chose one of these other options and God used them greatly. What happens more often (though not a lot) is that I identify a person who I think would be an incredible biblical counselor, and for various reasons the person chooses not to enter the training.

Getting from Here to There

There is no one way, no magic bullet that teaches how to discern who would be the best fit. You'll see below that our *Disciple-Making Champions* used a great diversity of means to select trainees. They also looked for a wide assortment of qualities and qualifications. You need to build your list of qualifications based upon your ministry MVP-C, profile, and philosophy. You need to build your selection process based upon your church history, your church culture, and your own personality.

Disciple-Making Champions

Building God's Team

As part of the *4E Ministry Training Strategy Questionnaire*, two dozen best-practice churches responded to the questions, "What qualifications are you looking for in those you train as biblical counselors?" and "What is involved in your selection, interview, and application process?" No one church listed all these qualifications or included all these elements in its selection process.

The Qualifications You Are Looking For

- A Christian, growing in Christ, and a church member (some churches specified the number of years as a believer and/or as a member).
- Commitment to the church values, mission, leadership covenant, doctrinal statement, and teacher assent form. Team player.
- Enthusiastic agreement with our counseling theology/philosophy and mission/vision.
- Biblically/doctrinally sound. Able to use the Bible for real-life wisdom and discernment.
- Spiritually and emotionally mature. Godliness. Evidence of Christlikeness. Growth in Christ.
- Growing demonstration of Christian character qualities such as the fruit of the Spirit and restoring others in a spirit of gentleness (Gal. 5:22–6:2).
- Demonstrated love for people. Highly compassionate. Experience with the pain of life. Non-judgmental. Relational skillfulness. Caring.

- Demonstrated ability to minister to people in informal one-another settings—shows a passion for and gift for counseling/encouragement based upon service in the church.
- Demonstrated ability to handle smaller commitments. Serving faithfully in the church.
- Meets the qualifications for an elder in 1 Timothy 3.
- Meets the qualifications for a deacon in 1 Timothy 3.
- FITS: Faithfulness in training and service; Intentionality in gospel growth; Teachable attitude; Skills demonstrated through small-group and one-on-one ministries.
- FAT: Faithful, Available, Teachable.

The Selection, Interview, and Application Process

- Prayer.
- Starts with self-selection: a sense of calling from Christ.
- Completion of a written biblical counseling ministry application form.
- Completion of church volunteer application form.
- Completion of a background check.
- Completion of a theology exam.
- Completion of a spiritual-gifts assessment.
- Submission of one to three personal references.
- Recommendation by a pastor, elder, deacon, ministry leader, or small-group leader.
- Completion of a personal interview.
- Personal relationship—observing the person's life in community.
- Observation of ministry during our "lower level" classes on informal one-another ministry.
- Completion of a commitment agreement/covenant.

The Qualifications/Qualities You Are Looking For

The material above lists thirteen different categories of qualifications used by best-practice churches. Most churches organized their list into about a half-dozen groupings. To be consistent, I find it best to align the qualifications you are looking for with the qualities you are trying to develop throughout your equipping. In my case, that means I am looking for a *baseline level of the 4Cs* of biblical content/

conviction, Christlike character, relational competence, and Christian community.

As I design the written interview form, ask questions in the in-person interview, examine references, and observe people in their daily life in our church, the 4Cs are always at the forefront of my thinking.

If you look at the list of qualifications on the previous pages, you can collate many of them into the 4Cs. I would associate the C of biblical content/conviction with the fourth bullet of biblically sound, able to use the Bible for real-life wisdom and discernment. I would also place parts of the second and third bullets under this rubric. Trainees don't have to have a Bible degree, but I am seeking to discern their level of commitment to, trust in, understanding of, and application of God's Word for real life.

The C of Christlike character fits into several of the bullet points, including the first through third, fifth and sixth, and ninth through eleventh. The starting baseline, of course, is salvation. From there I'm looking for evidence of Christlikeness *as the person interacts with others and with me.*

The C of relational competence also matches several of the bullet points, including seven through nine. I sometimes say to myself rather roughly, "Can this person relate his way out of a paper bag?" I don't mean to be crude or cruel. Rather, it's a baseline. Biblical counseling involves speaking the truth in *love.* If people demonstrate an underdeveloped ability to love others, then *at this point in their life* it may be wiser for them to receive biblical counseling rather than be trained to be a biblical counselor.

The C of Christian community is more difficult to quantify and to distinguish from relational competency. One of my students described it beautifully: "Community is the container for the other three Cs." You best learn biblical counseling in the context of community. The last sentence of the second bullet point captures part of this C: team player. The word "teachable" in the final two bullet points captures it also. As I interact with a candidate, I'm pondering, "Does Myron value relationships, how does he get along in groups, does he use his relational competency to draw others into community, or is Myron a lone ranger?"

The Selection, Interview, and Application Process

The selection, interview, and application process is how you "get at" or discern whether a candidate has the baseline level of qualifications deemed necessary to join your training. I collated thirteen common processes used by best-practice churches. Most mentioned at least half of these.

All leaders wisely and humbly mentioned prayer. "The harvest is plentiful but the workers are few. Ask the Lord of the harvest, therefore, to send out workers into his harvest field" (Matt. 9:37–38). God not only sovereignly gifts His people, but sovereignly calls and directs His people into specific fields of service. Without a daring confidence in the Lord of the harvest, it is impossible to match the right people to the right ministry.

Depending upon the history, background, size, style, and culture of the churches I have served, I have used several of the thirteen processes. In addition to prayer and self-selection, I always use a written Biblical Counseling Ministry Application Form (see Appendix 6.1) and the completion of a personal interview. You won't be surprised when you read the application form and detect the 4Cs. If you observed a personal interview, you wouldn't be surprised to hear those 4Cs woven throughout the interview in a natural, even spontaneous way. Nor will you be surprised when you see it contains a Redeemed Personality Inventory (see chapter nine and Appendix 6.1).

I value the input of others, so references are helpful, and recommendations from leaders in our church are beneficial. I value spiritual gifting, so a spiritual-gift assessment can be useful (more to indicate the style, feel, and focus of one's counseling rather than whether or not he or she would be a capable counselor). Legal and ethical issues are important to a counseling ministry, so a background check is wise.

Still, if you are skilled as a biblical counselor, if you relate with Scripture and soul (1 Thess. 2:8), and if your love abounds in knowledge

171

and depth of insight (Phil. 1:9), then nothing is more suitable and valuable than the in-person interview. The other sources of information provide the context and at times do the gatekeeping. The personal interview, especially if administered by a team of leaders, provides the connection that is central to building a biblical counseling team, a family. It helps you sense the connection between your team and the candidate. It helps you discern mutually and candidly if there is a good connection between this person and your biblical counseling ministry.

Commencement: Connecting from Start to Finish and Everywhere Between

How you start a ministry relationship has a great influence on the ongoing shape of that relationship. It was certainly true with Paul and the Ephesian elders. He told them at the start of his emotional farewell address, "You know how I lived the whole time I was with you, from the first day I came into the province of Asia" (Acts 20:18). Trace his ministry in Ephesus from Acts 19:1 on, and you'll see that Paul focused on connecting, relating, and speaking the truth in love from the onset to the farewell.

Consider what characterized the last moments of Paul's ministry to the Ephesians. "They all wept as they embraced him and kissed him. What grieved them most was his statement that they would never see his face again. Then they accompanied him to the ship. After we had torn ourselves away from them, we put out to sea" (Acts 20:37–21:1a).

That's the type of relationship that should characterize every church. A church *of* biblical counseling will be so saturated with spiritual friendships and spiritual conversations that it hurts when someone leaves. The church's biblical counseling ministry should be so connected that "grief" is the only word that describes the loss when someone leaves.

For some people, when they heard "enlisting," the words "relational" and "connecting" likely were far from their minds. Words like "recruiting," "screening," "processes," "procedures," "policies," and "paperwork" were likely embedded in their minds. I pray that notion is forever changed. Enlisting is about mobilizing ministers: nurturing a family and building a team.

172

What a foundation that lays for equipping! You've envisioned in community, you've enlisted as a community, and now you're ready to equip people for biblical content, Christlike character, and relational competence in the context of, within the container of, Christian community. I hope you can't wait. I can't.

Growing Together: Questions for Reflection, Discussion, and Application

1. What difference will it make in your attitude when you think of enlisting as connecting rather than as recruiting? When you move from asking, "How can we recruit more volunteers?" to "How can we connect committed people with our disciple-making vision?"

2. Regarding saturating your congregation with one-another ministry:
   a. Of the practical suggestions from the Disciple-Making Champions, which ones are you already using? Which ones would you like to add?
   b. How could you structure your church so that doing life together and speaking the truth in love *is* church?

3. As you assemble your dream team by calling people to connection:
   a. Which of the six steps (people, purpose, philosophy, profile, process, promise) do you think would be the easiest to create? The hardest?
   b. What changes would you make to the sample documents in Appendix 6.1 to adapt them for your situation?

4. In matching the right people to the right ministry:
   a. What qualifications/qualities are you looking for? Why are these central?
   b. Of the Disciple-Making Champions' list of options in the selection, interview, and application process, which would you use? Why? How?

5. A shift is on the horizon—from envisioning in community and enlisting as a community to equipping within community. How would you approach equipping so that you connect as deeply to your team as Paul did to his team?

PART 3

Equipping Godly Ministers for Ministry

The year was 1985—my first year out of seminary. Shirley and I had just moved to Elyria, Ohio, with our six-month-old son, Josh. We were thrilled that we would be living on a whopping $14,000 for my work at Open Door Christian School as the middle school and high school Bible teacher, school guidance counselor, and high school varsity wrestling coach. The $5,000 we saved during my four years in seminary became our down payment on our first home—a $42,000 three-bedroom, one-bath, two-car-garage, brick ranch home with a fenced backyard and a brand-new swing set for our son. Life was good.

Not only was I "Coach K" to three dozen young men on our wrestling team, I also launched my ministry as a coach-equipper of biblical counselors. I started PEP: the *Peer Encouragement Program*. I trained a dozen high school juniors and seniors in the basics of biblical encouragement and discipleship (that little manual eventually became my second book, *Spiritual Friends*). They met with upper elementary school and middle school students to listen, care, share, and encourage. Life was good.

Coaching and equipping are in my blood, in my DNA. It's who I am, who God designed me to be. Whether it's coaching wrestlers or coaching counselors, I am always thinking about a comprehensive foundation. Whether it's the first day of wrestling practice or the first night of counseling equipping, I always start with the Vince Lombardi illustration. Lombardi, the legendary football coach (1959–67) of the Green Bay Packers, was frustrated after his team played a poor first half. During halftime he held a football in his hands and said to these professional athletes, "Gentlemen, this is a football." They needed a reminder about the basics—Football 101.

In part three, I lay a comprehensive foundation for biblical counseling equipping—the 4Cs—that can constitute the focus of every biblical counseling equipping ministry.

- Biblical *Content/Conviction*: head/knowing—how to change lives with Christ's changeless truth
- Christlike *Character*: heart/being—how to reflect Christ
- Counseling *Competence*: hands/doing—how to care like Christ
- Christian *Community*: home/loving—how to grow together in Christ

In chapter seven we will learn how the 4Cs provide our biblical counseling training *goals and objectives*. This chapter answers the questions: "What is the purpose of biblical counseling training? What do nurtured graduates of biblical counseling training look like?"

In chapters eight and nine we will move from these broad goals and objectives to a focused discussion of biblical counseling training *curriculum and materials*. These two chapters address the question: "What should biblical counselors know, be, and do, and how should they relate?"

In chapter ten we will explore biblical counseling training *strategies and methods*. These suggest the how-to of shaping your training, and they present best-practice training methods for equipping biblical counselors.

This chapter tackles the question, "How do we structure our equipping so we effectively train biblical counselors to know, be, do, and love?"

A coach like Vince Lombardi loved specific goals. If he had written this section, his ROLOs (Reader-Oriented Learning Objectives) might sound like this: through your active reading and application of the four chapters in this section, you will be equipped to:

- Develop comprehensive four-dimensional training *goals and objectives* for equipping biblical counselors in the 4Cs of biblical content, Christlike character, counseling competence, and Christian community (chapter seven).
- Map out the focused *curriculum and materials* that will become your subject matter and lesson plans for equipping biblical counselors in content, character, competence, and community (chapters eight and nine).
- Apply transformational training *strategies and methods* that comprehensively equip your trainees for knowing (head/content), being (heart/character), doing (hands/competence), and loving (home/community) (chapter ten).

This 4C map has served me well—from my days as the PEP equipper, to my three churches as the LEAD equipper, and through my dozen years as a seminary professor. It has served hundreds of best-practice churches well also. This comprehensive biblical guide for equipping biblical counselors will be a tool for your church too.

7

Competent to Counsel

THE RÉSUMÉ OF THE
BIBLICAL COUNSELOR

Four years after I started my ministry at Open Door Christian School, I moved down the hallway 100 yards to begin my first pastoral ministry—Counseling and Discipleship Pastor at the Church of the Open Door (COD). Though the church was a mega-church of over 3,000, COD had never hired a counseling pastor. When they listed the position, all they knew was that they had scores of people asking for counseling and no pastors trained to counsel. The job description encompassed little more than having someone counsel people every week.

Being the guy with coaching-equipping in his veins, I prepared a packet of material proposing that they expand their vision and hire a Counseling *and* Discipleship Pastor. If hired, I would not only counsel and pastor; I would disciple and equip church members through the LEAD Ministry: *Life Encouragers And Disciplers*. I had taught, counseled, and coached the sons and daughters of half the board members, so even though I was the ripe young age of twenty-nine, they were enthusiastic about the vision and hired me. The year was 1989, and

I was shocked to be making $25,000, nearly double my pay just four years earlier. Life was good.

A Kid in His Dad's Suit

I will never forget the first evening of our first LEAD class. Among my twelve trainees was my wife, but everyone else was between five and twenty-five years older than me. It was back in the day when pastors wore a suit and tie even on a Wednesday night. I was just fine the first hour of our training—the lecture/interaction hour. Then, after a short break, we switched our chairs from rows to a circle and were about to have our first counseling small-group lab.

That was when an overwhelming image struck me. I pictured myself as a ten-year-old boy dressed in my dad's way-too-large suit, the sleeves dangling over my hands, and my feet too short to touch the floor. My first inclination was to ignore the image and pretend that I was fine. Then I made one of the smartest, bravest, most significant decisions of my young ministry. I shared my image with the class.

Rather than act like I had it all together, rather than fake it, I decided to walk the talk. I had told each of them during the enlisting process that we were going to get real and talk honestly about life. That first night we did, and we were never the same because of it. We jelled; connected; bonded. We spoke the truth in love. Person after person shared their story of trepidation. We laughed. We cried. We shared Scripture about our identity in Christ. We prayed. We went way over time . . . and nobody noticed (except the nursery worker who was watching our newborn daughter, Marie). Life was good.

A Portrait of Nurtured Graduates

That first night we experienced comprehensive equipping. In the context of community, we applied biblical content to our lives, encouraged one another to develop Christlike character, and began to cultivate biblical counseling competencies as we ministered to one another.

At that stage of my ministry, I wouldn't have called these goals and objectives 4C Equipping, but even then I was committed to comprehensive training. I had a picture in my mind—a portrait of a nurtured graduate of our LEAD biblical counseling ministry. I knew that I wanted to minister to the whole person—the head, the heart, and the hands in the context of God's home. Everything we did together for those two years we geared toward shaping one another into the image of that portrait.

Four-Dimensional Equipping Versus One-Dimensional Equipping

In my consulting, both in churches and in seminary settings, the primary weakness we identify involves training that lacks one or more of the 4Cs. In fact, many training programs, whether in churches or schools, tend to highlight one dimension (one of the 4Cs) to the detriment of the other components of comprehensive biblical counseling training.

Some biblical counseling equipping tilts almost exclusively to biblical content. Trainees know the Word, which is essential, but they are mostly head and little heart (truth minus love). Lacking the competency to relate truth to life, they end up preaching at counselees. They are unskilled at engaging counselees in scriptural explorations that empower counselees to apply truth to their lives.

Some biblical counseling training inclines the pendulum the other direction and focuses almost exclusively on counseling competency. Training consists of the meticulous practice of skills and techniques apart from an equal emphasis on biblical wisdom, Christlikeness, and loving engagement. Trainees have big hands, if you will, but underdeveloped heads and hearts.

Still other ministries focus on the character of the counselors and their spiritual formation, which is vital. But there is a mindset that somehow by osmosis the godly person will help others to become godlier. Churches and schools end up with trainees who are all heart but lacking in biblical insight and counseling abilities.

Additionally, some training in biblical counseling tends to be a tad tone-deaf to the community or relational aspect. Perhaps because of biblical counseling's appropriate emphasis on content and the Word, an inappropriate de-emphasis results. Training becomes classroom-like, didactic, and academic. Even the "lab" or skills component is more oriented to technique development or case study discussions than to relational depth and personal connection among group members. What is lacking is a nurturing environment that encourages group members to grow together through connecting with one another and communing with Christ. Since we counsel as we are trained, trainees end up more robotic than relational.

There are various explanations for one-dimensional equipping: the personality of the trainer, the training the trainer experienced, the educational philosophy of the trainer, and time limitations. Everything seeks to pull us away from comprehensive equipping.

This is why it is absolutely vital that we saturate our biblical counseling ministry with four-dimensional goals and objectives. The 4Cs should be like a neon light in our MVP-C Statement, our enlisting process, our scriptural foundation, our philosophy of education, our core learning objectives, our training itself, our evaluation of our trainees and our training, everything. We must commit to remain on the cutting edge of biblical counseling equipping by following Christ's disciple-making model of intentionally and comprehensively training the whole person: the head (knowing/content), the heart (being/character), and the hands (doing/competence) in the context of God's home (loving/community).

Our first task in equipping biblical counselors is to laser-focus on the four-dimensional biblical portrait. This chapter is your snapshot of the comprehensive résumé qualifications you seek to nurture in the biblical counselors you equip.

The Divine Counselor's Résumé Qualifications: God's Four-Dimensional Map

Imagine that you are forwarding your résumé to the Holy Spirit, the Divine Counselor. What items would you highlight to demonstrate your eligibility to enter the ranks of biblical counselors? What do the Scriptures say? What qualifies a person for biblical counseling? What qualities make your trainees eligible to claim the mantle of soul physician and spiritual friend?

Fortunately, for those of us who train biblical counselors, the apostle Paul already completed the résumé. "I myself am convinced, my brothers, that you yourselves are full of goodness, complete in knowledge and competent to instruct one another" (Rom. 15:14). In this verse, the surrounding context, and other biblical passages we discover the four résumé qualifications of a nurtured biblical counselor. They supply our biblical counseling equipping *goals and objectives*:

The Four Dimensions of Comprehensive Biblical Counseling Equipping

• Character	"Full of Goodness"	Heart/Being
• Content/Conviction	"Complete in Knowledge"	Head/Knowing
• Competence	"Competent to Instruct One Another"	Hands/Doing
• Community	"Brothers/One Another"	Home/Loving*

* See Appendix 7.1 for a fuller outline of biblical counseling 4C equipping goals.

Before we develop these characteristics, we need to consider a common reaction. The moment we start talking about training "lay" people as biblical counselors, we can expect push-back. People will raise numerous objections, sometimes vehemently, against our conviction that God's people can be competent counselors. We can respond to their push-back with God's Word, which settles the issue, and with research that validates the effectiveness of paraprofessional people helpers.

Confidence Based on God's Word: The Sufficiency of Christianity

Ponder who Paul is addressing in Romans 15:14 with his term "brothers." Are these apostles, pastors, elders, deacons, deaconesses, or former Jewish priests? Have they graduated from the exclusive training institutions of Paul's day? Are they the elite philosophers and scholars of Roman society?

No. They are "average, ordinary" Christians in Rome. "Brothers" was the common designation of a believer regardless of gender, status, position, or rank. Based upon the surrounding context (Rom. 16:1–16), Paul's addressees are members of small house churches spread throughout the city and dotting the countryside of Rome. These men and women, converted Jews and Greeks, slaves and free, Paul considers competent to counsel.

Based upon Paul's language, I conclude that Paul knew that his readers would be skeptical about their ability to counsel one another. I imagine them thinking, "Now, Paul, perhaps you, a super apostle, are competent to counsel. Perhaps the other apostles also. But not us!"

Paul is quite emphatic in his language. The NIV accurately translates his emphasis, "I myself." "You yourselves." Paul's addition of the personal pronoun produces emphasis by redundancy. Paul wants no mistakes. He is positive that they are powerful. "I, I myself. Inspired by the Divine Counselor, I am telling you that I am absolutely confident in you, you yourselves. Yes, you yourselves are competent to counsel one another."

Paul is not making an assumption here. He says that he is "convinced." He is confident in them, trusts them, and knows that he can count on them to counsel one another competently. He has faith in their spiritual ability, being inwardly certain because of external evidence. The evidence he offers provides the biblical prescription, the biblical résumé, for biblical counselors.

And the Survey Says: The Effectiveness of Paraprofessionals

While I was working on my doctorate, an article published in a major counseling journal sent shock waves through the counseling community. Its results called into question the efficacy of professional counseling training, while also distilling basic elements that qualify an individual to be an effective people helper.

The article traced the history of modern research into counselor effectiveness beginning with Durlak's work examining the results of forty-two studies that compared the effectiveness of professional help-ers to paraprofessionals (laypeople helpers). The data from the study indicated that lay helpers equaled or surpassed the effectiveness of the professional therapists.[1]

Hattie, Sharpley, and Rogers attempted to refute those findings by combining the results of forty-six studies. Their data, however, sup-ported Durlak's conclusions. Clients of lay helpers consistently achieved more positive outcomes than did clients of the professionally educated and experienced counselors.[2]

Berman and Norton reanalyzed Hattie's study. Their reanalysis indicated that lay counselors were equally effective as professional coun-selors in promoting positive change. They concluded that no research currently supported the notion that professional training, knowledge, or experience improved therapist effectiveness.[3]

Herman, in his review of these studies, indicated that research suggested that professional training was not the primary means for developing competence in helping people. Rather, the personal char-acteristics of the helper were the greatest factors leading to competence as a counselor. In other words, the studies demonstrated that maturity, love, genuine concern, empathy, humility, and vulnerability were more important than professional training.[4]

After the appearance of these studies, Tan noted that little research had been done to assess the effectiveness of church-based Christian lay counseling programs. He rectified that through a controlled study of a church-based lay counseling program. His findings indicated that the treatment group reported significantly more improvement on all measures than the control group, and they maintained their gains at significant levels. He concluded that

1. J. Durlak, "Comparative Effectiveness of Paraprofessional and Professional Helpers," *Psychological Bulletin* 86, no. 1 (1979): 80–92.

2. J. A. Hattie, H. J. Rogers, and C. F. Sharpley, "Comparative Effectiveness of Professional and Paraprofessional Helpers," *Psychological Bulletin* 95, no. 3 (1984): 534–41.

3. J. S. Berman and N. C. Norton, "Does Professional Training Make a Therapist More Effective?" *Psychology Bulletin* 98, no. 2 (1985): 401–7.

4. Keith Herman, "Reassessing Predictors of Therapist Competence," *Journal of Counseling and Development* 72 (September/October 1993): 29–32.

the study supports the effectiveness of Christian lay counseling in a local church context.[5]

Such descriptive research offers valuable support when people raise objections to the effectiveness of equipping biblical counselors for the local church. Of course, two thousand years earlier the apostle Paul offered all the biblical validation that we need when he affirmed that God's people in Rome were competent to counsel. We return now to our examination of the biblical qualifications that God's Word deems necessary for someone to be considered a competent biblical counselor.

Reflecting Christlike Character: Loving like Jesus— "Full of Goodness"

Is Paul saying that Christians who are far from Christ and unable to relate to others are powerful biblical counselors? Of course not. Competent biblical counselors have résumés with "full of goodness" as their first qualification.

"Goodness" is the same word Paul uses in Galatians 5:22–23 as one of the nine aspects of the fruit of the Spirit. When I first read Romans 15:14, I wondered why Paul would pick the fruit of goodness. Why not love, joy, peace, or any other fruit of the Spirit?

So I explored goodness. The Old Testament highlights the basic confession that God *is* good because His love endures forever (1 Chron. 16:34). It also emphasizes that our good God *does* good (Ex. 18:9). That is, He displays His goodness in active social relationships. Further, I noted Christ's statement that only God is good (Matt. 19:17). Then I noticed the linkage of goodness and godliness with godlikeness—with *Christlikeness* (Matt. 5:43–48; Eph. 2:10; Col. 1:10). In each of these passages, goodness displays itself in active, grace-oriented relationships, as when our good Father causes His sun to shine upon and His rain to fall on the righteous and the unrighteous.

5. Siang-Yang Tan and Yiu-Meng Toh, "The Effectiveness of Church-Based Lay Counselors: A Controlled Outcome Study," *Journal of Psychology and Christianity* 16, no. 3 (1997): 260–67.

Goodness is a virtue that reveals itself in social relationships, in our various contacts and connections with others. Biblical goodness always displays itself in relational contexts through undeserved kindness.

Equipping Christlike Counselors

Thus, in Romans 15:14, Paul is talking about *Christlike character* that relates with grace. The powerful spiritual friend reflects the ultimate Spiritual Friend, Jesus. We are powerful to the degree that we reflect the loving character of Christ. Paul is teaching us that the competent biblical counselor is the person who relates well, who connects deeply, who is compassionate, and who has the ability to develop intimate grace relationships.

In discussing goodness, Paul uses the modifier "full." "Full" pictures a net that breaks due to the stress and tension of too much weight and a cup that is so chock-full that its contents spill over. Paul pictures mature love and godly character flowing through Christ to us, then spilling over from us into our spiritual friend's life.

To the degree that our trainees increasingly reflect Christ and relate increasingly like Christ, to that degree they will be fruitful biblical counselors. The one who is good at relating is the person whose words and actions have deep impact.

Paul's first résumé qualification teaches that knowledge and skill without character is like one corpse practicing cosmetic surgery on another corpse. We witnessed this truth in a counseling lab when Amber shared her deep sorrow over the loss of her mother. As a male group member, Mike, attempted to connect, it became painfully obvious that Mike was badly misconnecting because he was trying to "practice skills" instead of relating deeply out of a good heart.

So we asked the question, "Mike, who would you be without your skills?" Mike was dumbfounded—sincerely wanting to help, but recognizing how truly unable he was to enter into Amber's world. With Amber and Mike's permission, we shifted our focus to Mike. One group member told his story of slowly learning to relate soul-to-soul. Another member simply hugged Mike, holding him while the dam of tears burst. A third individual painted a picture of Mike robbed of his toolbox and forced to break into his home to save his wife and children. He asked him, "Mike, what would you do if you did not have your toolbox of techniques?" One year later, Mike shared with us that our interactions with him not only changed how he offers biblical counseling, but transformed how he relates to his wife and children.

Equipping Counselors Whose Inner Life Increasingly Reflects the Inner Life of Christ

Who is qualified for the task of biblical counseling? The person who increasingly reflects Christ. Through the new covenant, God has implanted a new heart in the believer. However, as Peter reminds us, we must cultivate growth in Christ and the development of the Christian virtues.

> His divine power *has given us* everything we need for life and godliness through our knowledge of him who called us by his own glory and goodness. Through these he has given us his very great and precious promises, so that through them you may participate in the divine nature and escape the corruption in the world caused by evil desires. For this very reason, *make every effort* to add to your faith goodness; and to goodness, knowledge; and to knowledge, self-control; and to self-control, perseverance; and to perseverance, godliness; and to godliness, brotherly kindness; and to brotherly kindness, love. For if you possess these qualities *in increasing measure*, they will keep you from being ineffective and unproductive in your knowledge of our Lord Jesus Christ. (2 Peter 1:3–8)

We need to structure our equipping in biblical counseling to encourage our trainees to discipline themselves so that in humble cooperation with the Holy Spirit the implanted Christlikeness grows. Our biblical counseling training environment should be the greenhouse where these character traits blossom as our trainees cultivate and reflect the inner life of Christ.

Changing Lives with Biblical Content/Conviction: Thinking like Jesus—"Complete in Knowledge"

Is Paul implying that the best biblical counselor is the "touchy-feely" person who is never dedicated to serious study of the Scripture? Not at all. Remember that God calls us to love Him with our minds—with our brains (Matt. 22:37). This is why Paul lists "complete in knowledge" as the second qualification on the biblical counselor's résumé.

"Complete" does not suggest that our trainees become walking biblical encyclopedias with absolute knowledge of all theological truth. Only God has encyclopedic knowledge of all things actual and possible. Instead, by "complete" Paul means that we and our trainees become so filled with God's Word that it claims our entire being and stamps our whole life, conduct, attitude, and relationships. We are captured by God's truth.

Equipping Counselors Who Relate Truth to Life

What sort of knowledge does Paul emphasize? He could have chosen any of several words that highlight content or factual knowledge alone. However, Paul chooses a word for "knowledge" that highlights the combination of information and implication. Paul's word focuses upon insight and wisdom—the wisdom to relate truth to life.

Competent biblical counselors understand how to apply God's Word first to their own life. They also have the insight to see how God's Word relates to their friend's life. Additionally, they have the biblical vision to see how God is relating to their friend. They have discernment to see life from God's perspective.

In Philippians 1:9–11, Paul develops his philosophy of ministry, his conviction about what equips us for biblical counseling. "And this is my prayer: that your love may abound more and more in knowledge and depth of insight, so that you may be able to discern what is best and may be pure and blameless until the day of Christ, filled with the fruit of righteousness that comes through Jesus Christ—to the glory and praise of God."

Notice Paul's coupling of truth and love. For him, biblical counseling is never either/or—either we are loving, touchy-feely, heart people, or we are scholarly, academic, head people. Rather, ministry is both/and—we unite head and heart, love and truth in our personal ministry of the Word. When our love abounds more and more in knowledge, the result is insight—the ability to help our spiritual friends to discern not simply what is good, but what is best in their life situations.

189

Equipping Counselors Who Unite Scripture and Soul

We find this harmony of truth and love everywhere in Scripture. We already examined it in the core passage on local church equipping: leaders equip God's people to speak the truth in love (Eph. 4:15). We see it again in 1 Thessalonians 2:8. "We loved you so much that we were delighted to share with you not only the gospel of God but our own lives as well, because you had become so dear to us." Biblical ministry always unites Scripture and soul.

At the end of our training, we should be able to say what Paul said to Timothy at the end of his life. "You, however, know all about my teaching, my way of life" (2 Tim. 3:10a). That way we will not be hypocritical when we encourage our trainees the way Paul encouraged Timothy. "Watch your life and doctrine closely" (1 Tim. 4:16a). Everywhere we see teaching and life, truth and love, Scripture and soul, doctrine and relationship.

We need to structure our equipping in biblical counseling so that our trainees gain deep insight into people, problems, and solutions—from a biblical perspective. And our training needs to equip prospective biblical counselors with the wisdom to relate those biblical truths to people's daily lives and relationships—changing lives with Christ's changeless truth.

Caring with Counseling Competence: Serving like Jesus—"Competent to Instruct One Another"

Typical Christians in Rome with character and conviction are qualified to do what? Paul says they are competent to "instruct." The word "competent" means to have the power to accomplish a mission. It reminds me of Engineer Scotty on *Star Trek* yelling to Captain Kirk, "Capt'in Kirrrk. We ainta got da poworr! Our dilithium crystal, she's breakin' up!" Competence is the dilithium crystal, the warp drive, the fuel, the power necessary to fulfill God's call on our lives.

"Competent" also means to have the ability, capability, resources, and strength to function and relate well. Paul is confident that believers are capable and competent in Christ.

190

Equipping Counselors Who Are Competent to Disciple One Another

Powerfully competent to do what? Powerful to "instruct" (*nouthetein*). Jay Adams, founder of the National Association of Nouthetic Counselors (NANC), describes nouthetic counseling as confronting for change out of concern (see Adams, *Competent to Counsel, The Christian Counselor's Manual,* and *A Theology of Christian Counseling: More than Redemption*). "Instruct" contains this nuance, especially when the proposed change emphasizes inner heart change leading to relational change.

The foundational meaning of *noutheteo* comes from the root *noeo*, meaning to direct one's mind, to perceive, and from *nous*—the mind, heart, seat of spiritual, rational, and moral insight and action. The mind is the place of practical reason leading to moral action. The stress is not merely on the intellect, but also on the will and disposition. *Noutheteo* means to impart understanding, to set right, to lay on the heart. Nouthetic impartation of truth can take the form of admonition, teaching, reminding, advising, urging, encouraging, and spurring on.

Paul uses *noutheteo* in Colossians 1:20–29 to describe one aspect of his pastoral ministry. God commissioned him to present Christ's gospel of grace to people (1:20–25), infusing people with the hope of who they are in Christ (1:26–27), with the goal of presenting them mature in Christ (1:28), through personal, passionate, persistent involvement in their lives (1:28–29), by Christ's resurrection power (1:29). Believers who possess Christlike goodness (character) plus Christlike insight (conviction) are competent to disciple one another toward communion with Christ and conformity to Christ through the personal ministry of the Word—biblical counseling.

Equipping Counselors Who Are Competent to Comfort One Another

Paul never intended Romans 15:14 to be the final or only word on the nature of biblical counseling. Nor did he use *noutheteo* as the only or even the primary concept to describe the personal ministry of the Word. For instance, in 1 Thessalonians 5:14, Paul uses five distinct words for biblical counseling. "And we urge [*parakaleo*] you, brothers, warn [*noutheteo*] those who are idle, encourage [*paramutheomai*] the timid, help [*antechomai*] the weak, be patient with [*makrothumeo*] everyone."

Among the many New Testament words for spiritual care, *parakaleo* predominates. Whereas *noutheteo* occurs eleven times in the New Testament, *parakaleo* (comfort, encourage, console) appears 109 times. In 2 Corinthians 1:3–11, Paul informs us that we are competent to comfort (*parakaleo*) one another. Those who have humbly received God's comfort, God equips to offer comfort to others.

The word *parakaleo* emphasizes personal presence (one called alongside to help) and suffering with another person. It seeks to turn desolation into consolation through hope in God. The duty of comfort in Old and New Testament thinking fell not upon professional helpers, but upon close relatives, neighbors, friends, and colleagues. Comforters come alongside to help struggling, suffering people through personal presence coupled with scriptural insight.

When Christ ascended, He sent the Holy Spirit to be our *Parakletos*—our Comforter and Advocate called alongside to encourage and help in times of suffering, trouble, grief, injustice, and hardship. The Spirit performs His ministry by being in us and by revealing truth to us (John 14:16–17). As the Spirit of truth, His ministry is the exact opposite of Satan, who is the father of lies (John 8:44). Satan's name is "the accuser" (Rev. 12:10), and his core strategy is to speak lying words of condemnation to us. The Spirit's name is "Encourager" and "Advocate," and His strategy is to speak the truth in love about our justification and acceptance in Christ.

Think about what Paul is saying to *you and your trainees*. You don't have to have a Ph.D. in counseling to be a competent counselor. You have the *Resource* planted within you—the *Parakletos*, the Holy Spirit. You also have the *resources* planted within you—the ability to be a competent *parathetic* (combining *parakaleo* and *noutheteo*) biblical counselor who provides:

- Soul Care through *Parakaleo*: Coming alongside hurting people in their suffering and grief, weeping with them while offering hope through your personal presence coupled with scriptural insight. Offering them tastes of Jesus' empathetic care in the *sustaining* process so they know that it's normal to hurt. Sharing with them biblical encouragement in the *healing* process so they know that it's possible to hope.

- Spiritual Direction through *Noutheteo*: Entering the lives of people struggling to grow in their personal walk with Christ. Offering passionate, persistent, personal involvement in their lives as you assist them to see who they are in Christ and help them to live out their new life in Christ in communion with and conformity to Christ. Ministering to them in the *reconciling* process so they know that it's horrible to sin, but wonderful to be forgiven. Sharing Scripture and soul with them in the *guiding* process so they know that it's supernatural to mature.

We need to structure our equipping in biblical counseling so that our trainees develop the biblical counseling competencies of sustaining and healing (*parakaletic* counseling for suffering and progressive sanctification), and of reconciling and guiding (*nouthetic* counseling for sin and progressive sanctification). Our end goal is to equip our trainees to learn how to care like Christ.

Growing in Christian Community: Connecting in Jesus—"Brothers/One Another"

Every word Paul wrote about competent biblical counselors he penned in the plural—"brothers," "one another," "you yourselves." The effective biblical counselor is no "Lone Ranger" Christian. Competent biblical counselors live and grow together in community as they commune with Christ and connect with the body of Christ.

Paul sandwiches his words in Romans 15:14 around a one-another community context. In Romans 12:3–8, he writes of each member belonging to all the others, and of using gifts in the context of the body of Christ.

In Romans 12:9–21, the context reflects one-anothering. Be devoted to one another in love. Honor one another. Share with one another. Practice hospitality with one another. Rejoice with one another. Weep with one another. Live in harmony with one another.

In Romans 13, the context is loving one another: "Whatever other commandments there may be, are summed up in this one rule: 'Love your neighbor as yourself.' Love does no harm to its neighbor. Therefore love is the fulfillment of the law" (13:9–10).

Paul continues his one-anothering theme in Romans 14:1–15:13. Don't judge one another; instead, mutually edify each other. Bear with one another. Please one another. Build up one another. Be united with one another. Encourage one another. Accept one another. Worship with one another.

In Romans 16, Paul writes about meeting together with one another in house churches where believers connect intimately. Connecting in community is the context, before and after Romans 15:14. Effective training in biblical counseling is learned in community. Put another way, growth in character, content, and competence occurs in the context of community.

As I illustrated at the beginning of this chapter, small-group labs are a core aspect of my biblical counseling training. As part of the labs, I pair trainees as spiritual friends/encouragement partners. These relationships blossom into some of the most meaningful aspects of our biblical counseling training. For example, the pairing of Debbie, a mid-30s Caucasian woman, and Linda, an early-50s African-American woman, developed into a deep, lasting friendship. Not having known each other before September, they became so close that by December of that year, Linda asked Debbie to be her matron of honor at her May wedding. Not surprisingly, both Debbie and Linda are effective biblical counselors. They know how to connect.

One-to-one connection is vital, but so is small-group community, which is another component of the biblical counseling labs I lead. We learn to apply biblical truth, develop counseling competencies, and cultivate Christlike character as we connect in a caring community. In the context of a nurturing small-group environment, we participate in the horizontal one-another spiritual disciplines.

According to Paul, transformed lives occur as we connect together in the body of Christ (Rom. 12:3–16:27) *and* as we connect with Christ (Rom. 12:1–2). Conformity to Christ is the result of communion with Christ (2 Cor. 3:16–18; 4:16–18). Effective biblical counselors add another important qualification to their résumé: connection in community. We need to structure our equipping in biblical counseling so that our trainees relate, connect, and grow together in Christ.

Disciple-Making Champion:
Pastor John Henderson, Counseling Pastor,
Denton Bible Church

Pastor John Henderson oversees the Equipped to Counsel ministry used not only at the church where he serves—Denton Bible Church in Denton, Texas—but also in churches around the country. Pastor Henderson's equipping process models well the 4Cs.

Pastor Henderson described the goal of his biblical counseling equipping. "Our primary prayer for people who complete the equipped process is for them to experience a total paradigm shift in their view of God, the Scriptures, people, and counseling. We want people to be Christ-centered rather than man-centered in their understanding of everything. We want them to see counseling as a daily privilege and opportunity where they live, learning to apply the gospel in every detail of life, and making 'speaking the truth in love' a chief priority of their lives."

When asked what *content* objectives he wanted his trainees to address, Pastor Henderson replied, "We want to see consistent growth in: theology/truth/biblical knowledge and practical implications of these content areas; understanding of the gospel and how it speaks to daily life and struggles; understanding people and how to love, listen, and encourage them; common errors or false teachings that assault sound biblical counseling and how to answer these in a gentle, loving way from Scripture."

When asked what *character* objectives he wanted his trainees to master, Pastor Henderson shared, "I would like to see our people grow in their awe, wonder, and worship toward God. I pray that our hearts would be constantly stirred and moved by the gospel. I would like to see our people

195

deal honestly with the condition of their hearts and learn to minister the gospel to their own souls every hour. I pray that the Spirit would grow our love for Him and one another."

Pastor Henderson summarized the *competence* objectives he seeks for his trainees to gain. "Strong listening competencies, an ability to help people tell their stories and open up; being able to address personal struggles, sinfulness, and need for change in comfortable, warm, and gracious ways; learning to see where the gospel fits in someone's life; and how to make the gospel speak to others. I could probably list another twenty!"

Related to building *community*, Pastor Henderson explained, "We're constantly encouraging one another to apply what we are learning to our own hearts and lives and asking each other to face Christ in everything, and to listen together to Him through His Word. We leave room for good group discussion; I try to maintain a humble and transparent attitude as their pastor and teacher; we share testimonies and have people really open up during our training meetings."

A Word to Your Trainees: Confident Competency in Christ

When someone questions the legitimacy of equipping the body of Christ for biblical counseling, direct him or her back to the apostle Paul and Romans 15:14. When the people you are training share their trepidation, as our group did that first night, empathize with those feelings. But don't stop there. Provide them with the same biblical affirmation that Paul offers the believers in Rome.

Say to your biblical counselors, "I'm confident that your maturing Christlike character, increasing biblical content/conviction, and deepening Christian community connection make you competent to counsel. Most importantly, God is confident because your competence comes from Christ. Don't take a backseat to anyone!"

And then continue, "By the way, this means that we all have work to do. God is calling us individually and jointly to *grow* in wisdom, integrity, and love. There's work to do, but we are God's workmanship created in Christ Jesus to do good works that God has prepared

196

in advance (Eph. 2:10). There's work to do, but it is God who works in us to will and to act according to His good purposes (Phil. 2:13). Let's start growing!"

A Word to You as the Equipper: Growing in Christ/ Clinging to Christ

Here's my hunch. At times, you are breathing a sigh of relief. A plan is coming into focus. The 4C map gives you simple yet concrete handles as you begin to shape the goals and objectives of your training.

At other times, you are feeling very much like a ten-year-old kid in his dad's oversized suit. You are beginning to realize that you won't be able to hide behind the pulpit or the lectern. You're going to have to step out, step up, and step forward—warts and all, so to speak.

I would say to you what you said to your trainees. "Don't take a backseat to anyone!"

I would also say, as you said to your trainees, "There's work to do."

Imitate Christ

If we are honest, part of our trepidation arises because of a realization. If we are to equip others in the 4Cs, then we have to be growing in the 4Cs. We are to say to people what Paul said to the Corinthians. "Follow my example as I follow the example of Christ" (1 Cor. 11:1).

I don't have any secret steps or how-to shortcuts on that one. I will share this exhortation, however. Find a Paul and a Barnabas, or a Priscilla and a Ruth. In the classic threefold mentoring model, you already have a Timothy—a batch of them—your biblical counseling trainees.

As you build into them, who is building into you? Pray for a Paul or a Priscilla—an older, more mature saint who can disciple you. Pray for a Barnabas or a Ruth—a peer, a spiritual friend with whom you can share mutual encouragement. In conjunction with your personal walk with Christ and your relationships within the body of Christ, God will use your Paul/Priscilla and your Barnabas/Ruth relationships to mature you as a 4C biblical counselor/equipper.

Imitate Paul

I'm guessing that you realize something else. You're recognizing that you can't do this equipping stuff dispassionately, academically. As we already saw with Paul in 1 Thessalonians 2:8, equipping others requires that we give from the depths of our souls. It also requires a depth of relationship like the one we saw in the last chapter where Paul and the Ephesian elders had to tear themselves away from each other (Acts 20:36–21:1).

There's more. Listen to Paul's description of the equipping process in Galatians 4:19. "My dear children, for whom I am again in the pains of childbirth until Christ is formed in you." You might not have purchased this book if the title were *Equipping Counselors for Your Church: The Pains of Repetitive Childbirth*.

Paul describes that labor in more detail in Colossians 1:28–2:1a.

> We proclaim him, admonishing and teaching everyone with all wisdom, so that we may present everyone perfect in Christ. To this end I labor, struggling with all his energy, which so powerfully works in me. I want you to know how much I am struggling for you.

No. I am not trying to scare you. Well, perhaps I am. Equipping others should scare us into dependency—Christ-dependency. Like Paul, we need to cling to Christ and His unlimited power, not depend upon our own limited power.

Again, I have no easy formula to offer you. I will share this word of counsel, however. Practice the spiritual disciplines (1 Cor. 9:24–27; 1 Tim. 4:7). Engage in Bible study, prayer, biblical meditation, fasting, silence, solitude, Sabbath rest, fellowship, worship, and the other historic, biblical means of growth in grace. Abide in Christ so that you connect to Christ's resurrection power (Phil. 3:10).

Like your trainees, you can do it—in Christ. Be confident in your competency in Christ.

Commencement: The Soul Physician's Manual

I think back to those early days of PEP and LEAD equipping with fond memories. Life was good because God is good—all the time. But that doesn't mean life was easy, and it doesn't mean the equipping was a breeze. At times the training process felt like ongoing labor pains for me, just as it did for the apostle Paul.

If I was in ministry labor pains, at least there was a soul physician available—the Soul Physician. It was the Divine Counselor's 4C map that gave me hope and confidence. Sure, the birth process was messy, but at least I had access to the Soul Physician's manual that provided me with the goals and objectives I should emphasize in my equipping ministry.

It is to that manual that we again turn our attention, in even more detail, in chapters eight and nine. Now that we know that our biblical counseling training needs to address the 4Cs, we need to learn what content, character, competence, and community subject matter our trainees need to master. In the next two chapters we will put some meat on the 4C skeleton by examining biblical counseling training curriculum and materials.

Growing Together: Questions for Reflection, Discussion, and Application

1. As you think about equipping biblical counselors, what fears, doubts, or discouragement do you feel? How are you handling these feelings and thoughts?
2. Of biblical content/conviction, Christlike character, counseling competence, and Christian community:
   a. Which one do you think you are most inclined to emphasize? To deemphasize?
   b. When you were trained, which of the 4Cs was most emphasized? Least emphasized?

EQUIPPING GODLY MINISTERS FOR MINISTRY

   c. Which of the 4Cs do you think you are best prepared to equip others to learn?
   d. Which of the 4Cs do you think you are least prepared to equip others to learn? How will you strengthen this area?
3. How would equipping in biblical counseling be impacted if one of the following is over-emphasized? Deemphasized? Omitted?
   a. Biblical content/conviction?
   b. Christlike character?
   c. Counseling competence?
   d. Christian community?
4. How confident are you:
   a. That God's people can be equipped to be competent biblical counselors? On what do you base your confidence? What could increase your confidence?
   b. That God has equipped *you* to be a competent equipper of biblical counselors? What can you do to further develop your confidence in your competency in Christ?

8

What Makes Biblical Counseling Biblical?: Part One

THEOLOGY AND METHODOLOGY IN BIBLICAL COUNSELING

Two books are standard in any physician's office: *The Physician's Desk Reference* (*PDR*) and *The Merck Manual of Diagnosis and Therapy* (*Merck*). Both are considered "Bibles of medical knowledge and practice." With its 3,223 pages of prescription drugs, the annually updated *PDR* is the most comprehensive, widely used drug reference available. It details the usage, warnings, and precautions for more than four thousand prescription drugs. *Merck* is the most widely used medical text in the world. It provides the latest information on the vast expanse of human diseases, disorders, and injuries, as well as their symptoms and treatments. Intended for physicians, it is still useful for the layperson. As one sage has commented, "It is a must for everyone in a human body."

As the *PDR* and *Merck* are the manuals for physicians treating the body, so the Bible is God's authoritative, sufficient, relevant Word for physicians treating the soul. It is the *Soul Physician's Desk*

Reference (*SPDR*) manual for dispensing grace. It is "a must for any-one who has a soul." God's Word provides not only the latest, but the eternal, enduring information on the soul's design and disease, as well as its care and cure. For equipping in biblical counseling, the Bible not only guides the curriculum, but *is* our curriculum. As we read the pages of the *SPDR,* we learn what makes biblical counseling truly biblical.

Chapter seven introduced you to the broad portrait of what a nurtured 4C biblical counseling graduate looks like. Chapters eight and nine transition from big-picture *goals and objectives* to focused biblical counseling training *curriculum and materials.* These two chapters ask the question, "To speak the truth in love, what do biblical counselors need to know, do, and be in the context of com-munity (love)?"

Chapters eight and nine provide a best-practice map for answering that question biblically. If you want your graduates to claim the label "biblical counselor," then here are the areas you need to consider.

- Content areas you would seek to equip them to address (know)— chapter eight
- Competencies you would seek to equip them to develop (do)— chapter eight
- Character traits you would seek to equip them to cultivate (be)— chapter nine
- Christian community you would want them to participate in so they can lovingly embody God's truth (love)—chapter nine

The chart beginning on the next page provides the outline devel-oped in these chapters. Though the outline is detailed, I will *not* teach exactly what to communicate in each topic area. That would be like giving you a fish, but not teaching you to fish. Based on your gift-mix, your specific church, and your unique community, use these categories as a guide for designing the particular materials, content, and lesson plans that are the right fit for your trainees.

The outline changes the order of the 4Cs as described in chapter seven. The apostle Paul never intended one verse (Rom. 15:14) to communicate a linear, one-size-fits-all training sequence. In reality, we can't and shouldn't neatly separate the equipping components. This chapter addresses biblical counseling theology (content) and methodology (competence), while the next chapter highlights spiritual formation (character) and spiritual fellowship (community).

Core Proficiencies of the Competent Biblical Counselor

Content/Conviction: "Complete in Knowledge"—
Head/Knowing

How to Change Lives with Christ's Changeless Truth
Six Ultimate Life Questions That Every
Biblical Counselor Must Address

- God's Word: "What is truth? Where do I find answers?"
- The Trinity: "Who is God? How can I know Him personally?"
- Creation: "Who am I? What makes people tick?"
- Fall: "What went wrong? Why do we do the things we do?"
- Redemption: "Can I change? How do people change?"
- Consummation: "Where am I headed? How does our future destiny impact our present reality?"

Competence: "Competent to Instruct One Another"—
Hands/Doing

How to Care like Christ
Four Core Relational Competencies That Every Biblical
Counselor Must Develop

- Sustaining biblical counseling competencies: empathize and embrace—GRACE relational competencies
- Healing biblical counseling competencies: encourage and enlighten—RESTS relational competencies
- Reconciling biblical counseling competencies: expose and exhort—PEACE(E) relational competencies
- Guiding relational counseling competencies: empower and equip—FAITH(H) relational competencies

203

Character: "Full of Goodness"—Heart/Being

How to Reflect Christ
Four Marks of Christlike Character That Every
Biblical Counselor Must Cultivate

- Relating like Christ: loving God and others passionately
- Thinking like Christ: renewing my mind to view life from God's eternal perspective
- Choosing like Christ: dying to self and living sacrificially for others
- Feeling like Christ: facing life honestly and managing my moods biblically

Community: "Brothers/One Another"—Home/Loving

How to Grow Together in Christ
Two Kinds of Christian Community That Every Biblical
Counselor Must Participate In

- Communion with the body of Christ: horizontal spiritual disciplines—one-anothering
- Communion with Christ: vertical spiritual disciplines

Biblical Content: Six Ultimate Life Questions That Every Biblical Counselor Must Address

I just reviewed my LEAD training notes from 1989–92. Some evenings my handouts were so hot-off-the-presses that my class could literally feel the warmth from the copier. It wasn't that I didn't know what to say; it was that I had too much that I wanted to communicate. To avoid that dilemma, this section suggests the *core essentials* that you may want to cover.

You may give up before starting if you think you need to teach every fact that a biblical counselor might ever need to know. Remember, the ultimate Teacher is the Holy Spirit (John 14–16). Remember also, you are not in this alone. Focus on a *theology of and for biblical counseling* in your training. For *general theology*, which is essential for biblical counseling, depend upon the overall educational ministry of your church. Make it a prerequisite in your selection process that trainees have taken classes in your church such as theology and hermeneutics (principles of interpreting and applying the Bible).

If your church doesn't have such classes, then prayerfully your SWORD analysis will identify the need and motivate the creation of appropriate classes. If you still find in-house training to be lacking, then as part of the reading your trainees do, require a systematic-theology text and a principles-of-Bible-study text.

You might also become discouraged if you think you have to cover every possible counseling issue. Even the most robust training can't possibly do that. Those that try end up watering down their training with multiple one-hour (surface) sessions on every conceivable counseling topic.

Instead, do what best-practice training suggests. Focus on and spend the bulk of your training laying a deep foundation (see below). Then, in the second or advanced level of your training, address in detail one or two specific counseling issues, such as marriage, depression, or sexual abuse recovery. Do this with the specific purpose of *demonstrating to trainees how they can apply their foundational learning to specific counseling issues.* For one of their assignments, have them develop their biblical approach to a specific counseling issue using the methodology you modeled for them. Your SWORD Heart Exam will help you determine which specific additional counseling issues to highlight in your training.

Also recognize that you and your church are not the only training option. For example, two graduates of my first LEAD group identified early on that they wanted to launch a Beauty for Ashes sexual abuse recovery group. Since our additional training didn't cover that issue, they attended an intensive week-long Christian training seminar on the topic, read extensively, wrote their research paper on this issue, and received ongoing personalized supervision from me.

Six Foundational Biblical Counseling Concepts

Those two trainees were able to launch and lead a very effective sexual abuse recovery group because they had a solid foundation. They understood six biblical categories that are essential for seeing the life of the soul through the lens of Scripture: *God's Word, the Trinity, Creation, Fall, Redemption*, and *Consummation*. They examined them meticulously, as a med-school student examines the skeletal structure of the human body. They learned the framework that we are about to outline—the Great Physician's authoritative truth about six ultimate life questions that every biblical counselor must address.

To understand the logic and order of this framework, let's start by focusing on the middle three categories: *Creation—Fall—Redemption*. I still remember the day I was introduced to this way of thinking about life. It was the first day of my first Bible college class. More than a hundred intimidated freshmen awaited the arrival of Dr. Lawler. The bespectacled, diminutive Old Testament scholar's reputation preceded him. When he entered, all chatter ceased. Staring us down, he said, "Repeat after me: Creation. Fall. Redemption."

"Creation. Fall. Redemption," we mimicked in unison.

"Never forget those three words," he instructed us. "They summarize the entire story of the Bible."

These three categories also form the core of biblical counseling: *people, problems,* and *solutions.* Everyone involved in the personal ministry of the Word must ponder:

- Creation: How to understand *people* biblically—the nature of human nature.
- Fall: How to diagnose *problems* theologically—the root causes of sin and suffering.
- Redemption: How to prescribe *solutions* scripturally—the pathway to growth in grace.

Equipping in biblical counseling helps trainees acquire a biblical understanding of who we are—learning from the Creator who the creature is. It helps trainees develop a biblical diagnosis of what went wrong—why people do the things they do. It also helps trainees offer a biblical prescription of the source of true, lasting heart and life transformation—care and cure in Christ.

So, you wonder, "Why doesn't the outline start at creation?" Rephrase that question and the answer becomes clear: "Why start with God's Word?" There are two broad sources of information that we could depend upon to understand people, diagnose problems, and prescribe solutions—God's Word or human words. That's why it is wise to start biblical counseling training by addressing God's Word and the questions: "What is truth? And where do we find answers?"

Next, trainees need to know what happened *before* the beginning—in eternity past. They need to study the Trinity—the Creator of the soul. If your trainees are to understand people created in God's image, they first must understand the One in whose image people are created.

Then, just as you began before the beginning, end "after the ending." Help your trainees to think through the implications of the end of the story—consummation. How does our future destiny impact our present reality? Now we have our complete content outline: *God's Word, the Trinity, Creation, Fall, Redemption*, and *Consummation*.

God's Word: Nourish the Hunger of the Soul—Preventive Medicine ("What Is Truth? Where Do I Find Answers?")

As you develop your curriculum and content related to the Bible, ask, "How do my trainees need to view and use God's Word in order to speak the truth in love?" The following central categories help your trainees to think through answers to this question.[1]

The Necessity and Sufficiency of Scripture: Anchored in Scripture

Physicians of the body determine which nutrients the body needs to remain healthy. So it is with doctoring the soul. What does the soul need? "Man does not live on bread alone, but on every word that comes from the mouth of God" (Matt. 4:4). We must communicate to our trainees by how we live and by how we counsel that God's Word is absolutely necessary and totally sufficient (2 Tim. 3:16–17) for addressing all matters of the soul.

Our trainees need to feast on God's Word. They need to develop the conviction that the deepest questions in the human soul are God-questions, and that we find our deepest answers in God's Word.

---

1. For a detailed development of these concepts, see my *Soul Physicians: A Theology of Soul Care and Spiritual Direction* (Winona Lake, IN: BMH Books, 2007).

EQUIPPING GODLY MINISTERS FOR MINISTRY

The Reformers used the term *sola Scriptura* (by Scripture alone) to communicate their confidence in the robust wisdom for living found only in the Bible. Our equipping should help our trainees share Paul's certainty that in Christ are hidden *all* the treasures of wisdom and knowledge (Col. 2:3–10).

The Purpose and Nature of Scripture: The Narrative of Relationship

If our trainees are to use the Bible to nourish hungry souls, they must hear the Bible's story the way God tells it. And God tells it in story form, as a *narrative of relationship*. Over 75 percent of the Bible is narrative, and the rest of the Bible involves passionate psalms, wisdom applied to life, and personal letters to real people in real life situations and real relationships. The Bible is 100 percent relational (Matt. 22:34–40).

We need to trace the Bible's story with our trainees. The Bible begins by telling the story of relationship initiated and rejected (Gen. 1–3). After those first three chapters, the rest of the Bible tells the story of God wooing us back to Himself, all the while fighting the Evil One, who wants to seduce us away from our first love. Ever since Genesis 3, *life is a battle for our love*—the ageless question of who captures our heart—Christ or Satan.

Our trainees need to understand that their biblical counseling will be sterile and dead if they see the Bible as a textbook. But if they read and use the Bible as the story of the battle to win our hearts, then their biblical counseling will come alive.

The Relevancy of Scripture: Truth and Love Must Kiss

We want to communicate that the Word of God is profound—it deeply addresses the real life issues of real people in a really messy world. As we minister God's Word to people's suffering and sin, our trainees need to make truth and love kiss. Throughout your training, make Philippians 1:9–10 your prayer. "And this is my prayer: that your love may abound more and more in knowledge and depth of insight, so that you may be able to discern what is best."

Create in your trainees the longing to share Christ's changeless truth to change people's lives. Help them think through what that means. Does dispensing God's Word mean that they tell their counselees to "take two Scriptures and call them in the morning"? Does it mean that life is so simple that it consists of a one-problem-one-verse-one-solution formula? We need to train biblical counselors to use the Bible in *relationally relevant* ways.

The Trinity: Know the Creator of the Soul—The Great Physician ("Who Is God? How Can I Know Him Personally?")

As you develop your curriculum and content in this area, ask, "How can I help my trainees to know the Soul Physician personally in order to be a soul physician?" This question, like the others, is not simply about teaching content but about cultivating conviction through applying truth to life.

The Trinity as Our Model for Ministry: Before God Created, He Related

The Bible is our relational manual written by the most relational Being in the universe. By answering the question "Who is God?" we also answer the question "What is love?" Through exploring the eternal community within the Trinity, our trainees begin to see that they must relate soul-to-soul because God is Trinitarian (John 1; John 17).

The Character of God: Holy Love

A person's image of God is central to his or her growth in grace. Our trainees need to ponder how the character, attributes, and works of God the Father, Son, and Spirit impact their lives and the lives of their counselees.

The Person and Work of Satan: Spiritual Warfare

If there is a great story, then there must be a plot filled with conflict and a fiendish enemy. By beginning before the beginning, our trainees not only understand the Bible's Protagonist—Christ; they learn about His antagonist—Satan. Through probing the fall of Satan, we expose

209

the hidden spiritual warfare at work behind every temptation to sin. We learn not only the onset of the evil disease that infects image bearers, but also how Satan attempts to spread the virus of sin.

Creation: Examine the Spiritual Anatomy of the Soul— People ("Who Am I? What Makes People Tick?")

As you develop your curriculum and content in this area, ask, "How do my trainees need to view people in order to know, love, and minister to them God's way?"

Pursue God's Target: The Image of God

Sometimes in biblical counseling we start with the fall into sin and what went wrong. Instead, we would be wise first to explore with our trainees the creation narrative. It teaches how we were meant to live life with God and each other. It teaches God's original design for the soul—the nature of human nature as bearers of God's image. It enables us to answer the questions: "What is health? And what does a healthy image bearer look like?"

Knowing who God designed us to be provides us with our target, our purpose in life. The goal of biblical counseling is *our inner life increasingly reflecting the inner life of Christ*. Our goal is not simply symptom relief, but Christlikeness. Equip your trainees to be *soul-u-tion-focused*, not solution-focused.

Comprehensive Biblical Counseling: Understanding People

For our trainees to move others toward this target, they must grasp God's comprehensive original design for the human personality. We need to explore with our students the Bible's teaching about who we are as:

- Relational beings: created to love passionately
  1. Spiritual beings: created to love God
  2. Social beings: created to love one another
  3. Self-aware beings: created to know who we are in Christ
- Rational beings: created to think wisely

- Volitional beings: created to choose courageously
- Emotional beings: created to experience deeply
- Physical beings: created to live fully

Fall: Diagnose the Fallen Condition of the Soul—Problems ("What Went Wrong? Why Do We Do the Things We Do?")

As you develop your curriculum and content in this area, ask, "How do my trainees need to view suffering and sin in order to counsel people with compassion and discernment?"

Biblical Sufferology: Not the Way It's Supposed to Be

As important as it is to return to creation, we would be naive to end our journey there. God didn't. The true story of life must include the sad story of our descent into the abyss of sin.

Skip the fall and we skip relevant answers to real life questions. Our trainees need to understand that though sad and tragic, without this story they could never make sense of life. The fall is the only reasonable explanation for suffering and sin. By dissecting the fallen planet, trainees are able to diagnose the reasons for suffering and develop a biblical approach to grieving with hope.[2]

Diagnosing Sin Biblically: Why We Do What We Do

By dissecting the fallen *soul*, our trainees are able to diagnose the impact of sin on the human personality and predicament. Their biblical insight begins as you help them to see the depth of heart sin and the comprehensive nature of sin.

- Relational sin: idols of the heart/false lovers of the soul
- Rational sin: foolish beliefs
- Volitional sin: self-centered choices
- Emotional sin: ungoverned emotions

2. For a detailed development of a "biblical sufferology," see *God's Healing for Life's Losses: How to Find Hope When You're Hurting* (Winona Lake, IN: BMH Books, 2010).

Redemption: Prescribe God's Cure for the Soul—Solutions ("Can I Change? How Do People Change?")

As you develop your curriculum and content in this area, ask, "What comprehensive understanding of salvation do my trainees need to grasp in order to counsel people toward progressive sanctification?"

Our Complete Salvation: Justification, Regeneration, Reconciliation, Redemption

If the Bible ended with the fall, life would be hopeless and we would despair. Thankfully, God's story moves to *Redemption*. It addresses the questions we all want answered: "Can I change? How do people change?"

Our trainees need to understand that biblical counseling applies our salvation, comprehensively understood, to our progressive sanctification. At times, new biblical counselors mistakenly counsel Christians as if they were non-Christians. They view their spiritual friends only through the lens of depravity. That would be like a heart surgeon transplanting a perfectly healthy new heart into her patient, but then treating her patient as if he still had his old heart.

To avoid this, your trainees need to understand what took place at salvation. They need to grasp the fourfold nature of biblical salvation (justification, regeneration, reconciliation, and redemption) and the implications of each for daily growth in Christ. How do people change? By applying justification, reconciliation, regeneration, and redemption to their daily lives.

Progressive Sanctification: Reflecting the Inner Life of Christ

Our trainees need to think biblically about progressive sanctification. It involves the Christian's inner life increasingly reflecting the inner life of Christ relationally (spiritually, socially, self-aware), rationally, volitionally, and emotionally. Trainees need to understand the process of growth in grace, including issues such as mind renewal, putting on/putting off, and the spiritual disciplines.

212

The Role of the Church: Growth in Community

Trainees need to know that sanctification is neither a self-improvement project nor an individual process. We grow in community. Our trainees need the big picture of the relationship of biblical counseling to the rest of the life of the church.

Consummation: Envision the Final Healing of the Soul—Glorification ("Where Am I Headed? How Does Our Future Destiny Impact Our Present Reality?")

As you develop your curriculum and content in this area, ask, "How could reading the end of the story impact how my trainees live and counsel?"

Trainees need to see the big picture. Creation, fall, and redemption summarize life on planet Earth. However, we are everlasting beings. Just as we began with a look into eternity past, so now we peek into eternity future. When our trainees remember to read the end of God's story, then God opens the eyes of their hearts to see the day-by-day story in a new light. Our eternal future addresses the question, "Where am I headed?" The biblical answer to that question ought to impact drastically how our trainees live and counsel today. Heaven is not only the end of suffering and sinning; heaven is the motivation for endurance of suffering *today* and for fighting against sin *today*.

A Best-Practice Content Map

The preceding development of six ultimate life questions is only one map of foundational biblical content to emphasize. Two dozen best-practice churches add their perspective (see below). In the multitude of counselors there is much wisdom about biblical counseling. Your task is to weigh the combined advice in this chapter as you develop the curriculum that best matches your ministry context.

Disciple-Making Champions

Equipping for Biblical Counseling Content

As part of the *4E Ministry Training Strategy Questionnaire*, two dozen best-practice churches responded to the question, "What content (theology, truth, doctrine, biblical knowledge) do you want to equip your graduates to address?" The following list collates the most common themes.

- Sufficiency of Scripture: Distinctiveness of biblical counseling
- Relevancy of Scripture: How to relate truth to life, the Bible as living/dynamic
- Nature/Purpose of the Bible: Bible as story, relationship focus
- Hermeneutics: Principles of biblical interpretation and application
- God/the Trinity: Implications of the Trinity on biblical relationships, God's character
- Christology: Christ's sinless life, sacrificial death, resurrection, return
- Holy Spirit: Comforting and sanctifying work, power, filling, fruit
- Creation: God's design of the soul, understanding people, the image of God
- Fall: Sin, depravity, idols of the heart, rebelliousness, diagnosing problems
- Redemption: Salvation in Christ, the new heart/new person in Christ, prescribing solutions
- Gospel: Work of Christ, forgiveness, grace, faith, our complete salvation
- Sanctification: Progressive growth in grace, putting off/putting on, how people change, heart change, cure/care of the soul, the indicative (believing) and the imperative (obeying), repentance, forgiveness, mind renewal, loving God/others, prayer, spiritual disciplines
- Church: Body life, the role of the church in discipleship/counseling, church discipline
- Spiritual Warfare: Role of Satan, victory over the world/flesh/devil
- Counseling Issues: Marriage, parenting, anxiety, depression, sexual abuse, self-harm, sexual addiction, eating disorders, grief, and death and dying
- Common Errors: False teachings that assault sound biblical counseling
- Suffering: Biblical teaching, biblical hope and healing
- End Times: Heaven, hell, consummation, glorification, eternal perspective

Counseling Competence: Four Core Relational Competencies That Every Biblical Counselor Must Develop

We want our trainees to become soul physicians who understand people, diagnose problems, and prescribe solutions—biblically. A soul physician is like a doctor at a teaching hospital or a brilliant surgeon who can diagnose and treat the most obscure illness.

We all know of brilliant surgeons with horrific bedside manners, just as we all know of scholarly people who can't relate well. The *comprehensive biblical insights* of the soul physician must morph together with the *compassionate, competent Christian engagement* of the spiritual friend. This is exactly what Paul models in 1 Thessalonians 2:8. "We loved you so much that we were delighted to share with you not only the gospel of God [Scripture/truth] but our own lives [soul/love] as well, because you had become so dear to us."

Biblical counseling is not either/or: either a brilliant but uncaring soul physician, or a loving but unwise spiritual friend. God calls our trainees to be wise *and* loving soul physicians *and* spiritual friends. So now we consider what counseling competencies every trainee needs to develop in order to *care like Christ* by becoming spiritual friends who empathize with, encourage, exhort, and empower their counselees.

Twenty-Two Biblical Counseling Relational Competencies

Sustaining Biblical Counseling Competencies

Empathize and Embrace—GRACE Relational Competencies
- **G**: Grace connecting, committed involvement—Galatians 6:1–3
- **R**: Rich soul empathizing—Romans 12:15
- **A**: Accurate spiritual listening—John 2:23–4:43
- **C**: Caring spiritual conversations—Ephesians 4:29
- **E**: Empathetic scriptural explorations—Isaiah 61:1–3

Healing Biblical Counseling Competencies

Encourage and Enlighten—RESTS Relational Competencies
- **R**: Relational treatment planning—John 2:23–25
- **E**: Encouraging communication—Ephesians 4:29
- **S**: Story reinterpreting—Philippians 3:7–15
- **T**: Thirsting for spiritual conversations—Hebrews 10:24–25
- **S**: Stretching scriptural explorations—Ephesians 3:15–21

Reconciling Biblical Counseling Competencies

Expose and Exhort—PEACE(E) Relational Competencies
- **P**: Probing theologically—Ephesians 4:17–19
- **E**: Exposing through confronting wisely—2 Timothy 2:22–26
- **A**: Active softening of stubbornness—Hebrews 3–4
- **C**: Connecting intimately—2 Corinthians 6:11–13
- **E**: Enlightening spiritual conversations—Hebrews 3:12–19
- **E**: Empowering scriptural explorations—Hebrews 4:12–16

Guiding Relational Counseling Competencies

Empower and Equip—FAITH(H) Relational Competencies
- **F**: Faith-based interventions—2 Corinthians 5:17
- **A**: Activating envisioned maturity—2 Timothy 1:5–7
- **I**: Insight-oriented treatment planning—Colossians 3
- **T**: Taking action—Ephesians 4:17–32
- **H**: Holiness spiritual conversations—Romans 5–8
- **H**: Heroic scriptural explorations—Hebrews 10–11

One Map of Counseling Interventions and Interactions

In chapter seven, I outlined a biblical, historical (church history), and practical map: counseling for suffering through sustaining and healing (*parakaletic*), and counseling for sin through reconciling and guiding (*nouthetic*).[3] It is not *the model*, but *a map*. The suggested competencies listed with sustaining, healing, reconciling, and guiding are but one way to conceptualize the types of skills your training may seek to cultivate. Additionally, the idea is *not* that a biblical counselor uses those skills *only* within sustaining, or healing, or reconciling, or guiding. Life and counseling are much more complex and relational than that. Each competency is valuable throughout the entire biblical counseling relational process.

Frank Lake summarized ministry well when he wrote, "Pastoral care is defective unless it can deal thoroughly *both* with the evils we have suffered *and* with the sins we have committed."[4] Historically, biblical counseling has always dealt with *both* suffering *and* sin.

3. For a detailed training manual in sustaining, healing, reconciling, and guiding, see my *Spiritual Friends: A Methodology of Soul Care and Spiritual Direction* (Winona Lake, IN: BMH Books, 2007).
4. Frank Lake, *Clinical Theology* (London: Darton, Longman & Todd, 1966), 21, emphasis added.

Our trainees need to learn the art of comforting suffering people. This includes the competencies of *sustaining* where they listen to the earthly story of suffering, communicate that it's normal to hurt, and empathize with the agony of living in a fallen world. It also includes *healing* competencies where they stretch their spiritual friend to the heavenly, eternal story, communicate that it's possible to hope, and encourage people to find God in the midst of their suffering by looking at life with spiritual eyes.

Trainees also need to learn how to practice the art of counseling people battling besetting sins. This includes the competencies of *reconciling* where they expose the twofold truth that it's horrible to sin, but wonderful to be forgiven. It also includes *guiding* competencies where they empower people to live out the truth that it's supernatural to mature—through Christ's resurrection power, counselees can be victorious over the world, the flesh, and the devil.

Equipping in biblical counseling is much more than teaching a trainee how to implement a technique or skill. I prefer using the phrase "relational competencies." Rather than a mechanical technique we pull out of our toolbox of skills, relational competencies are wise and compassionate ways of speaking the truth in love.

Sustaining Biblical Counseling Competencies: Empathize and Embrace—GRACE Relational Competencies

What does it look like to engage and embrace a suffering person with wisdom and compassion that sustains his or her faith? The answer is easy to state, but takes a lifetime to develop. When trying to capture the essence of sustaining, I find it helpful to encourage my trainees to picture grace that helps others in their time of need.

> Therefore, since we have a great high priest who has gone through the heavens, Jesus the Son of God, let us hold firmly to the faith we profess. For we do not have a high priest who is unable to sympathize with our weaknesses, but we have one who has been tempted in every way, just as we are—yet was without sin. Let us then approach the throne of grace with confidence, so that

217

we may receive mercy and find grace to help us in our time of need. (Heb. 4:14–16)

What a perfect picture of sustaining relational competency, of grace relating. Jesus is not aloof, distant, or removed. In His incarnation, He went through the heavens to earth, sharing in our humanity, becoming like us, so that He might help us (Heb. 2:14–18). Jesus is touched with the feelings of our infirmities. He is able to suffer with and be affected similarly to us. He offers grace to help in our time of need—well-timed help, help in the nick of time, words aptly spoken in season and seasoned with grace. Our trainees can become Jesus with skin on.

In equipping for sustaining competencies, we train biblical counselors to address the question: "How can my spiritual friends and I experience GRACE relationships that sustain their faith through the trials of life?" GRACE summarizes five sustaining relational competencies.

- **G**: Grace connecting—Galatians 6:1–3
- **R**: Rich soul empathizing—Romans 12:15
- **A**: Accurate spiritual listening—John 2:23–4:43
- **C**: Caring spiritual conversations—Ephesians 4:29
- **E**: Empathetic scriptural explorations—Isaiah 61:1–3

Grace Connecting: Committed Involvement—Galatians 6:1–3

Grace connecting is personal involvement with a deep commitment to the maturity of another person. It includes connection through communication. Trainees have love in their hearts for their spiritual friends, but how do they convey it? Grace connection allows their passionate love to touch their spiritual friends through incarnational, face-to-face relating. Through grace connecting, trainees develop the relational competency of intimate interaction where they display the courage to talk seriously and to offer to go deeper.

Galatians 6:1–3 captures the attitude. Trainees restore others gently and humbly, carrying their burdens patiently and persistently.

They communicate, "I love you in Christ for the long haul, like a marathon runner."

Rich Soul Empathizing: Climbing in the Casket—Romans 12:15

Empathy is the ability to sense a person's inner response to external suffering and to communicate, "It's normal to hurt." It is the capacity to mourn with those who mourn.

I help trainees picture the depth of this concept by portraying it as "climbing in the casket." The apostle Paul needed such comfort when he wrote, "We were under great pressure, far beyond our ability to endure, so that we despaired even of life. Indeed, in our hearts we felt the sentence of death" (2 Cor. 1:8–9). Our trainees need to develop the capacity to share in the sorrows of others—communicating that they feel and experience their spiritual friends' pain.

Accurate Spiritual Listening: Faith-Drenched Alertness—John 2:23–4:43

Everyone who knows anything about counseling knows the value of listening. Biblical counseling trainees need to develop the competency of accurate spiritual listening: listening to God's Word as they listen to people's words.

Our training needs to demonstrate that words are meaningful (Prov. 18:4; 20:5) because they convey issues of the heart (Matt. 12:34) and, therefore, are worthy of soulful attentiveness (Prov. 18:13; James 1:19) because they reflect either God's interpretation of life or Satan's (Job 42:7). Our training also needs to help trainees develop basic components of competent spiritual listening.

- **L**: Loving motivation—Proverbs 21:13
- **I**: Intimate concern—Galatians 6:1–3
- **S**: Slowness to speak—James 1:19
- **T**: Timing—Proverbs 15:23
- **E**: Encouragement—Hebrews 10:24–25
- **N**: Need-focused hearing—Ephesians 4:29

Caring Spiritual Conversations: Sustaining Theological Trialogues—
Ephesians 4:29

In a monologue, I speak to you. In a dialogue, we speak to each other. In a trialogue, together we listen to God through His Word. In caring spiritual conversations, our trainees learn to use biblical wisdom principles to engage their spiritual friends in interactions that help them think through their external suffering and internal grief from God's perspective.

Trainees use sustaining spiritual conversations to help their friends face their suffering face-to-face with God. Spiritual conversations in sustaining encourage others to invite God into their casket.

Empathetic Scriptural Explorations: Sustaining Biblical Trialogues—
Isaiah 61:1–3

Spiritual conversations use *broad biblical principles* to prompt people to ponder their walk with God. Scriptural explorations use *specific applicable passages* to help people relate God's truth to their life.

Trainees need to learn to use sustaining scriptural explorations to help their spiritual friends lament to God candidly, crying out to God for His comfort. They need to learn not to use the Bible to preach at people in their suffering, instead exploring God's Word together to encourage people to relate God to their suffering.

Healing Biblical Counseling Competencies: Encourage and Enlighten—RESTS Relational Competencies

Through the sustaining relational competencies, trainees learn how to help their spiritual friends face the truth that life is bad and realize that in a fallen world it's normal to hurt. Having learned how to climb in the casket, trainees now need to learn how to celebrate the empty tomb. They need to develop healing relational competencies that help their spiritual friends see that even when life is bad, God is good—all the time—and realize that even in a fallen world it is possible to hope—because of Christ.

In equipping for healing competencies, we train biblical counselors to address the question, "How can my spiritual friends and I engage in RESTS relationships that heal their faith by offering hope in Christ?" RESTS summarizes five healing relational competencies.

- **R**: Relational treatment planning—John 2:23–25
- **E**: Encouraging communication—Ephesians 4:29
- **S**: Story reinterpreting—Philippians 3:7–15
- **T**: Thirsting fo spiritual conversations—Hebrews 10:24–25
- **S**: Stretching scriptural explorations—Ephesians 3:15–21

Relational Treatment Planning: Mutuality in Hope Building— John 2:23–25

Relational treatment planning is much more than altering symptoms or offering short-term solutions to circumstances and problems. In relational treatment planning the counselor and counselee cooperate with God in the process of sanctification, defined as moving toward communion with and conformity to Christ.

Our trainees need to develop the competency of helping people move from the smaller earthly story to the larger eternal story. They need to be able to assist counselees to expand their goals beyond changed circumstances and feelings to transformed hearts and relationships. They then need to learn how to journey with counselees toward progressive sanctification as they deal with suffering and sin biblically and practically.

Encouraging Communication: Hope-Based Interactions—Ephesians 4:29

Since people typically come to counselors with problem-saturated stories, our trainees must learn how to infuse hope. Though we encourage trainees to empathize with hurting people, we don't want them to join people in their shrunken perspective.

Encouraging communications infuse hope by putting Christ back into the picture. Satan attempts to deceive people into believing that since life is bad, God must not be good. Trainees must develop the competency of undeceiving people by helping them look at life with spiritual eyes, with faith eyes, with 20/20 spiritual vision.

Story Reinterpreting: Coauthoring Resurrection Narratives—Philippians 3:7–15

When the apostle Paul despaired of life, he came to understand that God allowed his struggles so that he would not rely upon himself, but upon God who raises the dead (2 Cor. 1:9). Biblical counselors need training in coauthoring resurrection narratives. From within the casket of despair, they encourage people to see life from God's eternal perspective. We equip trainees to develop the competency of story reinterpreting—using the benefit of faith to see the benefit of trials.

Thirsting for Spiritual Conversations: Healing Theological Trialogues—Hebrews 10:24–25

Created for paradise and now experiencing desert living, suffering people thirst. Satan desires to direct people in their thirst to broken cisterns that hold no water (Jer. 2:13). Thirsting for spiritual conversations encourages hurting people to recognize their deepest spiritual longing for God and enlighten them to see Christ as the only One who could ever satisfy their souls. Trainees in biblical counseling need to learn how to direct people to God, the Spring of Living Water.

Stretching Scriptural Explorations: Healing Biblical Trialogues—Ephesians 3:15–21

In stretching scriptural explorations, trainees learn how to explore together with counselees relevant biblical passages that enlighten counselees to see their suffering from a hope-filled and grace-focused perspective. Trainees need to learn to use healing biblical trialogues that encourage people to see what God is doing behind the scenes and what God might want to do in their hearts.

Reconciling Biblical Counseling Competencies: Expose and Exhort—PEACE(E) Relational Competencies

Training in biblical counseling should equip people to become soul caregivers who compassionately identify with people in pain and redirect them to Christ and the body of Christ to sustain and heal their faith (*paraka-*

letic counseling for suffering). Biblical counseling training should also equip people to become spiritual directors who understand spiritual dynamics and discern root causes of spiritual conflicts, providing loving wisdom that reconciles and guides people (*nouthetic* counseling for sinning).

In suffering, the goal is not less than dealing with symptoms, pain, and grief, it is more—helping people to find God even when or if they can't find relief. It is helping people to grow in grace as they face suffering face-to-face with Christ.

In sinning, the goal is not less than dealing with specific behavioral sins, it is more—helping people's inner lives to reflect increasingly the inner life of Christ. It is helping people to grow in grace in their relationships, affections, desires, thoughts, attitudes, motivations, actions, and emotions.

Biblical counseling for sin involves the twin processes of reconciling and guiding. In reconciling, trainees learn how to expose their spiritual friends' sin and Christ's grace. In guiding, trainees learn how to empower people to live out their new life through Christ's resurrection power.

In equipping for reconciling competencies, we train biblical counselors to address the question, "How can my spiritual friends and I engage in relationships that produce PEACE (shalom) as they experience reconciliation with God and others?" PEACE(E) summarizes six reconciling relational competencies:

- **P**: Probing theologically—Ephesians 4:17–19
- **E**: Exposing through confronting wisely—2 Timothy 2:22–26
- **A**: Active softening of stubbornness—Hebrews 3–4
- **C**: Connecting intimately—2 Corinthians 6:11–13
- **E**: Enlightening spiritual conversations—Hebrews 3:12–19
- **E**: Empowering scriptural explorations—Hebrews 4:12–16

Probing Theologically: Theory-Guided Awareness—Ephesians 4:17–19

Before trainees can expose sin, they have to understand biblical diagnostic categories of sin. Through the relational competency of probing theologically, trainees learn the art of relating the theology of the fall to

223

a person's life by diagnosing sin comprehensively and specifically. They learn how to interact with their spiritual friends to help them see that their sin is not a surface issue, but a heart issue that relates comprehensively to how they relate, think, choose, and feel.

Exposing through Confronting Wisely: Disclosing Discrepancies— 2 Timothy 2:22–26

Biblical confrontation has earned an undeserved bad rap. Trainees need equipping in loving, wise biblical care-fronting. They need to learn that confronting wisely helps people see where they are intoxicated by the lies of the world, the flesh, and the devil so they can come to their senses and escape the devil's trap.

Active Softening of Stubbornness: Loosening Resistance to Repentance— Hebrews 3–4

Confrontation attempts to help people see what they are unaware of. Softening stubbornness attempts to help people face things they are aware of, but refuse to change. Our trainees need equipping to help people when they resist the Spirit's work of conviction, change, and growth.

Connecting Intimately: Relating in the Moment—2 Corinthians 6:11–13

Perhaps one of the most difficult competencies to learn is also one of the most important ones to develop—connecting intimately. It is more caught than taught by how we relate to our trainees and by the environment we cultivate in our training groups and labs.

In connecting intimately, trainees learn how to handle what is occurring in their relationships right now with their counselees. They learn to discuss the here and now with a view toward the implications for the counselees' other relationships.

Enlightening Spiritual Conversations: Reconciling Theological Trialogues— Hebrews 3:12–19

Through enlightening spiritual conversations, trainees learn how to help their counselees see their own sin and their Father's amazing grace. This includes training in how to explore and apply biblical principles relevant to confession of sin, repentance, and receiving God's grace and forgiveness.

Empowering Scriptural Explorations: Reconciling Biblical Trialogues—Hebrews 4:12–16

Empowering scriptural explorations continue the process, but instead of applying general biblical principles of sanctification, trainees learn how to explore and apply specific biblical passages relevant to confession, repentance, grace, and forgiveness. Through this process, trainees learn how to help counselees apply God's living and active Word to their struggles with sin.

Guiding Relational Counseling Competencies: Empower and Equip—FAITH(H) Relational Competencies

In biblical guiding, trainees learn how to collaborate with counselees in applying principles and passages from God's Word to their lives and relationships. In equipping for guiding competencies, we train biblical counselors to address the question, "How can my spiritual friend and I engage in relationships that nourish FAITH active in love?" FAITH(H) encapsulates six guiding relational competencies.

- **F**: Faith-based interventions—2 Corinthians 5:17
- **A**: Activating envisioned maturity—2 Timothy 1:5–7
- **I**: Insight-oriented treatment planning—Colossians 3
- **T**: Taking action—Ephesians 4:17–32
- **H**: Holiness spiritual conversations—Romans 5–8
- **H**: Heroic scriptural explorations—Hebrews 10–11

Faith-Based Interventions: New Covenant Living—2 Corinthians 5:17

Having confessed the horrors of sin and received God's grace, counselees need biblical wisdom in applying progressive sanctification principles to their specific heart and relationship issues. Trainees need equipping in faith-based interventions that help counselees live out their new nature and their new relationship with Christ by putting off the old patterns of relating and putting on the new person in Christ.

225

Activating Envisioned Maturity: Stirring Up God's Gifts—2 Timothy 1:5–7

We need to equip our trainees to envision their spiritual friends walking in maturity and then to stimulate that maturity by stirring up the gift of God. Our trainees need to learn how to help people see their universal identity in Christ and recognize their unique calling from Christ.

Insight-Oriented Treatment Planning: Collaborative Spiritual Direction—Colossians 3

In insight-oriented treatment planning, biblical counselors work with their counselees to map out a personal spiritual growth process. Trainees need equipping in how to help their spiritual friends establish realistic and specific plans for ongoing growth in grace.

Taking Action: Homework That Works—Ephesians 4:17–32

Trainees need to master the art of helping their counselees apply new covenant truth to the specifics of their daily lives and relationships. Trainees need equipping in shaping homework that works in the real world by addressing specific issues of the heart and explicit patterns of relating.

Holiness Spiritual Conversations: Guiding Theological Trialogues—Romans 5–8

In holiness spiritual conversations, trainees learn how to explore with their counselees general biblical principles of growth in grace. How do they relate truth about the new creation in Christ to the specifics of suffering and sin?

Heroic Scriptural Explorations: Guiding Biblical Trialogues—Hebrews 10–11

Faith active in love involves trusting God while risking deep relationships with others. In heroic scriptural explorations, trainees learn how to empower their spiritual friends to be God's heroes. Trainees learn to explore with counselees specific, relevant biblical passages that help their counselees courageously apply God's truth to their relationships.

A Best-Practice Competency Map

The preceding development of four core relational competencies is only one map of foundational counseling competencies to emphasize. Two dozen best-practice churches add their perspective (see below). Your task is to weigh the combined advice in this chapter as you develop the curriculum that best matches your ministry context.

Disciple-Making Champions

Equipping for Counseling Competence

As part of the *4E Ministry Training Strategy Questionnaire*, two dozen best-practice churches responded to the question, "What counseling competencies (relational competencies, methods, skills, counseling abilities) do you seek to equip your graduates to develop?" The following list collates the most common themes.

- Four Stages: Love, know, speak, and do
- 4Es: Empathize, encourage, exhort, equip
- 6Ls: Love, listen, learn, label lies, lecture, launch
- Building Involvement: Developing a healthy helping relationship, caring interaction, building trust
- Empathy: Weeping or feeling with others; connecting or journeying with hurting people
- Providing Comfort
- Instilling, Building, and Offering Hope
- Drawing People Out: Helping people tell their stories
- Listening Skills: Understanding people and the complexities of their individual situations
- Gathering Data: Asking effective probing open-ended questions, note taking, using data well
- Interpreting Data: Compassionate discernment, interpreting personal information, observing verbal and non-verbal communication

- Isolating the Problem: Discovering where change is needed, determining direction
- Providing Biblical Encouragement: Helping people see life from God's eternal perspective
- Targeting the Heart: Drawing out the heart, discerning root issues, applying truth to the heart
- Biblical Discernment: Understanding biblical principles and how the Scriptures relate to the situation, seeing where God's Word fits into people's lives, seeing and using the Bible as God's authoritative, sufficient, relevant Word
- Spiritual Conversations: Connecting biblical principles to life, discussing biblical truths in personal and specific ways
- Scriptural Explorations: Exploring pertinent passages, discussing relevant verses
- Speaking the Truth in Love: Sensitive and gentle speech, blending grace and truth
- Providing Instruction: Leading the counselee to discover biblical truth and application
- Reconciling: Helping people see and confess sinful patterns, experience genuine repentance, and receive grace and forgiveness
- Confronting in Love: Care-fronting, opening blind eyes, graciously addressing personal struggles, sinfulness, and the need for change
- Guiding: Equipping people to put off and put on, helping people apply growth-in-grace principles
- Assigning and Assessing Homework: Extending the application process into day-to-day life
- Evangelism in Counseling: Understanding and sharing the love of Christ
- Prayer in Counseling
- Managing the Counseling Meeting
- Confidentiality in Counseling
- Group Leadership Skills

Commencement: A Robustly Healthy Trainee

When I teach on the 4Cs, I also like to use the imagery of the 4Hs—head, hands, heart, and home. That's not just because I like alliteration, but because the 4Hs help people picture what happens when an area is emphasized or deemphasized disproportionately. If I'm using a whiteboard or PowerPoint, I'll draw a stick figure or show a picture of a body with a huge head and a tiny heart, for example. That pictures training that is tilted too much toward academic content and not enough toward character development. Take a moment to imagine the other stick figures and body images that would depict a distorted training emphasis of any of the 4Hs.

Comprehensive training is not easy. It takes quality and quantity time. However, it is worth the effort because it results in a robustly healthy trainee—one whose head, hands, heart, and home are proportional. There's no distortion. That doesn't mean perfection, but it does imply holistic training. The whole person is equipped to minister the whole gospel to bring wholeness to hurting and hardened people.

Chapter nine continues our comprehensive, holistic training. Our trainees need to cultivate good heart health—Christlike character. They also need to participate in a healthy home—Christian community. Chapter nine will suggest the types of character traits and Christian community that complete our comprehensive training curriculum.

Growing Together: Questions for Reflection, Discussion, and Application

1. Of the six ultimate life questions and their content areas:
    a. Which ones surprise you? Why?
    b. Which ones have you taught on? How has your focus been different from the way that area was developed in this chapter? What would you teach in that content area?
    c. Which ones haven't you taught on? Why?
    d. What content area, if any, would you not include in your training curriculum? Why?
    e. What content area would you add for your training ministry? How would you develop it?
2. Of the collated list of biblical counseling content from the Disciple-Making Champions:
    a. Which ones surprise you? Why?
    b. Which ones haven't you taught on? Why?

    c. Which content area, if any, would you not include in your training curriculum? Why?

3. Of the four counseling areas and the twenty-two relational competencies that every biblical counselor must develop:

    a. Which ones surprise you? Why?

    b. Which ones have you equipped people for? How has your focus been different from the way that competency was developed in this chapter?

    c. Which ones haven't you equipped people for? Why?

    d. Which competency, if any, would you not include in your training? Why?

    e. What competencies would you add in your training? How would you develop them?

4. Of the collated list of counseling competencies from the Disciple-Making Champions:

    a. Which ones surprise you? Why?

    b. Which ones haven't you equipped people for? Why?

    c. Which competency, if any, would you not include in your training? Why?

9

What Makes Biblical Counseling
Biblical?: Part Two

Spiritual Formation and Spiritual
Fellowship in Biblical Counseling

Equipping Christians for biblical counseling requires the vision of Gutzon Borglum, the creative genius behind the presidential carvings on Mount Rushmore. Someone once asked him, "How did you ever create those faces out of that rock?" Borglum replied, "I didn't. Those faces were already in there. Hidden. I only uncovered them."

As equippers of Christians, we should never forget the freeing truth that the face of Jesus is already in every new creation in Christ (2 Cor. 3:17–18; 5:17). We don't have to drill in or implant the 4Cs. God simply calls us to stir up and fan into flame the gift of God that He has already implanted in every believer (2 Tim. 1:5–7).

This is especially true regarding the 2Cs of Christlike character and Christian community. Chapter nine continues our best-practice map of biblical counseling training *curriculum and materials*. If you want your graduates to claim the label "biblical counselor," then here are the types of:

- Character traits you would seek to equip them to cultivate (spiritual formation)
- Christian community you would want them to participate in so they can lovingly embody God's truth (spiritual fellowship)

Reflecting Christ's Character: "Full of Goodness"—Heart/Being

How to Reflect Christ: Four Marks of Christlike Character That Every Biblical Counselor Must Cultivate
- Relating like Christ: Loving God and others passionately
- Thinking like Christ: Renewing my mind to view life from God's eternal perspective
- Choosing like Christ: Dying to self and living sacrificially for others
- Feeling like Christ: Facing life honestly and managing my moods biblically

Growing Together in Community: "Brothers/One Another"—Home/Loving

How to Grow Together in Christ: Two Kinds of Christian Community That Every Biblical Counselor Must Participate In
- Communion with the Body of Christ: Horizontal spiritual disciplines—one-anothering
- Communion with Christ: Vertical spiritual disciplines

Christlike Character: Four Marks of Christlike Character That Every Biblical Counselor Must Cultivate

Consistency is essential in biblical counseling equipping. We need to maintain consistency between our stated theology and our stated practice. Recall that under the content category of Creation/People, we emphasized pursuing God's target—the image of God in Christ. We explained that the goal of biblical counseling is *our inner life increasingly reflecting the inner life of Christ.*

We further noted that for our trainees to move others toward this target, they must grasp God's comprehensive original design for the human personality, which we outlined, in part, as:

- Relational Beings: Created to love passionately
  1. Spiritual beings: created to love God
  2. Social beings: created to love one another
  3. Self-aware beings: created to know who we are in Christ
- Rational Beings: Created to think wisely
- Volitional Beings: Created to choose courageously
- Emotional Beings: Created to experience deeply

Then, related to Redemption/Solutions, we stressed that our trainees need to think biblically about progressive sanctification. Remaining consistent, we defined growth in grace as the Christian's inner life increasingly reflecting the inner life of Christ relationally (spiritually, socially, self-aware), rationally, volitionally, and emotionally.

So, to remain consistent in equipping our trainees for Christlike character, it is wise to focus on the four areas of their inner life increasingly reflecting the inner life of Christ. This chapter develops those four areas, while the next chapter describes training strategies and methods to use to help our trainees pursue that target—to cultivate Christlikeness.

Picturing the Spiritually Mature Christian[1]

Prior to developing those four areas, we need to consider some bigger-picture questions. What is our definition/description of a spiritually mature Christian? How do we measure spiritual maturity? What is our model, target, goal of spiritual maturity? How would we know a spiritually mature Christian if we saw one?

These seem like foundational questions, don't they? Yet often we attempt to equip biblical counselors without clear answers to these essential questions. Just as we often attempt to counsel Christians without a clear sense of the "end game." We haven't clearly and biblically thought through the purpose of biblical counseling. *We have failed to identify spiritual formation (transformation into the image of Christ) as the ultimate goal of biblical counseling.*

---

1. For a fuller development of a biblical theology of the spiritually mature Christian, see my *Soul Physicians: A Theology of Soul Care and Spiritual Direction* (Winona Lake, IN: BMH Books, 2007).

233

This is why all too often we end up working toward *solutions*—changing circumstances, improving feelings, or modifying surface behaviors. When, as we noted in chapter eight, we should be working toward *soul-u-tions*: comprehensive inner life transformation.

The underlying theme of salvation is Christ having transformed us from the inside out from self-worshiping, self-sufficient, self-centered, self-driven persons to Christ-worshiping, Christ-sufficient, Christ-centered, Christ-pursuing persons. The underlying theme of progressive sanctification is the ongoing transformation of our inner life from the old manner of life in sin and self to the new manner of life in Christ (Eph. 4:17–24; Col. 3:1–17).

- From relational sin (idols of the heart/false lovers of the soul) to relational purity (returning to my first love)
- From rational sin (foolish beliefs) to rational sanity (returning to God's eternal perspective)
- From volitional sin (self-centered choices) to volitional vitality (returning to other-centered purposes)
- From emotional sin (selfish ungoverned emotions) to emotional integrity (returning to managing our moods with a ministry focus)

It is to this fourfold transformation in our lives, in our trainees' lives, and in the lives of the people our trainees will counsel that we now turn our attention.

Relating like Christ: Loving God and Others Passionately

Relating like Christ is the first mark of Christlike character that every biblical counseling trainee must cultivate. In Matthew 22:34–40, Christ summarized the entire Old Testament with the two commands to love God wholeheartedly and to love our neighbor as our self. God created us as three-dimensional relational beings. We relate to Him (spiritual beings), to one another (social beings), and to ourselves (self-aware beings).

Spiritually, we want to help our trainees love God passionately. We want them to be cultivating a godly heart response to the question, "Like Jesus, do I increasingly exalt, enjoy, love, and find satisfaction in God more than any other?" Since God is triune, we also want our trainees to be cultivating a heart response to questions like the following:

- Relationship to God the Father: "Do I increasingly cling to God, running home to Him as my Father, like a faithful son or daughter?"
- Relationship to God the Son: "Do I increasingly enjoy Christ more than any other joy in life?"
- Relationship to God the Spirit: "Do I increasingly depend upon the Holy Spirit to sanctify me, make me holy, beautify me, empower and equip me?"

As social beings, we want to help our trainees love one another sacrificially as Christ models and Paul calls us to do in Philippians 2:1–18. We want our trainees to cultivate a godly heart response to the question, "Am I increasingly loving others deeply and sacrificially from the heart with grace?"

As self-aware beings, we are called by God to think of ourselves accurately according to who we are in and to Christ (Rom. 12:3). We want our trainees to cultivate a godly heart response to the question, "Am I increasingly resting confidently in who I am in and to Christ?"

Thinking Like Christ: Renewing My Mind to View Life from God's Eternal Perspective

Thinking like Christ is the second mark of Christlike character that every biblical counseling trainee must cultivate. God calls us to renew our minds so that as we relate to God, others, and ourselves, we "let this mind be in you which was also in Christ Jesus" (Phil. 2:5 KJV).

Rationally, mentally, we want our trainees to value what God values. The Reformers and Puritans called this "thinking God's thoughts after Him." We want our trainees to be cultivating a godly heart response to

235

the question, "Like Jesus, do I increasingly view life from the Father's eternal, gracious, and good perspective?"

We want our trainees to see life with spiritual eyes, with faith eyes, with 20/20 spiritual vision. We want God's Word to enlighten them to the reality that God's larger story interprets their smaller story (Rom. 8:17–18). We want the end of the story to impact how they live today (Rev. 7:9–17; 21:1–7).

We also want our trainees to be cultivating a heart response to questions like the following:

- Do I increasingly, together with all the saints, grasp the holy love of God?
- Do I increasingly allow God's eternal story to invade my earthly story?
- Do I increasingly renew my mind and stir up wholesome thinking?

Choosing like Christ: Dying to Self and Living Sacrificially for Others

Choosing like Christ is the third mark of Christlike character that every biblical counseling trainee must cultivate. Christ's life mission must become our life mission. "Whoever wants to become great among you must be your servant, and whoever wants to be first must be slave of all. For even the Son of Man did not come to be served, but to serve, and to give his life as a ransom for many" (Mark 10:43–45). "Greater love has no one than this, that he lay down his life for his friends" (John 15:13).

Volitionality relates to our will, choices, motivations, purposes— why we do what we do. Volitionally, we want our trainees to choose the courageous path of sacrificial living. We want them to cultivate a godly heart response to the question, "Like Jesus, do I increasingly die to self and live for God and others?"

We want our training process to empower our trainees so they are free to empower their counselees. We want our trainees to cultivate a positive heart response to questions like the following:

- Am I increasingly trusting Christ courageously and taking risks to minister to others?

236

- Am I increasingly finding my life by dying to myself, taking up my cross, and following Christ?
- Am I increasingly living to shepherd and minister to others?
- Am I increasingly serving Christ and others out of a pure heart, a good conscience, and a sincere faith?

Feeling like Christ: Facing Life Honestly and Managing My Moods Biblically

Feeling like Christ is the fourth mark of Christlike character that every biblical counseling trainee must cultivate. As I type that sentence, I imagine some push-back from readers. We have become accustomed, wrongly, to assuming that all feelings, all emotions, are bad. Nothing could be further from God's truth. God designed us as emotional beings. God is an emotional Being.

The issue is not whether we have emotions, but how we handle our emotions. This is true even for one of the most intense of emotions—anger. "In your anger do not sin" (Eph. 4:26). Jesus practiced what Paul preached. "He looked around at them in anger and, deeply distressed at their stubborn hearts, said to the man, 'Stretch out your hand.' He stretched it out, and his hand was completely restored" (Mark 3:5). Jesus experienced and expressed His emotions motivated by His commitment to minister to others.

Emotionally, we want our trainees to face life honestly and to manage their moods biblically. We want them to cultivate a godly heart response to the question, "Like Jesus, do I increasingly manage my moods with a ministry focus?"

Our training should assist our trainees to develop the emotional integrity to face all of life candidly, with all of its grief and hope, face-to-face with Christ. We want our trainees to cultivate a positive heart response to questions like the following:

- Am I increasingly developing emotional self-awareness: understanding my moods?
- Am I increasingly developing emotional self-mastery: soothing my soul in my Savior?

- Am I increasingly developing emotional maturity: managing my moods with a ministry focus?
- Am I increasingly developing emotional empathy: recognizing emotions in others?
- Am I increasingly developing emotional savvy: handling my relationships well?

A Best-Practice Character Map

The preceding development of four marks of Christlike character is only one map of foundational character to emphasize. In my training I also highlight the ninefold fruit of the Spirit. I mention and outline them here simply as another way to indicate that there is no one-size-fits-all character map. Biblical counseling training can also assist trainees to cultivate the fruit of the Spirit:

- Love: loving compassion
- Joy: joyful celebration
- Peace: peaceful integrity
- Patience/long-suffering: long-suffering resilience
- Kindness/gentleness: nourishing kindness
- Goodness: relational goodness
- Faithfulness/faith: grace-focused faith
- Gentleness/meekness: courageous meekness
- Self-Control: hope-based self-control

Two dozen best-practice churches add their perspective (see below). Your task is to weigh the combined advice in this chapter as you develop the character-training curriculum that best matches your ministry context.

Disciple-Making Champions

Equipping for Christlike Character

As part of the *4E Ministry Training Strategy Questionnaire*, two dozen best-practice churches responded to the question, "What Christlike character do you seek to equip your graduates to cultivate and manifest?" The following list collates the most common themes.

- Christlikeness: To be more like Jesus, growing mature in Christ, loving like Christ
- Reflecting Christ: To increasingly reflect the inner life of Christ
- Spiritual, Relational, Emotional Maturity/Intelligence
- Fruit of the Spirit: The character of Christ manifested through the fruit of the Spirit
- Spirit-Dependent: Filled with the Spirit
- Christian Virtues: Beatitudes, qualities of 2 Peter 1:5–8
- 1 Timothy 3 Character Qualities
- Love: Love God, His Word, and people; loving and serving others, loving the unsaved
- Worshipers: Growing in their awe, wonder, and worship toward God
- Compassion and Wisdom: Caring discernment
- Intimacy/Relationship with Christ: Face Christ in everything, speak to Him, listen to Him through His Word
- Gospel-Centered Lives: Dealing honestly with the condition of their hearts, ministering the gospel to their own souls, hearts stirred by the gospel, overwhelmed by grace
- Self-Counseling: Applying what they are learning to their own hearts and lives
- Living Faith: Living out faith in their families, churches, and communities
- Personal Holiness: Striving to live for God's glory, growing in grace
- Authenticity: Open, genuine, transparent, non-judgmental, forgiving, gracious, hopeful, faithful, having integrity
- Humility: Teachable

Christian Community: Two Kinds of Christian Community That Every Biblical Counselor Must Participate In

Just as we must maintain consistency between our theology and practice, we also need to maintain consistency between our definition of biblical counseling and our equipping of biblical counselors. Revisiting our definition of biblical counseling will make this clear.

Christ-centered, church-based, comprehensive, compassionate, and culturally informed biblical counseling depends upon the Holy Spirit to relate God's Word to suffering and sin by speaking and living God's truth in love to equip people to love God and one another (Matt. 22:35–40). It cultivates conformity to Christ and communion with Christ and the body of Christ, leading to a community of one-another disciple-makers (Matt. 28:18–20).

When I counsel someone, I always have the end in view. I want to help peole cultivate conformity to Christ—their inner life increasingly reflecting the inner life of Christ (spiritual formation). I also want to help people cultivate communion with Christ and the body of Christ (spiritual fellowship). Ultimately, I don't want to point people to myself or to never-ending meetings with me. I want to point them to the ultimate Spiritual Friend (Christ) and to ongoing spiritual friendships (within the body of Christ).

If that is what we want our trainees to do with and for their counselees, then it only makes sense that we would train them in the same way with the same goals. If the end goal of biblical counseling in the church is the creation of a community of one-another disciple-makers, then our biblical counseling equipping group must become a one-another community. We simply cannot effectively equip competent biblical counselors apart from the context of intimate biblical one-another community.

The old academic model must change, even in the academy. A word to professors—we must train people in the Christian college and seminary setting in the same way that we want students to train people in their churches. When we train pastors-to-be only in a didactic, lecture-oriented, brain-dump, content-exclusive model, then that's exactly what pastors will do *to* their people.

The model you are learning throughout this book is the identical model that I have implemented in three churches *and* that I implemented when I launched and led the MA in Christian Counseling and

Discipleship program at Capital Bible Seminary. The 4Cs, including the C of Christian community, have been the core components in each setting.

A word again to everyone—remember the imagery that one of my students used: "Community is the container for the other 3Cs." Christian community is the growth-enhancing context, the fertile soil, the healthy environment for equipping people in biblical content, counseling competence, and Christlike character. Every biblical counseling trainee must participate in two kinds of Christian community: communion with the body of Christ and communion with Christ.

Communion with the Body of Christ: The Horizontal Spiritual Disciplines

Don't take my word for it. Take God's Word and its teaching about one-another community. Consider the classic passage where Paul talks about God's bringing glory in the church and in Christ Jesus and doing so immeasurably beyond anything that we could ask or imagine. Notice the *container* in which that occurs. "I pray that you, being rooted and established in love, may have power, *together with all the saints*, to grasp how wide and long and high and deep is the love of Christ, and to know this love that surpasses knowledge—that you may be filled to the measure of all the fullness of God" (Eph. 3:17–19).

How do we understand who God is? How do we grasp His love? How do we become more like Christ? We do so *together with all the saints*. Sitting in rows and being lectured at for the entire training process does not count as *together with all the saints*.

Consider the classic passage about living out our new nature in Christ and being renewed in the image of Christ (Col. 3:1–17). How does that work itself out in the real world? By being united with one another across ethnic barriers, by bearing with one another, by forgiving one another, and by loving one another (3:11–14). It doesn't occur only through the pulpit ministry of the Word. In this passage Paul emphasizes the personal ministry of the Word. "Let the word of Christ dwell in you richly as you teach and admonish *one another* with all wisdom, and as you sing psalms, hymns and spiritual songs with gratitude in your hearts to God" (3:16). Progressive sanctification, whether for our counselees, our trainees, or ourselves, occurs in the context of one-another community.

Consider the classic passage that teaches how Christians experience victory over sin. "See to it brothers, that none of you has a sinful, unbelieving heart that turns away from the living God. But encourage one another daily, as long as it is called Today, so that none of you may be hardened by sin's deceitfulness" (Heb. 3:12–13). What softens the heart? What counteracts sin's lies? Daily one-another encouragement in Christian community.

Consider the classic passage that teaches how Christians experience healing hope in the midst of devastating suffering. "And let us consider how we may spur one another on toward love and good deeds. Let us not give up meeting together, as some are in the habit of doing, but let us encourage one another—and all the more as you see the Day approaching" (Heb. 10:24–25). In suffering and in sin, we need ongoing one-another community.

In the next chapter we learn best-practice biblical counseling training methods and strategies for cultivating community. There we will learn that we nurture community by being a community; we cultivate community in community.

In this chapter we focus on what our trainees need to experience in community. As a training small group, we want to experience one-another empathy (sustaining), encouragement (healing), exhortation (reconciling), and empowerment (guiding). We lead our group in such a way that together we experience group biblical counseling—group sustaining, healing, reconciling, and guiding.

We create and nurture a safe environment where we weep with one another—communicating that it's normal to hurt—and where together we explore life from God's perspective—communicating that it's possible to hope. We form and cultivate a grace environment where the faithful wounds of friends communicate that it's horrible to sin but wonderful to be forgiven and where we stir up one another, communicating that it's supernatural to mature. We are real and raw as we speak the truth in love to one another with authenticity and intimacy.

This soul-to-soul connecting doesn't imply any lack of curriculum, content, or materials about one-another ministry. In training groups I facilitate we explore more than a hundred one-another verses.[2] We also explore and apply passages such as the ones we just examined: Ephesians 3:17–19; Colossians 3:1–17; Hebrews 3:12–13; Hebrews 10:24–25; and many more.

Additionally, I always include, in either the in-class training or outside reading, teaching about the theology and practice of the spiritual disciplines.[3] Through individual supervision and through a writing project, I also have each trainee develop his or her own *Personal Spiritual Workout Routine/Plan.* The trainees craft a spiritual development plan that includes individual spiritual disciplines and group spiritual disciplines—all designed specifically for them and their current life situation.

Communion with Christ: The Vertical Spiritual Disciplines

Our definition of biblical counseling highlights not only communion with the body of Christ, but also communion with Christ. These vertical spiritual disciplines are essential to conformity to the image of Christ. Sometimes people assume that the vertical spiritual disciplines are always and only practiced individually. That need not and often should not be the case.

All four of the passages we examined in the previous section have elements of communion with Christ experienced together with the body of Christ. Hebrews 10:22, in the plural, exhorts, "Let us draw near to God with a sincere heart in full assurance of faith." In a training group, group communion with Christ in prayer should become an essential component—both planned and spontaneous. Many times our groups

---

2. See pages 29–31 of my *Spiritual Friends: A Methodology of Soul Care and Spiritual Direction* (Winona Lake, IN: BMH Books, 2007) for a chart listing these verses.

3. Donald Whitney, *Spiritual Disciplines for the Christian Life* (Colorado Springs: NavPress, 1991); R. Kent Hughes, *Disciplines of a Godly Man* (Wheaton, IL: Crossway Books, 1991); and Barbara Hughes, *Disciplines of a Godly Woman* (Wheaton, IL: Crossway Books, 2006) are among the books I have required.

have been engaged in counseling vignettes when it becomes obvious that one of the members is in need of prayer. The vignette stops and prayer begins.

The Colossians 3:15–17 passage merged seamlessly from one-another teaching and admonition to one-another worship through psalms, hymns, and spiritual songs with gratitude in their hearts to God. Many times I have been lecturing, a question is asked, a discussion begins, and spontaneous praise erupts. Other times I build in planned times of singing, praising, and group worship (more on this in the next chapter).

Again, this shouldn't imply that there's no curriculum, content, or materials about communion with Christ. In fact, creative Bible teaching should always relate truth to life. If we are talking about the Trinity and implications for biblical counseling, it is almost unimaginable that we wouldn't also discuss individual and group life application (again, more on this in the next chapter).

As described in chapter eight, biblical counseling values the role of homework. Just as one hour of counseling per week is not enough for ongoing growth in grace, so two hours of training is not enough. So, in conjunction with the training in spiritual disciplines mentioned above, trainees have homework assignments in the practice of the private and corporate spiritual disciplines that enhance their communion with Christ and help them tap into Christ's resurrection power.

Some private spiritual disciplines include Bible study, meditating on passages, prayer, fasting, solitude, silence, confession, Sabbath rest, and journaling. Some corporate spiritual disciplines include worship, service, stewardship/giving, evangelism, and fellowship.

A Best-Practice Community Map

Because of the nature of Christian community and because it is the container for the other 3Cs, it is difficult to outline a "curriculum." By talking about the two kinds of Christian community that every biblical counselor must participate in, I have outlined an atmosphere or attitude. Like the other 3Cs, even these two kinds of community are simply one map to address Christian community in biblical counseling training.

Two dozen best-practice churches add their perspective (see below). Your task is to weigh the combined advice in this chapter as you develop the community-building aspect that best matches your ministry context.

Disciple-Making Champions

Equipping for Christian Community

As part of the *4E Ministry Training Strategy Questionnaire*, two dozen best-practice churches responded to the question, "What community-building objectives and activities (group connecting, team-building, creating a home-like atmosphere, practicing private and corporate spiritual disciplines) do you seek to equip your training group to experience and your graduates to participate in?" The following list collates the most common themes.

- We work to create the proper atmosphere so that mutual one-another ministry takes place effectively in our training.
- Everyone is encouraged to experience and flourish in gospel community—a mutual care and bearing of burdens with one another both within and outside our training.
- Our training groups build on a church-wide culture of one-another discipleship.
- We strive to experience and practice the one-anothering that the apostle Paul wrote about so that every ministry member feels wanted, valued, respected, appreciated, and ministered to.
- Character is shaped in community over time, so we strive to cultivate a synergistic, productive group environment where there is trust and risk and whole-group involvement.
- We employ a body life approach and emphasize loving connection within our training.
- We call it "radical hospitality" and teach one another encouragement and community as a high value.
- We share testimonies of God's work in our lives through the training, and we encourage people to open up during our meetings.
- As leaders, we open our lives and struggles to encourage a community of authenticity.
- We strive to teach all our graduates how to employ small, authentic groups to help people grow and change.

245

- We create groups among our counselors-in-training and give them exercises to complete together in an effort to demonstrate the effectiveness and benefits of small group interaction.
- Within the group time we practice spiritual disciplines like corporate worship and prayer, mutual fellowship, and biblical encouragement.
- We consider the biblical one-another commands to be part of corporate spiritual disciplines—what we teach our trainees to do we experience together each time we meet.
- Outside the group time, we have our trainees read books on spiritual disciplines.
- Outside the group time, we encourage our people to practice spiritual disciplines such as silence, solitude, service, worship, confession, repentance, fellowship, biblical meditation, and frugality.

Outside Resources and Required Reading

Chapters eight and nine have focused on *curriculum and materials* with an emphasis on mapping out and outlining the categories to consider covering. It has been purposeful that these two chapters have not yet specifically focused on outside materials. It is unwise to highlight outside sources until you have decided what core 4C categories you believe your training ministry needs to cover.

To their credit, every one of the twenty-four best practice churches developed their own in-house curriculum materials: outlines, handouts, notes, manuals, or videos. Their typical best practice method was to use outside resources to supplement and fill in their in-house materials. See below for a detailed accounting of those outside resources currently used by twenty-four best practice churches. The average training ministry required four to five outside resources.

Disciple-Making Champions

Outside Materials

As part of the *4E Ministry Training Strategy Questionnaire*, two dozen best practice churches responded to the question, "What outside materials (books, articles, manuals, resources, videos) do you use in your biblical counseling equipping?" The following list collates in order of usage the most commonly used materials. The number after the resource denotes the number of churches using that resource as required reading or viewing.

- *Spiritual Friends* by Bob Kellemen: 9
- *Instruments in the Redeemer's Hand* by Paul Tripp: 7
- *How People Change* by Tim Lane and Paul Tripp: 7
- *Soul Physicians* by Bob Kellemen: 7
- Books by Jay Adams: 6
- Articles from *The Journal of Biblical Counseling*: 5
- *Equipped to Counsel* by John Henderson: 5
- Booklets from the Christian Counseling and Education Foundation: 4
- Counseling Video Observation Series from Faith Baptist Church, Lafayette, Indiana: 4
- Booklets from Faith Baptist Church, Lafayette, Indiana: 4
- *Idols of the Heart* by Elyse Fitzpatrick: 4
- *Counsel from the Cross* by Elyse Fitzpatrick: 4
- *God's Healing for Life's Losses* by Bob Kellemen: 4
- Observation Videos by the National Association of Nouthetic Counselors: 3
- *The Peacemaker* by Ken Sande: 3
- *The Self-Confrontation Manual* by John Broger: 3
- *Seeing with New Eyes* by David Powlison: 3
- *Speaking Truth in Love* by David Powlison: 3
- *CrossTalk* by Mike Emlet: 3
- *Systematic Theology* by Wayne Grudem: 3
- *Caring for God's People Video* by the American Association of Christian Counselors: 2
- *Beyond the Suffering* by Bob Kellemen: 2
- *Sacred Friendships* by Bob Kellemen: 2
- *Counseling* by John MacArthur: 2
- *The Heart of Anger* by Lou Priolo: 2
- *Disciplines of a Godly Man* by Kent Hughes: 2
- Other Books or Video Resources Noted One Time Each: 12

Commencement: How Do We Get from Here to There?

I thank God that the face of Jesus is already in every Christian we train to become a biblical counselor. I much prefer stirring up what God has placed within. "Old Faithful" at Yellowstone also communicates the idea of releasing something that is already within. Like clockwork, the geyser explodes upward because of the contents stored deep within.

When I taught that image in our church, one of our elders became extremely excited. "Men," he said to the rest of our elder ministry team, "do you understand this idea from 2 Timothy 1:5–7 that Pastor Bob is picturing with Mount Rushmore and with Old Faithful? *It's in there!* Our job as elders, coaches, and counselors isn't to put maturity into people. That would be impossible. Our role is to fan into flame and stir up the Christlikeness that's already in there!"

In chapters seven through nine we have seen "what's in there." In chapter seven we learned how the 4Cs provide our biblical counseling training *goals and objectives*. In chapters eight and nine we focused on the 4Cs of biblical counseling training *curriculum and materials*.

Because I have taught this so many times, I know what some of you are thinking: "All of that is great—it really is. It clarifies a lot for me. But . . . how do I move from goals, objectives, curriculum, and materials to the actual process of training folks in these four vital areas?"

Glad you asked. Chapter ten will explore biblical counseling training *strategies and methods*. We will address the question, "How do we effectively train biblical counselors to know, be, do, and love?" We will apply best practice transformational training concepts that comprehensively equip your trainees for biblical content, counseling competence, Christlike character, and Christian community.

Growing Together: Questions for Reflection, Discussion, and Application

1. Before reading this chapter, how would you have answered the following questions? What is your definition/description of a spiritually mature Christian? How do you measure spiritual maturity? What is your model, target, goal of spiritual maturity? Would you know a spiritually mature Christian if you saw one?

2. Now that you have read this chapter, in what ways, if any, would you answer those questions differently?

3. As briefly as possible, what would you say the ultimate goal of biblical counseling is?

4. Take a Redeemed Personality Inventory evaluating your current progress toward Christlikeness. Use a 10 for "Most Like Christ" and a 1 for "Least Like Christ."

_____ Like Jesus, I increasingly exalt, enjoy, love, and find satisfaction in God more than any other.

_____ I increasingly cling to God, running home to Him as my Father, like a faithful son or daughter.

_____ I increasingly enjoy Christ more than any other joy in life.

_____ I increasingly depend upon the Holy Spirit to sanctify me, make me holy, beautify me, empower and equip me.

_____ I increasingly love others deeply and sacrificially from the heart with grace.

_____ I increasingly rest confidently in who I am in and to Christ.

_____ Like Jesus, I increasingly view life from the Father's eternal, gracious, and good perspective.

_____ I increasingly, together with all the saints, grasp the holy love of God.

_____ I increasingly allow God's eternal story to invade my earthly story.

_____ I increasingly renew my mind and stir up wholesome thinking.

_____ Like Jesus, I increasingly die to self and live for God and others.

_____ I increasingly trust Christ courageously and take risks to minister to others.

_____ I increasingly find my life by dying to myself, taking up my cross, and following Christ.

_____ I increasingly live to shepherd others.

_____ I increasingly serve Christ and others out of a pure heart, good conscience, and sincere faith.

_____ I increasingly develop emotional self-awareness: understanding my moods.

_____ I increasingly develop emotional self-mastery: soothing my soul in my Savior.

_____ I increasingly develop emotional maturity: managing my moods with a ministry focus.

_____ I increasingly develop emotional empathy: recognizing emotions in others.

_____ I increasingly develop emotional savvy: handling my relationships well.

5. Of the four marks of Christlike character and their follow-up questions:
   a. Which ones surprise you? Why?
   b. Which ones have you taught on? How has your focus been different from the way those areas were developed in this chapter? What would you teach in those content areas?
   c. Which ones haven't you taught on? Why is that?
   d. What character area, if any, would you not include in your training curriculum? Why?
   e. What character area would you add for your training ministry? How would you develop it?

6. Of the two kinds of Christian community and their development in this chapter:
   a. Which ones surprise you? Why?
   b. Which ones have you focused on? How has your focus been different from the way those areas were developed in this chapter? What would you teach in those content areas?
   c. Which ones haven't you focused on? Why is that?
   d. What community aspect, if any, would you not include in your training curriculum? Why?
   e. What community aspect would you add for your training ministry? How would you develop it?

10

Equipping Competent Biblical Counselors

Transformational Training Strategies and Methods

I was profoundly impacted by the research and writing for the book *Beyond the Suffering: Embracing the Legacy of African American Soul Care and Spiritual Direction*. The book depicts the amazing one-another ministry of the black church during the horrors of enslavement. In chapter six ("The Old Ship of Zion"), my co-author and I describe the *Invisible Institution*—the hidden worship and fellowship meetings that occurred in the cabins and woods of the slave plantation.

Pastor Peter Randolph pictures the situation. "Not being allowed to hold meetings on the plantation, the slaves assemble in the swamps, out of reach of the patrols. They have an understanding among themselves as to the time and place of getting together."[1] Once gathered, Randolph explains their *spontaneous yet structured* gatherings.

---

1. Robert Kellemen and Karole Edwards, *Beyond the Suffering: Embracing the Legacy of African American Soul Care and Spiritual Direction* (Grand Rapids: Baker Books, 2007), 130.

Arrangements are then made for conducting the exercises. They first ask each other how they feel, the state of their minds, etc. The male members then select a certain space, in separate groups, for their division of the meeting. Preaching in order by the brethren; then praying and singing all around. . . . The preacher usually commences by calling himself unworthy.[2]

Their experience reminds us of the early church in Acts 2.

They devoted themselves to the apostles' teaching and to the fellowship, to the breaking of bread and to prayer. . . . Every day they continued to meet together in the temple courts. They broke bread in their homes and ate together with glad and sincere hearts, praising God and enjoying the favor of all the people. (Acts 2:42, 46–47)

If any two churches could have been all spontaneity and no structure, we might think it would have been the early church in Acts and the black church under American slavery. Yet we discover in both cases the art of *organizing the organism*. They made arrangements for conducting the exercises. They devoted themselves to the apostles' teaching. Though valuing spontaneity and the leading of the Spirit, they also treasured purposeful planning and ongoing training.

We so easily swing the ministry pendulum between structure *or* spontaneity, yet God's Word cherishes the *structured spontaneity of the organized organism* (Acts 6:1–7; 1 Cor. 14:26–40; 1 Tim. 3:5, 14–15; 2 Tim. 2:2; 4:2; Titus 2:1–8). God calls leaders to prepare His people for works of service so the body of Christ might be edified and equipped with the result that Christians speak the truth in love as the whole body joined and held together grows and builds itself up in love (the organized organism) (Eph. 4:11–16).

In my consulting ministry, I tend to see churches today swinging the pendulum toward the extreme of spontaneity without structure, organism without organization, and experiences without equipping. Relative to biblical counseling, that would result in being a church *of*

2. Ibid., 130–32.

one-another ministry (which is vital), but never becoming a church *with* an envisioned, enlisted, equipped, and empowered biblical counseling ministry. We should cultivate an environment where *informal one-another ministry* spontaneously saturates the entire congregation. We *also* should oversee a ministry where *equipping in formal biblical counseling* provides the entire congregation with access to believers who are competent to counsel. It is never either/or.

In chapter seven we learned how the 4Cs provide our biblical counseling training *goals and objectives*. In chapters eight and nine we moved from these broad goals and objectives to a focused discussion of biblical counseling training *curriculum and materials*. Now in chapter ten we explore biblical counseling transformational training *strategies and methods*. This chapter presents best practice answers to the question, "How do we *structure* our training so we comprehensively equip biblical counselors to know, be, do, and love?"

It is helpful to think through transformational strategies, methods, and structure using three broad categories.

- Organizing for 4C Equipping: Levels of training (informal versus formal models), length of training, and schedule, scope, and sequence of training
- Meeting for 4C Equipping: Transformational teaching-oriented training and transformational small group lab-oriented training
- Outside Training for 4C Equipping: Supervision, spiritual friendship, protégé meetings, and assignments.

Organizing for 4C Equipping

Before you read what I have to say about how to do it, remember this: *don't do it as I do it.* There is no cookie-cutter approach, no one-size-fits-all training model. I have already testified about how I blundered by trying to plop a successful large church model on a much smaller church. You will be reading principles and best practices that you need to interpret and implement to fit your biblical counseling ministry in your church.

Levels and Styles of Training: The Informal Model and the Formal Model

Several times in the book I have compared and contrasted training in informal one-another ministry and training in formal biblical counseling. Every member of every church should be equipped to speak the truth in love in small groups, in the foyer, over the backyard fence, at the dinner table, and at the diner—*the informal model*. Additionally, some members with gifting, passion, calling, and commitment may focus their ministry on intentional and intensive ongoing biblical counseling—*the formal model*.

While this chapter focuses on equipping in the formal model, it is important that we not forget the need to equip the entire congregation to speak the truth in love to one another. You may find it helpful to review the ideas from pages 159–60 and the Disciple-Making Champions section ("Saturating the Congregation") collated from twenty-four best practice churches.

I understand that it can seem daunting to add to your plate components such as those listed in chapter six when you are already equipping others in formal biblical counseling. Think long-term and think team. You don't have to do everything at once. *You* don't have to do it all yourself. Trained graduates gain wonderful experience by training others in informal one-another ministry.

Length of Training in the Formal Model

Informal training is typically of a shorter duration, more periodic, offered on an elective basis, and used in everyday life situations. Formal training, to which we now turn our attention, meets regularly over an extended period of time. How much training is enough; how much is too little; how much is too much? Initially, when you read the average length of training in best practice churches, you might be taken aback. Don't read ahead until you have considered some important points.

First, don't dumb down. Keep your expectations high. Formal biblical counseling is serious. People's lives matter. Comprehensive equipping is essential.

Second, factor in what a committed member would be doing if not in your training. Most committed members would likely be dedicating a couple of hours per week either to a ministry they were involved in or to a small group they participated in. Most would do so on an ongoing, open-ended basis—year after year.

Third, don't apologize. Don't be sheepish about insisting on commitment—both quality and quantity.

Fourth, communicate the amazing benefits of the training. Your meetings, done right and run well, will become the most powerful small group time that your trainees have ever experienced. Your trainees will say years later, "To this day, I miss our training small group and see it as the most amazing time of personal growth and group connection that I have ever experienced!"

Now that I have mentally prepared you . . . drum roll, please . . . for the twenty-four best practice churches, the average time spent meeting was one hundred hours.[3] That includes lecture, lab, and counseling observation. It does not include time spent outside the actual meetings in reading assignments, meeting with supervisors, and meeting with lab partners/spiritual friends. The lowest reported time in training was forty hours, the highest was one hundred fifty hours, and the mean was seventy-five hours of training.

The average length of training was one and a half years. The most frequent length was one year. The shortest length was three months—but that was intensive training meeting twelve hours each day, one day a week. The longest length was three years. Additionally, almost every best practice church also required ongoing supervision and/or continuing education as long as the biblical counselor still provided formal biblical counseling.

While I have structured my equipping ministry differently in each of my three churches, whenever I have offered formal training it typically ran two years, meeting once per week over nine months each year. That is one hundred forty-four hours of in-meeting time.

3. By comparison, in Tan's survey in 1991 (*Lay Counseling*), the average in-meeting time was 72 hours. The minimum was 40 to 50 hours. His own training of lay counselors lasted 108 hours.

Why meet that long? What do you do for that long? You comprehensively equip one another in the 4Cs of biblical content, Christlike character, counseling competence, and Christian community.

Is that too much for people? The attrition (dropout) rate is an excellent measure to use to answer that question. In my three churches, less than 4 percent have ever dropped out. Over 96 percent of the people who started the training continued for two years to graduation and beyond. Compare that to the percentage of people who stay in a small group for two years or, frankly, who do anything consistently for two years. The key to retention is careful selection, plus comprehensive equipping in the context of loving community that impacts the trainee's life so the trainee can impact the lives of others.

Schedule, Scope, and Sequence of Training in the Formal Model

Every time I have trained biblical counselors in the local church, my meeting schedule and training scope and sequence have been different. I offer the following schedule simply as one representative sample (it is from my first church LEAD biblical counseling equipping group). It was what fit best for that church with that MVP-C Statement with those trainees in our community.

We met every Wednesday night from September through May (other than holidays) for two hours for two years. We divided each year into semesters. I required attendance at 90 percent of all meetings. Our average attendance over the two years was 98 percent—our meetings became "can't miss."

LEAD Year One, Semester One

During our first hour we met for interactive, applicational lectures. We covered God's Word, the Trinity, and Creation (understanding people). During the second hour we met for intensive small group lab interactions focused on character and competence development. There we covered the counseling competencies associated with sustaining and healing.

Since that first training group, I have altered how I schedule each evening. Now I normally have the interactive lectures for two hours one evening (with a break between), and the next week I facilitate two-hour intensive small group labs. I have found that a two-hour slot for the labs is more conducive to relationship building, connecting, intense interaction, role-playing, and live counseling.

Another best practice alternative is to cover all the lecture/content material first—either the first year or the first semester—and then focus on the lab/competency area next. This method has the advantage of covering all the content first so that trainees are solidly grounded in biblical counseling theology/theory. However, in my thinking, that is outweighed by the disadvantage of an extended amount of time with a predominantly cognitive focus without the intimate relationship/community building time and without the focus on character and competence.

During this first semester, outside the meetings trainees averaged one hour per week in assigned reading. They were also required to meet every other week with an assigned encouragement partner/spiritual friend (of the same gender) from the class. Trainees also met with me (or another mentor/supervisor) every other week.

LEAD Year One, Semester Two

During the second semester our meeting schedule remained the same. The content focused on the fall (diagnosing problems), redemption (prescribing solutions), and glorification. Our training labs highlighted continued community building, character growth, and the development of the counseling competencies of reconciling and guiding. Trainees continued to spend one hour each week in outside reading, and continued to meet every other week with their encouragement partners and every other week for supervision. They also completed a project where they developed their personal spiritual disciplines/spiritual workout routine.

At the end of the first year every trainee was assessed in each of the 4Cs (see Appendix 10.1). They evaluated themselves, the group shared evaluations, their encouragement partner evaluated them, their supervisor/mentor evaluated them, and they completed a written exam. Each trainee then received a Level One LEAD Graduate Certificate in a formal ceremony during a church service.

LEAD Year Two, Semester One

The second year's meeting schedule remained the same. The content now focused on marriage and family/parenting, while the small group lab focused on marriage and family counseling. We based the decision to focus on marriage and family issues on our congregational and community assessments.

Trainees continued to spend one hour each week in outside reading. They now began approximately two hours each week in supervised ministry. Some provided individual counseling, some did marital or parental/family counseling, and some facilitated recovery/care/support groups. They learned how to lead groups by being a part of our intensive group labs. Trainees also met every other week for supervision. Most trainees voluntarily chose to continue meeting every other week (or even more often) with their encouragement partner, although they were now required to meet just once each month.

LEAD Year Two, Semester Two

The second semester's meeting schedule remained the same. The content and competence training now focused on depression and anxiety. The small group labs also continued to be a place where community was built and character was molded. We based the decision to focus on "mood disorder" issues on our congregational and community assessments. As I noted in a previous chapter, I believe trainees gain more from extensive training in one issue than they do from brief coverage of many issues. They learn how to study and use the Scriptures to develop a helping approach to other issues.

In addition to one hour each week in outside reading, trainees wrote a paper where they developed their model of biblical counseling theory and practice related to a counseling issue of their choice. They continued providing two hours each week of supervised ministry, either in individual, marital, or parental counseling, or in small group ministry. They also continued meeting for supervision and meeting with their encouragement partner for mutual spiritual friendship.

At the end of the second year, every trainee was again assessed in each of the 4Cs through self-assessment, group assessment, encouragement partner assessment, assessment from his or her supervisor, and a written exam (see Appendix 10.1). At the end of the training, each graduate received a Level Two LEAD Graduate Certificate.

Meeting for 4C Equipping

For simplicity of communication we can divide our thinking about in-person group meetings into teaching-oriented training and small group lab-oriented training. However, they often morph into one another. In a lesson where truth is applied to life in the context of community, the class sometimes shifts spontaneously to a lab-like counseling time. At other times the class shifts purposefully to a small group discussion time or partner role-play time. Also, in a ministry where God's Word is viewed as relevant and sufficient, small group labs have content components and material to cover, meaning that, at times, teaching modes are included in the lab training.

Transformational Teaching-Oriented Training

A confession: I do not like the word "lecture." It connotes being talked at—listening to a monologue. Too often that is our image of training in biblical counseling. That needs to change.

One section of one chapter can't address everything that a transformational teacher might want to implement. What it can do, and what I will do, is share five foundational transformational teaching principles that can shape how we equip our biblical counseling trainees. (See Appendix 10.2 for a sample lesson plan and lesson outline.)

Transformational Bible Teaching Is Comprehensive

We need to start with a definition of transformational teaching:

> *Creative, interactive, engaging joint-exploration and two-way com-munication of truth (content) related to life (character) and ministry (competence) in the context of relationship (community).*

Notice in this description that teaching is not simply about covering content. It much more comprehensively addresses all 4Cs. To train biblical counselors we must think like and teach like biblical counselors—always relating truth to life in the context of relationships.

Transformational Teaching Is Student-Oriented

Notice also from the definition that transformational teaching is not teacher-oriented, but student-oriented. Just as each section of this book begins with a list of ROLOs (Reader-Oriented Learning Objectives), so every lesson we teach should start with a list of SOLOs (Student-Oriented Learning Objectives) (see Appendix 10.2).

Those SOLOs should complete the following sentence for the 3Cs in the context of the fourth C. In the context of community, and based upon active engagement and participation in this lesson:

- The student will be able to know (content) . . .
- The student will be able to do (competence) . . .
- The student will be able to be (character) . . .

By thinking like this, we shift our focus from information to transformation. We no longer ask, "What information do I need to dump and download into my student's brain?" Instead, we pray, "Father, how can our time together (home) transform our heads, hearts, and hands?"

Transformational Bible Teaching Is Big-Picture Focused

What's the big idea? That is not the question asked by an agitated friend. Instead, it is the question asked by Professor Haddon Robinson in his classic text on biblical preaching, which we can relate to biblical teaching.[4] Effective communication demands a single theme. While your lesson will engage students in thinking about many ideas and applications, and while it will address all 4Cs, each lesson needs cohesiveness. What is the dominant idea or theme that unites the various points of the lesson?

For example, when I teach on the Trinity, I start with a simple big idea. *The Trinity is our model for biblical counseling ministry.* We discuss that single idea from a host of different perspectives, looking at a number of different passages. But everything zeroes in on how the relationship within the Trinity models the soul-to-soul connecting required of the caring, competent biblical counselor.

Transformational Bible Teaching Is Life-Changing

Thirty years ago I learned four rhyming words that sound like a line from a Dr. Seuss book: *Hook, Book, Look, Took.* This little memory device from Larry Richards has shaped my teaching for three decades.[5]

Hook engages students in considering the "why" question: "Why is this lesson important to me? Why should I even listen?" In a sermon, it is the riveting illustration that introduces the vital importance of the message. In a lesson, it is the opening discussion/interaction question that helps students to ponder the real-life significance of the upcoming lesson material.

When teaching about the Trinity as our model for biblical counseling ministry, I tell my students about sixteen-year-old Aminah McKinnie of Madison, Mississippi, who confesses in *Newsweek* that she is beset by feelings of isolation mixed with longings to be connected.[6] I then propose that the solution to her disconnected soul is nothing less than Trinitarian theology. Next, I have students divide into pairs or small groups to discuss the following questions:

4. Haddon Robinson, *Biblical Preaching: The Development and Delivery of Expository Messages* (Grand Rapids: Baker Books, 1982).
5. Lawrence Richards and Gary Bredfeldt, *Creative Bible Teaching* (Chicago: Moody, 1998).
6. Sharon Begley, "A World of Their Own," *Newsweek*, May 8, 2000, 52–56.

- Who do you know that is like Aminah—experiencing fleeting, fragmented relationships?
- To what degree does it shock you that Trinitarian theology is the solution to disconnected, unanchored souls?

Prepared to ponder the relevancy of the topic, we next turn to *the Book* (the Bible) and address what Richards calls *book*. This answers the "what" question: "What does the Bible say about our topic? What does the Bible teach about the Trinity?"

Likely this is the part of a lesson that most of us think about when we think about teaching. It is the main thing, but it is not the only thing. It is central, but it is not exclusive.

Even with the content/book aspect of the lesson, creativity and engagement are essential. It still is not simply a lecture (see below for an introduction to creative Bible teaching methods).

Theologically speaking, this part of the lesson is *academic* theology—the vital foundation for teaching in biblical counseling. It includes *systematic* theology where you outline the entire New Testament's teaching on the Trinity. It includes *biblical* theology where you explore one author's teaching on the Trinity (I typically highlight John). It includes *exegetical* theology where you explore in depth the teaching about the Trinity from one or two central passages (I typically highlight John 1 where we examine the mutual intimacy within the Trinity and John 17 where we explore the mutual glory shared by the Trinity). It also includes *lexical* theology where you examine specific words used to describe the relationship within the Trinity ("glory" used numerous times in John 17 being one example).

As vital as *book* is, we don't stop there. Instead, interspersed throughout the lesson is the *look* element. Look addresses the "so what" question: "So what difference should this make to my life? What personal application could I make to my life?" I use PDQs—Prompting Discussion Questions—built into every lesson outline to help students ponder either individually or together how to apply the truth to their lives.

In theology this is known as *spiritual* theology. It is a missing ingredient in much theological education. It links the head and the heart. It moves from information about God and the Bible to transformational application of the Bible to my life and relationships. I might ask a PDQ like "Think of someone you could begin to enjoy more fully. How could that relationship more fully reflect the mutual enjoyment of the Trinity as described in John 1 and John 17?"

The *took* aspect of the lesson asks the "what now" question: "What could I do with this truth now in my ministry? What are the ministry implications of this truth?" (This is different from Richards's use of *took* where he makes it a more specific application of the more general *look* implication.)

Theologically, this is *practical or pastoral* theology. It relates truth not just to our lives, but to how we do ministry. When we explore John 17, we note that the Trinity is an eternal mutual admiration society. Father and Son in John 17 are passionate about spreading each other's fame. We summarize that by noting that *It's All About Him.* Life is not ultimately about us. So in a *took* ministry implication, we ponder a question such as, "How would our counseling look different if we realized that counseling is not about us or about our counselee, but ultimately about helping our counselee to glorify God in the midst of his or her struggle with suffering and sin?"

Transformational Bible Teaching Is Creative

The methods for creative Bible teaching are almost limitless. It is less important that we master all of them than it is that we are aware that lecturing is only one method among many. A few select methods for creative Bible teaching in biblical counseling training follow.

- *Lecture:* Done well—with handouts, PowerPoint, illustrations, audio/CDs/music, video/DVDs, teaching to the right brain and left brain, personal sharing, and passion—the lecture method is one of the most efficient ways to communicate truth.
- *Student Interaction:* I have already noted many examples such as opening *hook* discussions, interspersed *look* PDQs, and lesson ending *took* ministry application questions. You can group

263

students in pairs or in small groups, or have the entire class interact. You can have prepared questions and/or allot time for spontaneous questions and answers.

- *Student Teaching:* We learn best what we teach, so assigning students parts of lessons to study, prepare, and present is very effective.
- *Student and Teacher Sharing:* Personal examples, stories, and illustrations enhance acquisition of knowledge, skill, and character.
- *Case Studies, Role-Play, and Counseling Observation:* While sometimes reserved for lab learning, I often incorporate these into the teaching-oriented training.
- *Fellowship and Worship:* Again, these are at times reserved for lab settings, but I include prayer/praise, cheers/tears, worship CDs and DVDs, and testimony times in the teaching component.
- *Outside Assignments:* Required reading, research projects, personal application projects, ministry implication projects, and written papers are all effective methods to enhance learning.
- *Assessments:* Quizzes and exams keep students accountable and stretch their learning, especially when questions go beyond mere rote learning to depth of concept understanding and application.

Transformational Small Group Lab-Oriented Training

Two questions will help us organize our thinking about transformational small group lab training. What is the climate or environment we hope to develop and how do we cultivate it? What training methods can we use and how do we implement them?

The Transformational Small Group Lab Climate and How to Cultivate It

I have used the terms "lab," "small group," and "small group lab" interchangeably. Used alone, "lab" can have a clinical feel to it. Instead of real life lived together and *experiential* learning, it might picture artificial, forced connection, and *experimental* learning. Saying "small group-oriented training" might cause some to think that we are training people only or primarily to be small group leaders. The phrase "small group lab" is meant to convey what I have said numerous times: *community is the container for equipping in content, character, and competency.* The authentic, intimate small group environment provides the fertile soil in which we nurture competent biblical counselors.

In teaching, if we become overly dependent upon the lecture mode and content communication, we suck the life out of our biblical counseling training. In small group labs, if we become overly dependent on skill development, we suck the air out of the one-another community environment. The lab as a place only to discuss case studies, or only to observe experts counsel, or only to practice skills through role-playing, becomes a sterile environment. Those are essential components of lab work, but they must exist within a genuine, secure small group community.

So, in lab training, my first goal is to cultivate a climate where we experience biblical counseling together. We grow more like Christ as we receive *parakaletic* soul care for our suffering and as we receive *nouthetic* spiritual direction for our struggle against sin. We become more competent biblical counselors as we sustain, heal, reconcile, and guide one another.

How do we do this? It begins with a mindset, with a vision communicated consistently. The vision is that we are not a pack of lab rats. We are image bearers. We are here not simply to learn skills, but to minister to one another.

As leaders, we must model that vision. I did that when I shared with my first training group my image of myself as a ten-year-old boy in my father's oversized suit. In my very first seminary small group lab two of my students had so caught the vision that on the first day they invited me to open up. One was a pastor's wife, one was a pastor, and as the lab began they asked me what the transition was like from pastor to professor and who was currently building into my life.

Rather than dismiss their care and concern so I could focus on the lesson plan, I shared openly. The group focused on me. I was on what became affectionately known as "the hot seat." "The hot seat" refers to anytime the group shifts its focus from discussing the material to offering sustaining, healing, reconciling, and guiding to an individual.

By responding to their invitation, I modeled the priority of "presence"—staying in the moment, dealing with what is happening in the room, focusing on the people in the group and the relationships among group members. Whether in the seminary setting or the local church setting, I have found that you rarely need to role-play because when you prioritize presence, you experience and engage in live biblical counseling with one another.

Authentic community is caught and learned by experience more than taught or read. When I consult, churches often bring me onsite to lead a small group lab. In a lab we will talk about a question from *Spiritual Friends* or dabble in a role-play assignment. I'll say something like "Bill, that question seems like it really hits home for you. Would you like to talk about it a bit more at a personal level?" After an hour of counseling Bill on "the hot seat," he'll say, "Wow! In an instant we went from talking about counseling to my being counseled. That was amazing and so helpful personally." And someone else will chime in, "Bill, thank you for your courage to be so vulnerable and open. Not only did it help you personally, but I learned more in one hour of watching you being counseled than I would ever learn in hours of reading about counseling."

This also illustrates the need to invite intimacy, not to force intimacy. While some labs stay clinical forever, I have observed others that are so bent on experiencing deep relationships that people feel guilty if they are not ready to go deep, or feel coerced into going deeper faster than they are ready. Knowing the difference is not always easy, but it begins with creating a safe environment—safe to go deep or safe not to until a person is ready.

The Transformational Small Group Lab Methods and How to Implement Them

Don't think that "the hot seat" is *the* method you use. That turns a spontaneous, divinely appointed connection into a method. A grace-

266

oriented community where group members feel safe to speak the truth in love is the context for using a variety of lab-based methods.

Some methods are best used in conjunction with a training manual or book. I will use my biblical counseling training book *Spiritual Friends* to illustrate some of these methods and how to use them.

- Trainees come to class having read assigned content sections of *Spiritual Friends*. I facilitate discussions and respond to questions about principles and methods of biblical counseling. Often these quickly morph into real life counseling situations.
- Before class, trainees complete a series of character development questions. We use this section of *Spiritual Friends* in several ways. Sometimes students pair up with their encouragement partners to share. Other times we start with a particular question, and the discussion soon morphs into "the hot seat." Other times I simply invite people to share: "Is there a particular question that raised something in your heart and life that you want us to help you with?" Again, these often shift spontaneously into "hot seat" interactions.
- Before class, trainees complete questions related to competency development. Some of these require the students to share how they might respond to a person with a particular issue. Others ask students to evaluate or discuss a case study. Still others suggest role-plays that they can practice with their encouragement partner or with the group.
- The important principle to remember with any book or training manual is that it is your servant, not your master. It is a guide to prompt discussion, not a list of questions you must cover in an allotted amount of time. Allow the material to prime the pump and get the discussion going, and then use your biblical counseling skills to invite people to go deeper.
- Hold one another accountable for having read and engaged the material thoroughly before class, and then you don't have to be sure you cover everything in class. You can accomplish this

through the honor system, through quizzes covering the material, or through trainees showing you, their encouragement partner, or the group that they have completed the chapter questions.

We can categorize additional lab training methods by thinking through increasing levels of on-the-job-training.

- *Discuss Case Studies:* Facilitate a discussion of a case study with background information and presenting problem and have the group explore relevant biblical principles (theory) and how they would intervene and interact (methods).
- *Practice "Meta-skills":* Give students specific, brief assignments to practice specific skills such as listening, or spiritual conversations. Often it is helpful to do this in triads: one person is the counselor, one person is the counselee, and the other person provides feedback. Then you rotate so that each person has occupied each role.
- *Use Triad Role-Play Counseling:* This combines and goes beyond case studies and meta-skills. Share a prepared case study, then one student plays the counselee, another student plays the counselor, and a third student provides feedback.
- *Use Group Observation Role-Play Counseling:* Here, instead of just one person observing, the entire class observes one student role-play counseling another, and then they all provide feedback.
- *Use Observation of Live Counseling by the Trainer:* A class member, a church member, or a member of the community is counseled live by the trainer while the class observes. After the session ends, the trainer/counselor, the counselee, and the class interact about what they observed and learned and ask questions for clarification and instruction.
- *Use Live Counseling by the Trainee with the Trainer Sitting In:* The class observes while a trainee counsels another class member, a church member, or a member of the community. The trainer/supervisor is in the room and periodically offers feedback, shares

probing questions, and occasionally and briefly counsels and then hands things back to the trainee. Everyone interacts about the counseling afterward.

- *Use Live Counseling by the Trainee without the Trainer Sitting In:* The trainer and the class observe the student counseling someone live, and all interact at the end of the session.[7]

Some of the live counseling is pre-planned and may occur in a room with a microphone and a one-way mirror, if your facilities allow for that. At other times, the live counseling occurs spontaneously through "the hot seat" method described previously.

Frequently during the discussion of the live counseling, the trainee/counselor ends up on "the hot seat." A group member might note, "Barb, you seemed a tad disengaged in the session. Did you sense that at all?" Perhaps Barb acknowledges her disengagement and the group invites Barb to ponder with them what may be happening in her heart that she wants to work on.

Or, going even deeper, perhaps Barb does not acknowledge that she was relationally distant. Other group members express a similar experience of Barb's keeping them at arm's length. As the discussion unfolds, Barb disengages from the group. As the leader you may discern that the timing is not right and you need to address this later. Or you may invite Barb either to discuss it now with you in front of the group or later in supervision. "Barb, it seems that you may be disengaging a bit with us even while we give you feedback about disengaging. Would you like to talk with me about that now, would you and I like to interact about that later during supervision, or would you like to think about it, ponder it, pray about it, and maybe share with us next week?"

Now your small group lab has gone full circle. You created a safe place to speak the truth in love. Barb spoke the truth in love to her counselee, but it raised issues in Barb's life. Now you have invited Barb to allow you and the group to enter her life. This is the essence of transformational small group lab-oriented training in biblical counseling.

7. See Appendix 10.1 for a sample *Biblical Counseling Competency Evaluation Form.*

Outside Training for 4C Equipping

Teaching related to real life and small group labs that experience real life are foundational for equipping in biblical counseling. To that foundation we add training that occurs outside the context of your meetings. Two categories summarize this area: meetings with a Paul, a Barnabas, and a Timothy, and completing outside training assignments.

Transformational Meetings with a Paul, a Barnabas, and a Timothy

I have always used the time-honored, biblical three-fold equipping model. It involves meeting with a supervisor/mentor (a Paul or a Priscilla), meeting with a spiritual friend/encouragement partner (a Barnabas or a Ruth), and meeting with a protégé (a Timothy or a Euodia—Phil. 4:2).

Depending on the size of your group and whether you have trained any co-trainers, you may be the only supervisor. If you are, then keeping your training group to a maximum of twelve is essential. You will meet every other week with each person, in addition to all your other ministry commitments. Additionally, twelve is an ideal maximum size for the joint small group meetings.

If you have co-trainers, then you can train more than twelve people at one time since you can divide the supervisory roles. Where possible, it is helpful if each trainee at some point in the course of his or her training has access to each supervisor. It is also helpful if each supervisor/trainer facilitates each small group at some point.

Transformational Supervision Meetings

In my model of supervision the supervisory role is multifaceted, and it evolves over the two-year period. I am always working to help each trainee mature in each of the 4Cs. We meet every other week and spend time discussing questions about the content we have covered and its application to life. During these meetings I provide sustaining, healing, reconciling, and guiding—biblical counseling. These meetings assist in the development of Christlike character. They also develop counseling competencies because one of the best ways to learn to be a biblical counselor is to be counseled by a biblical counselor.

During consultation I am sometimes asked, "Are your trainees really open to being counseled? Do mature people like this really have enough issues to work on?" Once you start teaching about truth applied to life, once you start opening up illustratively about your own life, and once you create a safe small group atmosphere, trainees open up. And when we realize that biblical counseling is simply intensive and intentional focused discipleship, we know that we all have enough issues to work on until we reach heaven.

By the second semester of training, encouragement partners counsel each other on tape. Much of supervision now involves listening to portions of tapes and helping trainees to assess and develop their counseling. As with the labs, many times the way trainees relate as a counselor opens up windows to their own heart issues, and listening to a tape can quickly shift to talking about the trainee's own life.

By the second year, trainees are being taped offering live counseling to church and/or community members. Supervision focuses on these tapes in similar ways to the tapes with their encouragement partners.

Transformational Spiritual Friendship Meetings

During the first year I have trainees meet with their encouragement partners every other week. The first semester trainees develop their spiritual friendships with each other. They also provide mutual sustaining, healing, reconciling, and guiding (these are not taped the first semester).

By the second semester they are more focused on developing counseling competencies. At times they work through role-play assignments from *Spiritual Friends*. Most of the time they take turns counseling one another on tape—with real life issues.

As I noted earlier, the second year they are required to meet only once per month. They decide what they want to focus on. Typically they have built such strong spiritual friendships that they meet almost weekly and continue to discuss and apply content, encourage one another in

Christlike character development, and develop their counseling competencies—often by continuing to counsel one another.

Transformational Protégé Meetings

Normally I do not have trainees meet with protégés until the end of the first year. (I discuss in the next two chapters the appropriate paperwork and safeguards once these meetings begin.) These meetings involve live taped counseling. I screen and assign all counselees based upon their issues and the expertise of the trainee.

The trainees listen to their tapes and evaluate themselves. I listen to portions of the tape with the trainees, and we assess and evaluate their counseling competencies. Often this discussion shifts to issues in the trainee's life, and we shift back to their character development.

In consultation I am asked, "But will people really agree to counsel with a 'lay' person?" Most do, especially when they understand the level of training, know it is supervised, and understand that the supervisor can become involved if needed. I am also asked, "Don't people feel squeamish about being counseled on tape?" Some may at first, but they barely think about the tape once the session begins. They know how we safeguard the tapes and how the tapes assist their biblical counselor to help them more.

Transformational Training Assignments

I have used a wide variety of outside training assignments. Required reading is standard all four semesters. Completing assignments from *Spiritual Friends* is standard the first year. Periodic quizzes are typical, and year-end exams are standard each year.

Homework assignments vary from semester to semester and group to group. The first year students develop their own spiritual disciplines/spiritual workout routine. The final semester of the final year, students research and write a twelve- to fifteen-page project on a counseling issue they choose. By choice many students attend local, regional, or national counseling conferences or our own weekend conferences.

While it is not an "assignment" per se, once each semester we plan a fun event. It might be attending a sporting event, dining out together, enjoying a cookout at someone's home, or throwing a seasonal party. Counseling is serious ministry. Counselors need to have fun. And counseling training groups need to understand that they don't have to "go deep" every second.

Disciple-Making Champions

Transformational Training Methods

As part of the *4E Ministry Training Strategy Questionnaire*, two dozen best-practice churches responded to the question, "What equipping methods/means/style do you use to accomplish your content, competence, character, and community objectives?" The following list collates the most common themes.

- *Transformational Teaching:* Creative PowerPoint lectures, discussion groups, video presentations, question and answer sessions, case studies, brainstorming, personal application, ministry implications, Bible studies, quizzes, exams, student teaching
- *Transformational Small Groups/Labs:* observing experienced counselors, observing one-another counseling, studying case studies, role-playing, completing practice exercises employing counseling principles, doing life together, one-anothering, sharing authentically, being counseled, doing personal growth exercises/interactions, triads, and sharing personal stories, prayer, and praise
- *Transformational Outside Equipping:* Meeting with supervisors/mentors; completing homework assignments, required reading, and research papers; completing personal improvement projects and personal sanctification projects; having accountability partners; creating self-counsel projects; counseling under supervision; fellowshipping and scheduling fun times; attending outside conferences; journaling

Commencement: Organizing the Organism

Pastor Peter Randolph described how in the *Invisible Institution* arrangements were made for conducting the exercises. Following in their heroic footsteps, this chapter has helped us to organize the organism and structure for spontaneity. In fact, the whole book has offered that focus.

Tracking where we have been so far, we have learned how to help an entire congregation catch and cast a vision for informal one-another ministry and formal biblical counseling (envisioning). We have learned how to cultivate a climate where the entire congregation owns the MVP-C vision and how to nurture a family and build a team (enlisting). We just learned how to oversee comprehensive, transformational 4C training (equipping).

From my research and consulting I can guarantee you that if you have taken your church this far, you are far ahead of the vast majority of churches. I can also tell you that many of the churches that get this far experience a bit of panic once their first group graduates and they start training their second group. They think, "Too many spinning plates! How do we shepherd our graduates while we also train our second equipping group? Help!"

Help is on its way. We now shift to our fourth E: Empowering/employing godly ministers for biblical counseling ministry. In the chapters to come, we will learn how to oversee the ongoing organizing of the organism by leading ministries that are built to last, that grow from good to great, and that leave a legacy of loving leaders.

Don't panic. By God's grace, in His strength, and for His glory others have succeeded—and so will you. Not somehow, but triumphantly.

Growing Together: Questions for Reflection, Discussion, and Application

1. On the continuum of spontaneity and structure, where would you place yourself? How might that impact how you process and apply this chapter?
2. Regarding the average length of training in biblical counseling:
   a. How surprised are you at the typical duration (one hundred hours over one to two years)? How do you think your congregation would respond to that? How could you prepare them?
   b. As you reflect on your biblical counseling training in your church, what duration do you think is most appropriate? Why?

3. Of the five elements of transformational teaching-oriented training:
   a. Which do you think are most important?
   b. Which is already naturally your strength? Which might you need to work on and how?
4. Regarding the transformational small group lab training:
   a. How surprised are you by the relational focus of the lab training? How similar or dissimilar is it to what you have experienced? To what you would have anticipated?
   b. What elements of the lab training would you most want to incorporate? Why? How will you do that?
5. Concerning the three-fold equipping model:
   a. How have Paul/Priscilla, Barnabas/Ruth, and Timothy/Euodia relationships impacted your life and ministry?
   b. How could you use each of these transformational relationships in your biblical counseling training?

PART 4

Empowering/Employing Godly Ministers for Ministry

W hen I arrive at the fourth E in my seminar on *The 4E Ministry Training Strategy*, I show two PowerPoint slides that picture two forces fighting against the successful oversight of equipped biblical counselors. One slide pictures spinning plates; the other slide pictures an elephant in a living room.

Spinning Plates and Organizing the Organism

When I talk about spinning plates, I share that I have good news, bad news, and more good news. The good news: if you have progressed through envisioning, enlisting, and equipping, then you are far ahead of the curve. Your church will be one of the few that comprehensively address envisioning, enlisting, and equipping.

The bad news: the few that do get this far sometimes crash and burn shortly after takeoff. Why? No one has thought through what it means to "organize the organism."

Not one to end on bad news, I share more good news: there are answers to practical questions about overseeing biblical counseling ministries. Questions like the following: "Now that we've launched the ministry, how do we keep it running—especially while we have a myriad of other plates spinning? How do we balance structure and spontaneity? How do we nourish the relational/community focus while addressing procedural and policy issues?"

Chapter eleven portrays the relational processes that help churches to deploy and employ empowered ministers for ministry to the congregation and community. It explores the proactive mindset that is necessary to move from training to implementation, from implementation to ongoing growth, and from growth to passing the baton of ministry. It demonstrates how to oversee the biblical counseling ministry by organizing the organism through launching ministries built to last, leading ministries from good to great, and leaving a lasting legacy of loving leaders.

Elephants in the Room and Protecting Ministries

No one likes to talk about ethical and legal concerns. They are often the unspoken elephants in the room that motivate church leaders to squelch biblical counseling ministries. While we cannot allow the unwise and unnecessary fear of man to stop us from serving God, we must take ethical and legal concerns seriously. Even more importantly, we must take seriously God's law of love that demands that our ministry remain above reproach.

Chapter twelve explains that by following sound principles of ethical behavior, legal norms, wise practices, and biblical standards, churches can confidently launch and lead biblical counseling ministries. Chapter twelve teaches us how to care carefully.

Empowered by God for God's Glory

I intend the words "empowering/employing" to indicate that our work is not done after we have envisioned, enlisted, and equipped our biblical counseling team. We need to deploy them into ministry. We need to develop the type of ongoing ministry structure that enables them, through God's empowering, to employ their gifts for God's glory.

With this understanding in mind, one final time we can consider our ROLOs: Reader-Oriented Learning Objectives. Through your active reading and application of the two chapters in this section, you will be equipped to:

- Oversee the ongoing organizing of the organism through God's empowering for God's glory by administrating ministries, mentoring/supervising ministers, and passing the baton of ministry (chapter eleven).
- Care carefully by following sound principles of ethical behavior, legal norms, wise practices, and biblical standards (chapter twelve).

How do you oversee people in a caring way that builds community as you impact your community? How do you care carefully? Part four teaches us how.

11

Overseeing Ministries
for God's Glory

ORGANIZING THE ORGANISM

I was the ripe young age of thirty-one when our initial two-year LEAD biblical counseling group graduated. All twelve members who started, finished. All twelve spent at least the next two years ministering to members of our church and community.

One graduate led our New Hope Fellowship group, ministering every week to twenty people who were seeking to overcome various addictions. Two graduates launched and led a Beauty for Ashes group, working each week with ten women who had been sexually abused. Another graduate led a weekly Parenting Adolescents group, ministering to twelve parents each week. One graduate became my co-trainer for the next round of teaching. He ministered to twelve trainees and counseled two counselees per week. The other seven graduates provided an average of just over two biblical counseling sessions per week, for a total of fifteen people counseled weekly. That's more than seventy people ministered to each week by our biblical counseling team (more than one hundred if you include the people I was counseling, training, and supervising).

I share this story to illustrate that:

- By God's empowering, it can be done—and you can do it too.
- Even with God's empowering, there's still work to be done.
- To oversee the work that needs to be done, we need to organize the organism—for His glory.

You may think, "Well, Bob, your process was made much easier by the fact that you were in a large church." Perhaps. Yet a host of circumstances made it a wild ride as we simultaneously sailed and refitted our ship. Our church had never before had a counseling pastor, much less tried to launch a counseling ministry. At the time there were few books or churches we could turn to for wisdom. We weren't quite making it up as we went along, but it was close.

Though my title was Counseling and Discipleship Pastor, only 25 percent of my time was allotted to the LEAD ministry. The other 75 percent included my schedule of counseling twenty people per week, leading an Adult Bible Fellowship (a church within a church) of more than four hundred people, performing all the traditional pastoral-shepherding functions, and that dreaded M-word: meetings. In addition to ongoing supervision of the twelve LEAD graduates, one graduate and I were co-leading a second group of twenty-four LEAD trainees.

While I enjoyed the blessing of excellent secretarial assistance, her role was part-time and she served two other pastors. She was able to devote three hours each week to the LEAD ministry.

We had no budget. Paperwork costs came out of a general staff fund, and the only biblical counseling resources we had were books I bought and donated to the church library.

Now you may think, "Okay, Bob, I guess the process wasn't all that easy. In fact, now you're scaring me. How in the world can people pull off the oversight of a biblical counseling ministry?"

You Are Not Alone

If that is your thinking, then you are not alone. At the end of the *4E Ministry Training Strategy Questionnaire*, I asked the two dozen best practice churches to share the strengths and weaknesses of their equipping ministries. By far the greatest weakness related to overseeing people once they moved from trainees to graduates. Leaders shared struggles such as the following:

- We give a good start to those interested in biblical counseling, but the ministry seems to fizzle after the initial equipping push.
- Overseeing the ministry is an area of particular weakness for us right now.
- Our greatest weaknesses relate to administrative structures and systems.
- We have grown quickly, which has allowed many things to slip through the cracks, and we don't feel that we are where we need to be in terms of ongoing oversight.
- We don't really have the organizational skills or administrative personnel to oversee our growing ministry as well as we would like.
- We don't have the policies and procedures in place yet that allow us to provide the type of oversight that we know we need.

Clearly there is a need for organizing the organism. It does no good and wastes valuable time to envision, enlist, and equip, only to stop short of the ongoing administrating of the ministry. Without mobilizing and deploying, those we equip can become consumers rather than ministers; they soak in without serving; they take in without giving out.

God-Sized Dreams Bring Glory to God, Not to Us

Clearly the challenge is great. It is a challenge so large that we have no hope of achieving it apart from God's empowering. That is why *before* God calls us to equip His people (Eph. 4:11–16), He reminds us that He "is able to do immeasurably more than all we ask or imagine, according to his power that is at work within us" (Eph. 3:20). He also reminds us that it's not about us. It's all about Him. "To him be glory in the church and in Christ Jesus throughout all generations, for ever and ever! Amen" (Eph. 3:21).

Yes, we will explore our role in overseeing the biblical counseling ministry. However, we must see our role as God-glorifying, Christ-centered, and Spirit-dependent. We don't empower, employ, and deploy people in our power. We empower people with and through God's empowering for God's glory.

We have these trained biblical counselors, and now we need to learn how to oversee the shepherding of these ministers. As we do, we can shape our thinking about organizing the organism around three relational practices.

- Launching ministries built to last: administrating ministries
- Leading ministries from good to great: mentoring and supervising ministers
- Leaving a lasting legacy of loving leaders: passing the baton of ministry

Launching Ministries Built to Last: Administrating Ministries

While perhaps grammatically incorrect, I sometimes hyphenate the words "ad-ministrating" and "ad-ministering." In doing so, I am indicating that there is nothing inherently non-ministerial or non-relational about administration. Paul penned the Pastoral Epistles to mentor Timothy and Titus to be relational overseers. "I am writing you these instructions so that, if I am delayed, you will know how people ought to conduct themselves in God's household, which is the church of the living God" (1 Tim. 3:14–15). "The reason I left you in Crete was that you might straighten out what was left unfinished and appoint elders in every town, as I directed you" (Titus 1:5).

Administrating a biblical counseling ministry requires that we proactively and relationally address unfinished matters left after our envisioning, enlisting, and equipping. As we employ and deploy biblical counselors, we need to:

- Evaluate: testing ministers
- Graduate and congratulate: commissioning and affirming ministers
- Designate: connecting ministers to assigned ministries
- Create: implementing new ministries
- Automate: organizing ministry policies and procedures
- Formulate: developing a ministry budget
- Communicate: telling your ministry story

Evaluate: Testing Ministers

In organizing the organism, it helps to think chronologically and sequentially. Imagine that you have just concluded your last meeting of your nine-month or two-year equipping ministry. Now what? What needs to happen before you can deploy your equipped counselors?

First, you need to evaluate them to be sure that they are indeed equipped counselors. There are many reasons to assess trainees before they become graduates, and there are many potential areas of assessment to consider. Nothing tells us why to assess and what to assess better than Romans 15:14. Remember that in this verse Paul says he is convinced that the believers at Rome are competent. "Convinced" means to be inwardly certain because of *external evidence*. While Paul does not tell us how he assessed their competency, he does tell us what evidence he looked for—the 4Cs of biblical content, Christlike character, counseling competence, and Christian community.

Yes, there are legal/ethical reasons to evaluate trainees (see chapter twelve). You want to be able to demonstrate, objectively, their level of qualification for biblical counseling. Yes, there are practical reasons for assessing trainees. When you see weaknesses, you can focus on helping them to grow and mature in those areas. When you see a pattern of weaknesses, it helps you to assess the effectiveness of *your* training.

285

It demonstrates areas where you need to grow as a trainer, in ongoing supervision and in the next round of training.

Yet there is no better reason to evaluate trainees than the biblical reason. Before you say to someone, "I am convinced that you are competent to counsel," you need to be able to back up those words with external evidence. And there is no better assessment model than the biblical 4Cs.

That said, if in your training you use something other than the 4Cs, be sure to communicate your training goals throughout the enlisting and equipping process. From your profile of a nurtured graduate (see Appendix 6.1) onward, everyone should know what a successful graduate looks like. That portrait of a nurtured trainee becomes your gatekeeper, your standard that you use to evaluate trainees.

Evaluating Biblical Content

As chapter 10 illustrated, at the end of each year of training, every trainee is assessed in each of the 4Cs (see Appendix 10.1 for sample assessments). Quality assessment must focus on the specific student-oriented learning objectives and specific content taught during the training. In the case of my training, that means addressing all the material related to life's six ultimate questions.

Written assessment can include objective sections such as true/false, multiple choice, fill-in, and matching. They can also include subjective sections with short answer and essay questions that seek to discern how well the student relates truth to life and ministry (as Appendix 10.1 demonstrates, this is the focus of my exams). In addition to written assessment, you can also measure content acquisition and application through your observation of the trainees during lab and through listening to your trainees' taped sessions.

Evaluating Counseling Competence

Once again, your evaluation will target the areas of competency that you focused on in your training. In my setting, that means assessing how well trainees demonstrate the sustaining GRACE relational competencies, the healing RESTS relational competencies, the reconciling PEACE(E) relational competencies, and the guiding FAITH(H) relational competencies (see Appendix 10.1).

There are several effective ways to measure relational competencies. During your group time, if you have both role-play and live counseling, then you and the entire group can offer immediate, specific feedback of strengths and weaknesses. Additionally, at the last meeting of each year, your group can spend the entire time sharing candid feedback about the competency growth you have seen and the areas of growth you believe each person needs to develop further.

If you pair your trainees with partners for role-play or live counseling, and if these are taped, then you, the partner, and the trainee can all share both oral and written feedback. If during your training trainees provide any live counseling on tape, then you, the trainee, and the counselee can all provide feedback. (See Appendices 10.1 and 11.1 for sample evaluation forms.)

Evaluating Christlike Character

There are various tests that seek to measure levels of spiritual maturity. In my training I do a pre-training, mid-training, and post-training comparison using the Redeemed Personality Inventory (RPI) that builds upon my training focus (see Appendix 6.1). Trainees complete a self-assessment at the three points noted. Their encouragement partner and I also complete an RPI assessment of the trainees at the end of the first and second year of training.

Given the relational component discussed in chapters eight and nine, I also use feedback from the trainer(s), the encouragement partner, and the group. Throughout the training, as different trainees are on "the hot seat," they receive loving feedback about perceived areas of spiritual maturity—both strengths and areas for further growth. As with competency issues, at the last meeting of each year we spend our entire time sharing candid feedback about Christlike character growth and development.

Evaluating Christian Community

While somewhat subjective, there are ways to "get at" a trainee's level of growth in Christian community. Measures include attendance, attitude, and engagement in the lab small groups, in the supervision meetings, and in the encouragement partner meetings. Assessment in this area addresses more than whether trainees are *practicing* the skills of sustaining, healing, reconciling, and guiding. It evaluates how well, in a *one-another context*, the trainees are *embodying* sustaining, healing, reconciling, and guiding.

My definition of Christian community emphasizes the horizontal spiritual disciplines of communion with the body of Christ and the vertical spiritual disciplines of communion with Christ. Therefore, I ask each graduate to assess how well he or she is implementing the *Personal Spiritual Workout Routine* (see chapter nine and see Appendix 10.1).

What If a Trainee Is Not Approved?

This chapter focuses on the formal model of equipping trainees for ongoing, intensive biblical counseling. In the informal model of saturating the congregation with one-another ministers, I don't suggest a pass/fail assessment. If there is any assessment, it should focus on assessing the quality of the training so it can be continually improved.

In the formal model, if the trainee is approved, then we joyfully move to the next step of graduate and congratulate. But what happens if your various means of evaluation blend together to suggest that the trainee is not ready to become a graduate?

First, pre-warn. Even in the initial interview process you should make it clear that graduation is based upon assessment in the 4Cs. Then, throughout your training, discuss any patterns of weaknesses and co-create a plan of growth. It should never come as a surprise to trainees that their graduation is in jeopardy.

Second, be gentle. Affirm their growth and worth in Christ. Lovingly explain the objective and subjective measures that indicate any lack of readiness. Help them to assess their own self-assessment. Do they think they are ready? Are there areas they think they need to work on?

Third, plan together the possible next steps. If it is a personal or character issue, then receiving biblical counseling may be in order. If it is a competency issue, then perhaps retaking the training would be suggested. Or it is possible that the person should be matched with another ministry. The person could still use his or her training in one-another ministry, but would not offer ongoing biblical counseling under your ministry.

All that being said, in my three church ministries I have never had a trainee not graduate. I have had situations at the end of the first year where both the trainee and I saw red flags that needed to be addressed. By God's grace they were addressed, and the trainee graduated and was greatly used by God.

What If a Trainee Drops Out?

On a few rare occasions I have had trainees stop the training. If that occurs, the first response should be a candid conversation discussing the trainee's reasons for wanting to stop along with a reminder of the initial commitment that the trainee made. In some cases the person may recommit at this point. If not, then an "exit interview" is important. Seek to be sure that no bridges are burned, and seek to learn what your ministry might be able to do better in the future.

Graduate and Congratulate: Commissioning and Affirming Ministers

The more likely and likable occurrence involves your trainees' becoming graduates. That requires celebration! At the very least provide them with a certificate or diploma. If at all possible, offer a public commissioning in a church service with prayer and testimonies.

As I noted in the Introduction, some churches provide a full-blown graduation ceremony. While I have never done that, I have always hosted a party for graduates and their families.

Designate: Connecting Ministers to Assigned Ministries

When someone graduates from high school, college, or graduate school, the obvious questions are: "What's next? What am I qualified to do? And where and how do I use my training?" The same is true with your biblical counseling graduates.

To answer those questions, return to a form like the Profile of a LEAD Nurtured Graduate (Appendix 6.1). What were the initial options—individual counseling, marital counseling, family/parental counseling, small group leadership, or something else?

Within those parameters, you want to garner a mutual decision between the graduate and yourself about the best fit for him or her in the biblical counseling ministry. Based upon your church and community assessments, where are the needs? What is the graduate passionate about and best gifted and equipped to offer?

Create: Implementing New Ministries

In some cases, the placement answer may be simple. Individual counseling may be the extent of your biblical counseling ministry— and that is wonderful. In other cases, as has often been the case with my graduates, we determined that they should start a new ministry— normally a group-focused ministry.

I have previously mentioned two female graduates who used their LEAD training to launch and lead a Beauty for Ashes group for women who had been sexually abused. Since our church never had such a ministry, we were creating an entirely new ministry. So we used a modified 4E process in launching that new ministry. In three months they worked through the envisioning and enlisting process.

For further equipping they immersed themselves in an intensive one-week Christian training course on sexual abuse recovery. They had each done their second-year research project on this issue, and they continued to read and develop their awareness. They also spent time that summer observing me counseling people who had been sexually abused.

For the fourth E of empowering/employing/deploying, we developed expectations, reporting responsibilities, paperwork, policies, and procedures. We obtained approval from the church for the launch of this new ministry. We decided how they would lead the group and what materials they would use. We obtained a place to meet that would maintain privacy and confidentiality. We developed a plan for how they would communicate about the group's launch, purpose, and function. And we created a safe, confidential system for women who were interested to contact them. We also organized our plans for my ongoing supervision of these two graduates. Three months after graduation they launched Beauty for Ashes and ministered to ten women every week.

Automate: Organizing Ministry Policies and Procedures

"Automate" may seem like an odd label. However, I use it to stress that organizing ministry policies and procedures streamlines your process *so that you have more time for people.* This is where many people get confused and many training ministries make a major mistake. The false mindset says, "I don't want to focus all my time on paperwork. I just want to do people-ministry." I would counter, "Get your systems in place and they will run themselves so you can focus your time and energy on people—organize the organism."

Appendix 11.1 provides a thorough, detailed *Policy and Procedure Manual.* Since every church situation is unique, no policy and procedure manual fits everyone, so simply view Appendix 11.1 as one sample. The *Policy and Procedure Manual* highlights three areas: intake procedures, welcome form/consent form, and record keeping. Since these are detailed in the appendix, the following material simply highlights how they are used and why they are important.

Intake Procedures: Triage

I think of intake procedures as triage—who is counseled, by whom, when, and why? Through the Intake Procedures Form, the Initial Intake Form, and the Ministry Guidelines Form (see Appendix 11.1), you develop a step-by-step policy that determines how you handle requests for counseling. Intake policies and procedures should include:

- *Who is counseled?* Only church members/attendees? People from the community?

- *How are counseling requests prioritized?* By severity of the issue? By ability, giftedness, and training of the team members? By whether the person is a member/attender or from the community? By the availability of the counseling team?
- *Who provides the counseling and why?* Is referral made to one of the staff pastors? The counseling pastor? One of the trained LEAD counselors? An outside counseling agency? A medical doctor?
- *Who makes the decisions?* The counseling pastor/LEAD director? A trained administrative assistant? (I have always required my administrative assistant to complete the LEAD training.)
- *What steps are taken when a counselee is assigned to a LEAD counselor?* What are the step-by-step procedures that the counselee must take? That the trainer, director, or administrative assistant must take? That the LEAD counselor must take?
- *What forms must be completed?* Who completes which forms? Where are they kept? Who sees which forms and why?
- *What is the reporting structure?* How is information about counseling cases conveyed and to whom?
- *Where do counselors and counselees meet?* What is the policy regarding proper meeting etiquette, safeguards, privacy, meeting with a person of the opposite gender, and confidentiality?
- *What is the supervision policy?* Who sees whom and how often?

Welcome Form/Consent Form

Chapter twelve expands upon the legal and ethical issues related to informed consent—counselees have a right to know the scope and nature of the biblical counseling you offer. Appendix 11.1 contains a Welcome Form, a Consent Form, and a Consent to Minister to a Minor Child Form. The forms must be read, explained and discussed, completed, signed, dated, and kept in the counselee's file.

The Welcome Form describes in two pages or less your philosophy and practice of biblical counseling. Through the Welcome Form and Consent Form, prospective counselees gain an introduction to what type of counseling you offer, your definition of biblical counseling, what you call your counseling, what your goals are, your confidentiality policy, your appointment structure, the training level of your counselors, what commitments you make to your counselee, and what commitments you expect of your counselee.

Record Keeping

Proper record keeping not only maintains ethical and legal standards, but enhances communication and streamlines your processes. I include the following record keeping forms in my *Policy and Procedure Manual* (see Appendix 11.1):

- LEAD Biblical Counseling Ministry Goals Form
- LEAD Biblical Counseling Ministry Personal Information Form
- LEAD Biblical Counseling Ministry Permission to Record and Review Form
- Authorization for Release of Information (to Your Counseling Ministry)
- Authorization to Release Information (from Your Counseling Ministry)
- LEAD Biblical Counseling Record Sheet
- LEAD Biblical Counseling Tape Self-Evaluation
- LEAD Individual Biblical Counseling Evaluation
- LEAD Marital Biblical Counseling Evaluation
- LEAD Family Biblical Counseling Evaluation
- LEAD Biblical Counseling Commencement Summary

Formulate: Developing a Ministry Budget

As I noted, in my first ministry we barely had a budget. In fact, that has been the case in each of my three churches. I am not saying that this is the best practice model, but I am saying that you can run an excellent biblical counseling ministry on a limited budget.

Other churches have a more extensive budget designated for their biblical counseling ministry. Faith Baptist Church in Lafayette, Indiana, organizes its budget around initial expenses, annual counseling budget, and next steps.

Initial Counseling Ministry Expenses

Under initial expenses, budget categories might include:

- Resource library for counselors
- Resource library for counselees
- Counseling training handouts/notes
- Counseling filing cabinet for secure storage of confidential counseling files
- Pastoral/trainer salary/stipend
- Secretarial/administrative support salary/stipend

Keep two things in mind in these categories. First, start slow to grow large and stay long. For example, you don't need the Library of Congress when you start. Based upon your needs assessment, purchase books that are most pertinent to the needs of your congregation and community. Second, be creative. For example, ask for donations of quality biblical counseling books. With secretarial support, many ministries can begin with volunteer staffing. Some churches ask their trainees to pay for the cost of producing counseling training notes.

Annual Counseling Budget

Related to your annual counseling ministry expenses, budget categories to consider may include:

- Insurance increase due to counseling liability (you should expect numbers in the hundreds, not numbers in the thousands, for these changes)
- Paper and copying costs for counseling forms
- Expanding the resource library for counselors
- Expanding the resource library for counselees
- Pastoral/trainer salary/stipend
- Secretarial/administrative support salary/stipend
- Additional training for trainees, graduates, and trainers
- Advertising
- Attorney/consulting fees

Next Steps Budget

For larger counseling ministries, a few additional budget line items might include:

- A dedicated phone line
- A director of counseling (part-time/full-time scheduler/organizer)
- Expanded advertising—mailings, business cards, brochures

Counseling Ministry Income

In chapter twelve related to legal issues, I recommend that charging for counseling services is an unwise best practice for a local church ministry. However, there are a few other potential sources of counseling ministry income.

Some churches charge a "cancellation fee." Some churches generate some income through donations to the counseling ministry. Other churches cover their resource expenses through selling resources at cost to counselees. However, most churches cover their counseling budget through specific ministry line items in their overall annual church budget.

Communicate: Telling Your Ministry Story

With the word "communicate," I address what some would call advertising, marketing, or ministry-based brand marketing. I like to describe it as telling your ministry story.

The primary way to share your story is word-of-mouth through counselees whose lives have been changed (perhaps we should call it word-of-life). I have never had to advertise my local church counseling or the counseling of a LEAD ministry. More than enough referrals came via word-of-mouth.

It can be beneficial, however, in communicating clearly and with excellence, to create a ministry brochure. Most of what can appear in a brochure comes directly from your MVP-C Statement. Add to that your ministry name and logo, include testimonials, share contact information, and you have a ready-made ministry brochure.

Most local newspapers have a free section to inform the community about church events, group ministries, and seminars. Such advertising of free or low-cost events can create awareness and tell your story of changing lives with Christ's changeless truth.

Leading Ministries from Good to Great: Mentoring and Supervising Ministers

Continuing our chronological journey, we have evaluated and graduated our biblical counselors. We have designated where they will serve and in some cases co-created their new ministry. Behind the scenes we have automated the ministry policies and procedures and formulated the ministry budget. With everything in place, we have communicated to a congregation and community in need of biblical counseling ministry.

Now your trainees have moved from graduates to ministers. They are flying solo for the first time, likely with trepidation. However, you remind them that they are not alone—Christ is always with them, you are there for them, and they are there for each other. There are two primary means of ongoing training to help scared soloists grow into confident and even more competent pilots: mentoring through continuing education, and supervision in individual and group formats.

The Disciple-Making Champions (see below) demonstrate that there are many creative ways to ensure that graduates keep growing. I meet with each new group of graduates and say, "Our goal is to nurture your 4C growth by combining mentoring and supervision while respecting your time." Within those parameters, we decide together how best to accomplish that goal.

Disciple-Making Champions

Continuing Education and Ongoing Supervision

As part of the *4E Ministry Training Strategy Questionnaire*, two dozen best practice churches responded to the question, "Once trainees become graduates, what ongoing training and continuing education do you offer?" The following list collates typical responses.

- Four times per year we have a four-hour continuing education session.
- We offer three all-day in-services annually.
- We encourage our graduates to attend a biblical counseling conference every year.
- Graduates attend thirty hours of training per year.
- We have periodic "supper seminars" for our team, which includes discussion of topics, case studies, and ongoing training.
- We require our graduates to read selected resource books.
- We offer specialized training classes on an as-needed basis.
- We offer training videos.

As part of the *4E Ministry Training Strategy Questionnaire*, two dozen best practice churches responded to the question, "Once trainees become graduates, what modes of supervision do you offer?" The following list collates typical responses.

- They meet with our Director of Biblical Counseling in individual supervision once per month.
- Once per month we sit in on their counseling and provide feedback after the session.
- We have group supervision that they attend bi-monthly and share their cases with their trainers and their peers.
- We provide periodic supervision sessions and on-call assistance.
- Before graduation they are supervised for fifty hours. After graduation they receive supervision every other week for the first year.
- We meet once a month for two hours for team meetings to talk about cases.
- Graduates sit in on my counseling sessions.
- We developed a system of tiered peer supervision and accountability.

Mentoring through Continuing Education

You can divide continuing education options into in-house or outsourced opportunities, ongoing or specialized opportunities, and reading/researching or listening/viewing opportunities. There are several advantages of in-house training. You can tailor your continuing education to the specific expressed and observed needs of your counselors, it is typically free for your counselors, and it avoids travel time and expense. The disadvantage is that you have to either create the training experience or organize bringing someone in to provide the continuing education. Your in-house training can be periodic—meeting whenever a special need arises, or offering a periodic seminar. Or it can be ongoing—meeting at planned times and intervals.

Out-sourced training tends to be much easier for the trainer (you), but can be more time-consuming and costly for the graduate counselor. However, it can expose your counselors to the best training in the country, and it allows them to hear different perspectives. With outside training, counselors can choose to attend a general conference or a specialized seminar on a specific counseling issue.

In today's ever-changing world, the "reading/researching" and "listening/viewing" options are ever-growing. Your graduates can "attend" webinars from the comfort of their home computer, listen to books on tape, view taped sessions of expert counselors, and much more.

Individual and Group Supervision

While continuing education can be obtained in a host of ways with great flexibility, I tend to be more structured with supervision. I have found tremendous value in monthly group supervision combined with twice monthly individual supervision.

The group supervision has several advantages. It allows continued development of the group cohesion experienced during your training phase. Graduates consistently express that ongoing group supervision is a cherished time of reconnecting. They also articulate how helpful it is to receive feedback from people who are committed to the same approach to counseling and who know each other so well.

Typically we meet for at least two hours. We start with one individual sharing one of his or her counseling cases (whether in individual counseling or small group ministry). Just as in the training labs, sometimes the focus is on case wisdom (how to apply truth to life), sometimes it is on counseling intervention, and sometimes it shifts to the life of the counselor. Even though only one or two individuals may share their cases during the meeting, everyone benefits from the joint discussion about applying biblical principles to counseling situations.

In individual supervision we often listen to sections of taped counseling. As was the case during the training phase and in group supervision, the individual supervision might focus on content application, counseling competency and intervention, or the life of the counselor.

In addition to group and individual supervision, it is necessary to maintain crisis availability. Counselors must have access to a trained supervisor 24/7. If you are the only supervisor in your church and you will be unavailable, then you need to make arrangements for someone from outside the church to be available. That sounds more drastic and time-consuming than it normally is. Emergencies, by their very name and nature, don't happen that often.

This raises the issue of the ratio of supervisor to counselors. You can understand why twelve to one is a maximum ratio. This also raises the issue of training other trainers—of raising up additional supervisors, which is our next area of focus.

Leaving a Lasting Legacy of Loving Leaders: Passing the Baton of Ministry

We need to practice what we preach regarding every member a disciple-maker. We do that by making it our goal to identify at least one person from every training sequence to whom we can pass the baton of ministry.

In my first church, my co-trainer was a high school guidance counselor at the time of our ministry. Since that time he has become a church planter with a focus on equipping equippers. In my second church, my co-trainer was my administrative assistant. A dozen years later, I now have the privilege of consulting with her and her associate pastor as they launch a fresh version of biblical counseling training in their church. I understand now what the apostle John meant when he said, "I have no greater joy than to hear that my children are walking in the truth" (3 John 4).

I have found that there are five fundamentals to leaving a lasting legacy of loving leaders. We need to evaluate the ministry, scope out qualified leaders, offer on-the-job training, de-parent, and leave well.

Evaluate the Ministry

This chapter has emphasized evaluating your trainees as they become graduates. We also need to be humble learners willing to turn that process around by asking our trainees and graduates to evaluate our training (see Appendix 11.2 for a sample LEAD Biblical Counseling Ministry Evaluation Form). How our counselees evaluate us is certainly an important aspect of evaluating our overall equipping ministry. Yet who is better prepared to offer us feedback on our 4E equipping for 4C ministry than those we have been training?

Perhaps you are wondering, "What does ministry evaluation have to do with passing the baton of ministry?" We want to be sure that what we pass on is as effective as possible. We want to lay a solid foundation for others to build on.

Scope Out Qualified Leaders

Like Paul in 2 Timothy 2:2, we scope out and equip those who are qualified to equip others. From the onset of the enlistment process, I am always praying that God would give me wisdom to identify potential future trainers.

Once I have identified someone, I am not shy about sharing my vision with him or her. Typically people are shocked, humbled, terrified, and honored when I say, "Would you be willing to pray about my training you to become a co-trainer?" Since the person is already motivated to be trained as a biblical counselor, you can imagine how this enlarged vision keeps the person focused throughout the training process.

Offer On-the-Job Training

I'm also not shy about telling the rest of the group that I have identified a group member whom I will be mentoring for future co-leadership. I share that others in the group may sense a calling and giftedness for that role. I never want to exclude anyone God may lead into a leadership role.

Anyone I train as a future co-trainer receives all the regular mentoring of other trainees. In addition, during our supervisory meetings the first semester we discuss the 4C training process. I want to help this person begin looking at equipping through the eyes of a trainer.

Depending on the person, by the second semester of the first year or by the second year, the person is participating in some leadership roles. He or she leads sections of a lab, teaches portions of a lecture, and offers supervision of another trainee. This on-the-job training is vital.

I never have the person move directly into the training role unless he or she has already counseled or is simultaneously counseling others. I don't want people moving from being trained to counsel to training others to counsel without having counseled others. During the next round of training, this person becomes a co-trainer. Under my supervision, he or she shares in all the training leadership roles.

De-parenting

With co-trainers I always think about "de-parenting." Or, as I put it, "De-Kellemenizing." Yes, I have a 4E and a 4C structure. And, yes, I have a curriculum. However, it can be improved upon, and it should be taught and shared out of each person's giftedness, teaching style, and unique personality.

When co-trainers are teaching a lesson, I insist that they "make it their own." They need to do their own biblical study of the topic. They must craft their own lesson outline, illustrations, and interactions. If they lead a small group lab, they need to do it their way, not Kellemen's way. We are not creating clones. We want to model our best way of equipping so that co-trainers develop their best way of equipping.

Leaving Well

We all like to think that our ministry will continue forever. Yet we all know that is impossible. Our ministry description may change.

Our mission or vision may change. God may call us to another place of service.

When any of those occur, we need to leave well. We have prepared the way for that by passing the baton of leadership throughout our training. Now we need to make that final handoff in a mature, God-honoring way.

Circumstances always vary, but where possible it is helpful to have a final meeting with all past trainees and graduates and all current trainees. Gather the entire team. Explain the reason for your departure from this ministry. Remind the team of the thorough training that their new leader has had. Exhort the team to love, honor, and respect their new leader the way they have you. Remind everyone that their ultimate leader is Christ. Pray for their new leader. Then share a good-bye time akin to Paul's farewell to the elders at Ephesus (Acts 20). This allows people to grieve the departure of one leader and begin to transfer ownership to a new leader.

Commencement: Pictures of the Children and Grandchildren

Yesterday my wife and I received a Christmas card from someone I trained in my first LEAD group—over two decades ago. The connection and bond is even closer because she and my wife were encouragement partners. She included a note in her card thanking us for our ministry in her life and saying that to this day the training was life-changing. She went on to say that she and a pastor at her church are now co-leading a grief recovery group and that she's using her training from our LEAD group.

As I did at the beginning of this chapter, I share this story for God's glory. It never ceases to amaze me how God empowers us to empower others. There is great joy in having children and grandchildren in the ministry. As Sister Ellen said in the Introduction, "These are your grand-babies, Dr. Kellemen!"

It would be fun to stop writing right here. Grandbabies could be the bookends around this book. However, there's that elephant in the room yet to be considered: legal and ethical issues. It would be self-centered of me to end with fun if that meant I had not fully equipped you to address that elephant. So let's address the elephant one bite at a time, and then find another way to end with fun!

Growing Together: Questions for Reflection, Discussion, and Application

1. As you think about the ongoing oversight (organizing the organism) of your biblical counseling ministry:
   a. What excites you about the process?
   b. What scares you about the process? How could the material in this chapter help you address those fears?
2. Regarding launching ministries built to last:
   a. Of evaluate, graduate, designate, create, automate, formulate, and communicate, which do you think you need to work on the most? Why?
   b. What one or two specific action steps do you need to start with in each area of evaluate, graduate, designate, create, automate, formulate, and communicate?
3. Regarding leading ministries from good to great:
   a. What continuing education opportunities do you believe are best for graduates of biblical counseling ministries?
   b. What forms of group and individual supervision have you experienced? What would you want to replicate from those experiences? What would you want to change?
4. Regarding leaving a lasting legacy of loving leaders:
   a. Of evaluating the ministry, scoping out qualified leaders, offering on-the-job-training, de-parenting, and leaving well, which one do you think is most important? Why?
   b. What could you do right now to begin the process of passing the baton?

12

Practicing Ethical and Legal Wisdom in Ministry

CARING CAREFULLY

In my consulting, I have found that it is easy for churches to cascade into polar extremes regarding biblical counseling and the law. One extreme causes churches to retreat in paranoia because of the fear of lawsuits. In response, they decline to launch church counseling ministries and refer everyone to outside help. In the other extreme response, churches ignore legal issues and place at risk their church, their counseling ministry, and the people to whom they minister.

We overcome our extreme reactions to legal requirements (either fearing them or ignoring them) by understanding that they are a mere shadow of the far higher ethical standards of God's law. We must obey the law of God and the law of the land in the fear of God and not the fear of man.

The Law of Love

Paul taught us to submit ourselves to God-established authorities—the law of the land (Rom. 13:1–7). In the very next breath, Paul writes about the law of God—the law of love. "Let no debt remain outstanding, except the continuing debt to love one another, for he who loves his fellowman has fulfilled the law" (Rom. 13:8). Paul then explains that "whatever other commandment there may be, are summed up in this one rule: 'Love your neighbor as yourself.' Love does no harm to its neighbor. Therefore love is the fulfillment of the law" (Rom. 13:9–10).

The precept "First, do no harm" is not simply a principle of medical ethics. It is a foundational principle of Christian life and ministry. Jesus reserves His most scathing judgment for ministers who abuse their power by abusing those to whom they minister. His list of woes to unethical, unloving shepherds in Matthew 23:1–39 should cure every ministry leader of a lax attitude toward ministry relational standards. Jesus warns of certain and severe judgment for anyone who mistreats the little child (Matt. 18:1–9) or fails to minister to the little lost sheep (Matt. 18:10–14).

Jesus and Paul contrast the hireling and the true shepherd, the savage wolves and the good shepherds, the true apostle and the false apostle (John 10:1–21; Acts 20:13–38; 2 Cor. 10:1–12:21). Paul and Peter, in outlining the requirements of God's shepherds, highlight godly character and ethical conduct (1 Tim. 3:1–16; 1 Peter 5:1–5).

These specific law-of-love requirements flow from the most foundational requirement of God. "What does the LORD require of you? To act justly and to love mercy and to walk humbly with your God" (Mic. 6:8). Even more importantly, all ethical ministry behavior flows ultimately from the very character of God. "Just as he who called you is holy, so be holy in all you do; for it is written: 'Be holy, because I am holy'" (1 Peter 1:15–16). This God-like holiness has specific life, ministry, and relationship application. In the same text, Peter writes, "Now that you have purified yourselves by obeying the truth so that you have sincere love for your brothers, love one another deeply, from the heart" (1 Peter 1:22).

I do not pen this chapter in a spirit of "legalese." Practicing ethical and legal wisdom in ministry is nothing less than being Christlike in how we practice biblical counseling. It is nothing less than ensuring that every possible safeguard is in place so that the hurting people we minister to are helped and not harmed. It is nothing less than overseeing that our biblical counseling ministry fulfills God's law of love. When we do that, fulfilling the law of the land, while still necessary, will be undemanding in comparison.

So, as you read this final chapter, suppress the thought, "Ugh, not legal stuff!" Emphasize the thought, "I can't wait to learn more about how to oversee that our biblical counseling ministry cares carefully by loving biblically!"

Practicing What We Preach

We need to practice what we preach about God's law of love and about the law of the land. Regarding God's law of love, be a good Berean Christian (Acts 17:11). Search the Scriptures to determine how God's law of love applies to your unique biblical counseling ministry in your specific church and community.

Regarding the law of the land, I need to practice what I preach with this preliminary disclosure statement.

> As the author of this chapter, I am not a legal expert. The reader should not consider this chapter legal counsel personally or for any specific church or ministry. I provide this chapter simply as a synopsis of my research of best practices designed to help readers become more aware of some basic ethical and legal considerations. I encourage readers to take responsibility for remaining current, as legal interpretations change over time. I encourage churches to contract with an attorney who is an expert on the pertinent laws in their state, as laws vary from state to state. I encourage churches to maintain and provide malpractice and liability insurance covering the church, pastors, trustees, elected leaders, and those trained in the biblical counseling ministry.

The nature of your training ministry (informal one-another ministry or formal biblical counseling) will play a significant role in how you address these issues. The information in this chapter is for the formal implementation of biblical counseling in the local church.

Pertinent Legal History and the Legal Climate: The Law and Church Counseling

Before exploring specific wisdom principles, it is helpful to gain a "lay of the land." What is the recent history of the legal system and church counseling, and what is the legal climate relative to the church?

The Records Show

We can trace the current concern about church counseling and the law back over three decades to the case of *Nally v. Grace Community Church of the Valley*.[1] On April 1, 1979, twenty-four-year-old Kenneth Nally committed suicide. Four years earlier Ken had begun seeing a secular psychologist. In 1978 he began a discipleship relationship with one of the pastors at Grace Community Church.

The records show that in the two-month period between February 1979 and his death, Ken saw at least four physicians, one psychiatrist, a psychologist, and a psychologist's assistant, and had several counseling sessions with pastors at Grace Community Church. Ken's parents, Walter and Maria Nally, could have sued anyone who had seen their son over the few months prior to his death, but they chose Grace Community Church.

They charged, among other things, wrongful death based upon "clergyman malpractice" and negligent counseling. They alleged that following a suicide attempt, the pastors "actively and affirmatively dissuaded [Ken] from seeking further psychological and/or psychiatric care."[2] Despite the records showing that the pastors encouraged Ken to keep his appointments with physicians and outside counseling professionals, the case went through the California court system twice before the Supreme Court of California exonerated the church in November 1988.

---

1. *Nally v. Grace Community Church of the Valley*, 763 P.2d 948 (Cal. 1988). Information on this case is summarized from Steve Levicoff, *Christian Counseling and the Law* (Chicago: Moody, 1991), and from George Ohlschlager and Peter Mosgofian, *Law for the Christian Counselor: A Guidebook for Clinicians and Pastors* (Dallas: Word, 1992).

2. Levicoff, *Christian Counseling and the Law*, 18–19; *Nally v. Grace*, 763 P.2d at 952.

Levicoff explains, "The key question was whether the pastors, as spiritual counselors, had a duty to refer Ken Nally to professional secular counselors to help prevent his suicide. The Court of Appeal ruled that 'nontherapists [nonlicensed] counselors—*both religious and secular*—have a duty to refer suicidal persons to psychiatrists or psychotherapists qualified to prevent suicides.'"[3]

Levicoff continues, "In reversing the Court of Appeal, the state Supreme Court rejected the imposition of a broad 'duty to refer,' not only for the defendants, but for nontherapist counselors in general."[4] Addressing pastoral counselors specifically, the court stated:

> The Legislature has exempted the clergy from the licensure require-ments applicable to marriage, family, child and domestic counselors and from the operation of statutes regulating psychologists. In so doing, the Legislature has recognized that access to the clergy should be free from state imposed counseling standards and that the secular state is not equipped to ascertain the competence of counseling when performed by those affiliated with religious organizations.[5]

Expanding their holding to non-therapist counselors in general, the court noted:

> By their very definition, nontherapist counselors are not professional medical experts on suicide. Their activities are undertaken pursuant to doctrines explicitly left unregulated by the state.[6]

Levicoff concludes, "The good news is that, in addition to religious counselors, the decision protects peer counselors."[7]

The Nallys appealed the case to the United States Supreme Court, which refused to hear the case, thus allowing the California Supreme

3. Levicoff, *Christian Counseling and the Law*, 19; *Nally v. Grace*, 763 P.2d at 954, italics in the original.
4. Ibid.
5. Levicoff, *Christian Counseling and the Law*, 20; *Nally v. Grace*, 763 P.2d at 959–60.
6. *Nally v. Grace*, 763 P.2d at 958–59 n.7.
7. Levicoff, *Christian Counseling and the Law*, 20.

Court opinion to stand. Levicoff summarized his conclusions based upon this case and other case law.

> Legally, Christian counseling falls under the general term *spiritual* or *religious* counseling and enters a realm that civil courts are neither prepared nor permitted to adjudicate. In terms of the law, the primary difference between spiritual and secular counseling is in the area of regulation. While secular counseling can be regulated by the government or licensing board, spiritual counseling deals with religious beliefs, and the courts are precluded from making value judgments as to the truth or falsehood of those beliefs.[8]

The Legal Climate Today

Levicoff does not believe that Christians and churches should be naive. He explains that in 1989 the American Bar Association sponsored a seminar called *Tort and Religion*. It was touted for "attorneys who want to be on the leading edge of an explosive new area of law."[9] The purpose of the seminar was, in effect, to train attorneys in how to sue churches.[10]

Jay Quine, a lawyer, pastor, and seminary professor, bluntly opines, "Law school professors are not friends. They have one goal: to make you a shrewd lawyer. Lawyers are trained to think with one word: LAW! Law is competitive, cut-throat, brutal. Lawyers are different. They have no qualms about suing your church. The law is the law."[11]

Perhaps you are thinking, "Bob, if your goal is to reassure me, then I'm not sure it's working." My goal is not reassurance. My goal is wisdom. Wisdom requires that we face facts, that we not be naive. Churches are not immune from lawsuits. They can be sued for a divot in the parking lot that causes Aunt Sally to fall and break her hip, but the answer is not to eliminate all parking lots. The answer is to take care of our parking lot *because we care about Aunt Sally*. That said, there is

8. Ibid., 33–34.
9. Quoted in ibid., 23.
10. Ibid.
11. Jay Quine, *Legal Issues for Christian Workers and the Church* (seminar notes presented at Lancaster Bible College, Lancaster, PA, 1998), 1: quotes derived from lecture notes.

nothing anyone or any organization can do to guarantee they will never be sued. However, there is much that we can do to practice ethical and legal wisdom that seeks to do no harm and do much good.

Scope of Care: Communicating Honestly and Accurately about Your Ministry

The first law-of-the-land and law-of-love issue that biblical counseling ministries must address relates to informed consent. Technically, informed consent means that the caregiver has a duty to disclose fairly the scope and nature of the care provided and alternative modes of care so that the person seeking care can make an informed voluntary decision. Adequacy of disclosure is judged by what a reasonable person would want to know to make that informed decision.[12]

Practically speaking, this means that with our biblical counseling ministries we need to communicate honestly and accurately who we are, what we offer, and what we do *not* offer. In other words, we never hold out our graduates to be more than they are trained and qualified to be. In the event of a legal action, the standard our graduates will be held to in a court of law is that which we held them to in public.

In Appendix 11.1, you will find three forms (LEAD Biblical Counseling Ministry Welcome Form, LEAD Biblical Counseling Ministry Consent Form, and LEAD Biblical Counseling Ministry Consent to Minister to a Minor Child) that express ways to communicate informed consent in local church biblical counseling. The second form states, in part:

I have been informed that the spiritual care I will be receiving from _____ (Name of Biblical Counselor) at _____ (Name of Church) is Christian and biblical in nature. I have also been informed that _____ (Name of Biblical Counselor) is an encourager and discipler trained at _____ (Name of Church) as a biblical counselor and spiritual friend in the church's

12. Ohlschlager and Mosgofian, *Law for the Christian Counselor*, 154.

310

LEAD (Life Encourager And Discipler) Biblical Counseling Ministry. Under supervision from one of the LEAD trainers, _____ (Name of Biblical Counselor) offers to provide biblical encouragement and discipleship on personal and relational matters from a spiritual perspective guided by biblical principles. He/she is *not* trained, authorized, or licensed to provide professional counseling, psychological treatment, or psychological diagnosis. I understand that if and when I desire and request professional counseling, then I will be encouraged to seek such outside assistance. I give my consent to _____ (Name of Biblical Counselor) to discuss any and all of the information that I talk about in our meetings with his/her supervisor(s) in the LEAD Biblical Counseling Ministry.

Clearly Communicate Who You Are

From Appendix 11.1, you will note several important aspects. First, the forms carefully label the type of care being offered. In the sample forms, "biblical counselor" is the primary label chosen and defined. It is supported by other terms such as "spiritual friend," "encourager," "discipler," "soul care," and "spiritual direction." Second, the forms repeatedly use terms like "ministry," "discipleship," and "local church" to highlight the non-licensed, spiritual nature of the help offered.

Practitioners in best practice churches often debate whether or not to use, in any form, with any modifiers, the term "counseling" or "counselor." Some people choose to avoid terms such as "lay counselor," "Christian counselor," "biblical counselor," and "spiritual counselor" because of the possibility of someone mistaking this non-professional, non-licensed counseling for professional licensed counseling. Instead, they choose other legitimate words and descriptions used in the Bible or in church history—words with less potential for causing confusion to the person seeking care. Others strongly desire to claim and even reclaim the mantle and label of "biblical counselor," seeing it as a legitimate scriptural description that the church should not allow the world to usurp. They then carefully explain what they mean and do not mean by their terms. See below for how twenty-four Disciple-Making Champions address this issue.

Whatever term you use, never label your graduates something they are not trained to do. Regardless of which term you choose, the vital issue is how you describe and define your terms.

Clearly Communicate What You Offer and What You Do Not Offer

A central aspect of defining your label involves stating what goals you aim to address and what goals you do *not* aim to address. What is the scope and nature of the care you offer? The LEAD Biblical Counseling Ministry Welcome Form outlines specifically what I mean by "biblical counseling," using the biblical and church history categories of sustaining, healing, reconciling, and guiding.

The LEAD Biblical Counseling Ministry Consent Form (all those who receive care must read, discuss, and sign both forms) clearly distinguishes between what is offered and what is not offered, what the biblical counselor/ spiritual friend is and is *not* qualified to do. LEAD biblical counselors offer to provide biblical encouragement and discipleship on personal and relational matters from a spiritual perspective guided by biblical principles. They are not trained, authorized, or licensed to provide professional counseling, psychological treatment, or psychological diagnosis.

To maintain this distinction, I recommend never charging fees for counseling services. Once a fee is mandated, then an implied professional relationship is established. At that point, both the state and the individual receiving counseling would likely perceive you to be offering professional counseling.

Chapter eleven noted that some churches charge a cancellation fee (with a clear statement of the nature of that fee), some accept donations toward the counseling ministry or the church, some ask people to cover the costs of texts or handouts, and some ask people to cover the cost of resources such as books. I have never participated in any of those practices. I have always covered the cost of the counseling ministry budget through line items in the church budget. When we had a church bookstore, transactions of counseling related books took place separately from the counseling ministry. I have never charged a cancellation fee for missed appointments.

312

Disciple-Making Champions

What Do You Call Your Ministry?

As part of the *4E Ministry Training Strategy Questionnaire*, two dozen best-practice churches responded to the question, "What do you call what your graduates do? Is it 'counseling,' 'biblical counseling,' 'lay counseling,' or do you avoid the word 'counseling'? If so, what do you call it?" The following are the most common answers. The number after the answer indicates how many of the twenty-four best practice churches used that term (some churches use more than one term).

- Biblical Counseling: 11
- Spiritual Friendship: 6
- Soul Care: 4
- Lay Counseling: 3
- Lay Biblical Counseling: 3
- Discipleship: 3
- Spiritual Direction: 2
- Biblical Discipleship Counseling: 1
- Spiritual Counseling: 1
- Gospel Counseling: 1

Quality of Care: Building Safeguards in Your Ministry

We can compare scope of care and quality of care in a non-technical, non-legal sense.

- Scope of Care: Claim to do only what you are trained to do.
- Quality of Care: Do with integrity and propriety what you claim to do.

In terms of legal theory, quality of care relates to negligence and/or malpractice. Both Levicoff and Ohlschlager see overlap in negligence and malpractice; even the definitions they provide are similar. Malpractice is an act or omission by a professional practitioner in the treatment of a patient or client that is inconsistent with the reasonable care or skill usually demonstrated by ordinary, prudent practitioners of the same profession, similarly situated.[13] Negligence can be defined as an act or omission to act that was unreasonable in light of an established duty of care, which was breached, resulting in harm of another.[14] There are four elements of a negligence suit:

- *Duty of Care:* The caregiver's responsibility to ensure the safety and welfare of the person receiving care.
- *Breach of Duty:* The caregiver either does something he/she should not do (for example, sexual involvement with a counselee), or does not do something he/she should have done (for example, failure to refer when necessary or failure to inform a third party in danger of harm from the counselee).
- *Injury:* Harm done to a person's physical or mental well-being, reputation, pride, rights, and privileges (lawsuits in this area may include issues related to church discipline and public disclosure of information).
- *Proximate Cause:* The counselor's breach of duty of care was the proximate (or direct) cause of the injury.[15]

While these matters can seem technical and even intimidating, they involve practical and necessary safeguards. Seven pertinent issues summarize the quality of care matters that every biblical counseling ministry should address: propriety, humility, referral, confidentiality, church discipline, documentation, and supervision.

Propriety in Biblical Counseling Ministry

We have all heard the horror stories of sexual temptation and sexual involvement between a counselor and a counselee. Obviously, the motivation for safeguarding this area must be much greater than simply avoiding a lawsuit. Propriety should be motivated by our desire to honor God and to minister in healthy, helpful ways to hurting, vulnerable people. Safeguards include:

13. Ibid., 17.
14. Quine, *Legal Issues for Christian Workers and the Church*, 2.
15. Levicoff, *Christian Counseling and the Law*, 84–85.

- Perform background checks on all trainees. This is increasingly a common, necessary, and expected practice in all church ministries. It should be standard as part of the enlistment process for a biblical counseling trainee.
- Do not allow counseling sessions off premises.
- Require all counseling sessions to meet in a building when others are around.
- Require that counseling sessions meet in rooms that have doors with windows. While this can be problematic in some buildings, it is worth the cost.
- Discourage mixed gender sessions without a third person present. Have a trainee or staff member present.[16]

These safeguards protect everyone. Of course, we want to protect the hurting person in need of trustworthy care. We also want to protect the caregiver. All it takes is one false accusation or one moment of succumbing to temptation to destroy a person's reputation, family, and ministry.

Humility in Biblical Counseling

God's Word commands us not to think more highly of ourselves than we ought, but rather to think of ourselves with sober judgment according to our gifting and training (Rom. 12:3; 15:14). We all have limits and limitations. Thus, we should never allow any of our graduates (or ourselves) to counsel beyond their competence, ability, or training. A detailed intake policy and procedure (see Appendix 11.1) provides a safeguard so that the person needing care is assigned to a person qualified to care for that individual with that specific issue.

We should never give cross-disciplinary advice (advice related to any profession for which we are not trained, such as law, medicine, or psychiatry). Regarding medications or physical issues, defer and refer to qualified medical personnel. It is a wise best practice to maintain a

---

16. We should not assume that eliminating all mixed gender counseling removes all possibility of sexual temptation or inappropriate behavior. Same-sex counselor/counselee attraction and seduction must also be guarded against.

consulting relationship with trusted medical professionals. Those who lead the biblical counseling ministry need to have access to other pastors, counselors, and educators with whom they can confer and consult.

Seeking certification from national biblical counseling ministries for your counselors or for your counseling ministry can be another sign of humility. It communicates that you are part of a group larger than yourself, it typically provides opportunities for outside continuing education, and it often offers collegial relationships and supervisory connections.

Referral and Biblical Counseling Ministry

Referral is one specific way that we demonstrate humility in biblical counseling. No one is equipped to minister to everyone. No training program has the time to equip trainees for every possible issue. Your informed consent form should list the areas where your ministry will focus. Counseling issues outside those areas should be referred to others with pertinent expertise. It is imperative that your ministry identify professional resources to refer people to when issues arise beyond the competency of your team.

Related to referral are the issues of wrongful termination, abandonment, and follow-up care. The duty of care operates continually until the counseling relationship is validly terminated. If the counselee desires continued counseling but the counselor believes that ongoing counseling would no longer be effective, the counselor is responsible to recommend an appropriate referral.

Ideally, the decision to end counseling should be made mutually. If the decision is made because the initial issues that brought the person to counseling have been satisfactorily addressed, then the counselor should complete a Commencement Summary (see Appendix 11.1). The final counseling session should address a summary of the initial goals, a summary of the growth resulting from the meetings, insight concerning any unresolved areas, suggestions for further growth (including appropriate follow-up care), and the reasons for commencement. The counselee should complete a Biblical Counseling Evaluation Form (see Appendix 11.1). Counselees should know that if an issue returns or new issues develop, they are invited to contact your offices again. Often it is helpful at commencement to schedule another appointment three months later (or a mutually determined time) for a "check-in/check-up."

Confidentiality in Biblical Counseling Ministry

Like each of the quality of care issues, confidentiality has legal meanings as well as biblical/ethical implications. In the legal realm most states do not recognize a confidentiality privilege for lay Christian counselors who are not pastors. Privileged communication is codified in the law and means that a minister acting in his professional capacity as a spiritual adviser cannot be forced to reveal the content of confidential communications to any outside party, including a court of law. Confidentiality, on the other hand, is an ethical decision not to reveal what is learned in the context of a professional relationship, and it does not have legal protection.[17]

Our focus is on the ethical and relational nature of confidentiality in biblical counseling and on a counselee's expectation of confidential communication. Each biblical counseling ministry must develop clear organizational policies. These policies need to be in writing, explained to the counselee at the start of counseling, and signed. Embedded within The LEAD Biblical Counseling Ministry Welcome Form (see Appendix 11.1) is the following statement:

> Confidentiality is an important aspect of the biblical counseling relationship, and we will carefully guard the information you entrust to us. All communications between you and our LEAD Biblical Counseling Ministry offices will be held in strict confidence, unless you (or a parent in the case of a minor) give authorization to release this information. The exceptions to this would be: (1) if a person expresses intent to harm himself/herself or someone else; (2) if there is evidence or reasonable suspicion of abuse against a minor child, elder person, or dependent adult; (3) if a subpoena or other court order is received directing the disclosure of information; (4) if/when LEAD

17. Levicoff, *Christian Counseling and the Law,* 71–73.

biblical counselors consult with their supervision; or (5) if a person persistently refuses to renounce a particular sin (habitual unrepentant rebellion against the Word of God) and it becomes necessary to seek the assistance of others in the church to encourage repentance, restoration, and reconciliation (see Matt. 18:15–20 and our Church Discipline Policy). Please be assured that our counselors strongly prefer not to disclose personal information to others, and that they will make every effort to help you find ways to resolve a problem as privately as possible.

Some people assume that discussing and signing a policy like this would have a chilling effect on a person's willingness to share personally. However, every legitimate counseling organization and ministry will have such a statement, so counselees will not find this out of the ordinary. By discussing this openly at the outset, you put counselees at ease.

Church Discipline and Biblical Counseling Ministry

As noted in the confidentiality statement, church discipline is one of the exceptions to confidentiality. The potential legal ramifications include invasion of privacy, defamation of character, publication of private facts, and infliction of emotional distress.[18] Biblically, God's Word contains guidelines designed to restore errant believers by bringing them to repentance and reconciliation with Christ and the body of Christ (within or outside the context of a formal biblical counseling ministry).

Within the context of biblical counseling, counselees frequently bring to counseling their struggles to overcome besetting sins. Struggling against sin is not a cause for increased levels of church discipline intervention. However, persistent refusal to renounce a particular sin (habitual unrepentant rebellion against the Word of God) can lead to the initiation of a church restoration/discipline process.

Churches should create a written Church Discipline Policy (see Appendix 12.1). It should be discussed with and signed by every new member, and it should be read at least once a year at an official church meeting. The policy should clearly spell out the biblical principles and

18. Ibid., 105–15.

practices, the spiritual motivations and goals, and the step-by-step process to which every member agrees to adhere.

To date, case law seems to support a church's right to discipline members who have agreed to such discipline as part of the membership process. However, when members under discipline remove themselves from membership, at least some case law suggests that this withdraws the person's consent to participate in a spiritual relationship. Therefore, disciplinary actions no longer have First Amendment protection.[19] Some would suggest that you discipline only members.[20] Others would suggest that the church discipline policy explain that resignation from membership after the initiation of church discipline does not void the church's responsibility to carry on the church discipline process.[21]

If a counselee evidences continued unrepentant rebellion, it is essential that the church restoration/discipline policy be followed carefully. Each step of the process should be documented. If the process continues to the step of public discipline, the discipline announcement should be discreetly shared at a members-only meeting.

Documentation and Biblical Counseling

Chapter eleven addresses many of the issues related to appropriate documentation. Documentation serves both to organize the organism and to assist in caring carefully. If scope of care or quality of care issues arise, it will be extremely helpful if you have carefully documented your *training*. Maintain a basic outline of your 4E/4C structure, have available copies of your training materials, and keep copies of your completed evaluations of trainees (see Appendix 10.1).

You should also document each counseling relationship with basic case notes (see the Biblical Counseling Record Sheet in Appendix 11.1). Case notes should include the name of the person seen, the date, the session number, a review of the previous session, goals for the current session, an in-session summary, a list of post-session

19. Ibid., 110.
20. Quine, *Legal Issues for Christian Workers and the Church*, 5.
21. Levicoff, *Christian Counseling and the Law*, 114.

homework, and the next meeting date and time. On the back of this form include a treatment plan that matches your training model (the sample contained in Appendix 11.1 uses the "map/model" of sustaining, healing, reconciling, guiding, relationally, rationally, volitionally, and emotionally). In this way, all record keeping stays consistent with the training received. In case notes, ensure that your graduates do not use psychological labels and diagnostic categories. Typically they lack training for this. Additionally, the use of such labels could be perceived as movement away from spiritual care to psychological and even licensed counseling.

Keep these records on site in a secure location—they should never leave the building. There is no clear, uniform standard for how long to keep such records. Best practice ministries tend to keep them for three years, after which they are destroyed.

There are also no clear standards regarding who keeps the records if the "lead trainer" departs the ministry or moves to another church. If the baton has been passed well, as discussed in chapter eleven, then I recommend that the notes pass to the next lead trainer. If, on the other hand, the ministry for some reason disbands when the lead trainer leaves, then that trainer should maintain the notes for three years before destroying them.

Supervision and Biblical Counseling

All graduates must be supervised by qualified individuals. As part of supervision, the supervisor should discuss all counseling evaluation forms completed at commencement (termination), and these evaluations should be maintained. The supervisor should also document and keep records of all continuing education.

Count the Cost: Prudence and Commitment

I am not naive. This is not an easy chapter. However, I don't like to pretend. We have to address these "elephants in the room." They deal with the law of the land to which God commands us to submit, and they deal with the law of love that God commands us to obey.

God calls us to be prudent in regard to our responsibilities to abide by and respect the law. And He calls us to be loving and above reproach as we minister to people. We are to be shrewd and wise as snakes and innocent and harmless as doves (Matt. 10:16).

There is nothing we can do to prevent someone from suing us. We can only provide the best practices possible to defend our actions before the legal system and, more importantly, before our God. Nothing can, or should, prevent us from ministering to the body of Christ. Yes, we need to count the cost (Luke 14:28–33). And yes, we need to serve God even when there will be a cost—as there always will. We can never allow the fear of man to stop us from serving God.

Commencement: Changing Lives with Christ's Changeless Truth

You know by now that I'm a *Nike* type of guy—just do it. As we conclude and commence, not just this chapter but the entire book, I want to say to you, "Just do it!"

My prayer is that this book persuades people—like *you*—to launch and lead 4E training ministries. It can be done; others have, and so can you. "Just do it!"

Since this book has been a collegial process with two dozen best practice churches participating, it seems only fitting to conclude/commence not only with my words but also with their words. My final question to these Disciple-Making Champions in the *4E Ministry Training Questionnaire* was, "What advice would you like to offer others who are about to launch a biblical counseling training ministry?" The following five pearls of wisdom and words of encouragement summarize themes I heard repeatedly:

- Pray like crazy. The Spirit of God will have to bring it about as you submit to Him. Focus on a few key men and women in the early going. Go for quality, not quantity. Pour into those key men and women, getting them firmly rooted in the gospel, the Word, and a Christ-centered counseling paradigm.

321

- Pray, pray, and pray. Ask others for advice and helpful input. Seek God's Word for solutions to common problems so that you can be biblical in your approach to see the Holy Spirit transform lives, which is pleasing to God.
- To borrow the old Peace Corps motto: It's the hardest job you'll ever love. My advice is . . . do it! And enjoy the challenge and the growth that God will bring about in your life.
- Is it hard? Sure. Is it seemingly easier to ignore the problems of sin and suffering in the body of Christ? Certainly. Can we please God, though, and not do what is hard or not deal with sin and suffering? Absolutely not. So begin by personally engaging your neighbors and fellow believers where you live. Then grow your ministry to teach others the joy of what you are doing as well.
- Do it. Start small. Do not wait until you have everything figured out—start and adjust as you go.

What themes did you hear? I heard: pray, build upon God's Word, and "Just do it!" That's pretty good advice in my book.

Do you want to change lives? Do you want to change lives like an Ed Sullivan? Do you want to leave a legacy of loving leaders? Do you want to birth some spiritual grandbabies? Then change lives with Christ's changeless truth by equipping God's people to speak the truth in love.

Growing Together: Questions for Reflection, Discussion, and Application

1. When you think about legal and ethical issues, which extreme do you tend toward: fearing them or ignoring them? Why?
2. Before getting too caught up in the details of this chapter, ask yourself how you could apply the big picture of this chapter: *Obey the law of God and the law of the land in the fear of God and not the fear of man.*
3. How does it change your perspective, attitude, and mindset about legal and ethical issues when you realize that they:

    a. Are just a mere shadow of the deeper requirements of God's law of love?

    b. Flow ultimately from the very character of our holy God?

4. What specific biblical counseling ministry applications do you need to make relative to scope of care and communicating honestly and accurately about your ministry?

5. What specific biblical counseling ministry applications do you need to make relative to each of the seven quality of care matters: propriety, humility, referral, confidentiality, church discipline, documentation, and supervision?

6. Will you just do it? No, that's not what I want to ask with my last question. How and when and with whom will you start 4E training?

Appendices

Practical Equipping Resources

Below is a list of the appendices found in this section of the book. The number of each appendix indicates which chapter it is linked to.

- Appendix 1.1: A Listing of the Twenty-Four Best Practice Disciple-Making Champions
- Appendix 2.1: Congregational SWORD Heart Exam
- Appendix 3.1: A Church-Wide MVP-C Statement
- Appendix 3.2: A Biblical Counseling Ministry-Specific MVP-C Statement
- Appendix 3.3: An Elder Ministry Team MVP-C Statement
- Appendix 4.1: A Personal Ministry MVP-C Statement
- Appendix 4.2: A Sample Discussion Guide: Discovering Our Biblical Counseling Mission
- Appendix 4.3: A LEAD Biblical Counseling MVP-C Statement
- Appendix 4.4: Vision-Catching Probes
- Appendix 5.1: A Formal Congregational Vote
- Appendix 6.1: LEAD Information Packet
- Appendix 7.1: Biblical Counseling 4C Equipping Goals
- Appendix 10.1: LEAD Biblical Counseling Trainee Assessments
- Appendix 10.2: LEAD Sample Lesson Objectives and Lesson Outline
- Appendix 11.1: LEAD Ministry Policy and Procedure Manual
- Appendix 11.2: LEAD Biblical Counseling Ministry Evaluation Form
- Appendix 12.1: Church Discipline Policy

Appendix 1.1

A Listing of the Twenty-Four Best Practice Disciple-Making Champions

I greatly appreciate the following two dozen best practice churches and para-church agencies. Each thoughtfully completed a thorough nine-page, seventy-three question *4E Ministry Training Strategy Questionnaire*.

- Dr. Ernie Baker: Professor of Biblical Counseling, The Master's College and Seminary, Santa Clarita, California; Director of Men's Ministry, Crown Valley Community Church, Acton, California.
- Pastor Brad Bigney (Senior Pastor) and Pastor Ken Long (Pastor of Small Groups/Counseling): Grace Fellowship Church, Florence, Kentucky.
- Pastor Dwayne Bond: Lead Pastor, Wellspring Church, Matthews, North Carolina.
- Dr. Kevin Carson: Pastor, Sonrise Baptist Church, Ozark, Missouri.
- Dr. Robert K. Cheong: Pastor of Care and Counseling, Sojourn Community Church, Louisville, Kentucky.
- Pastor Greg Cook (Soul Care Pastor) and Leigh Ann Stull (Soul Care Minister): Christ Chapel Bible Church, Fort Worth, Texas.
- Dr. Howard Eyrich: Pastor of Counseling Ministries, Briarwood Presbyterian Church, Birmingham, Alabama.
- Julie Ganschow: Biblical Counselor, Faith Community Church, Kansas City, Missouri.

- Brad Hambrick: Executive Director, Crossroads Counseling, Augusta, Georgia.
- Maurice Harton: Missionary, Grace Baptist Church, Bowie, Maryland.
- Pastor John Henderson: Counseling Pastor, Denton Bible Church, Denton, Texas.
- Dr. Garrett Higbee: Executive Director of Biblical Soul Care, Harvest Bible Chapel, Elgin, Illinois; Executive Director, Twelve Stones Ministries, Helmsburg, Indiana.
- Pastor Isaac Huang: Pastor of Chinese Ministries, Chantilly Bible Church, Chantilly, Virginia.
- Pastor Derek R. Iannelli-Smith: Elder, Oasis Church, Goose Creek, South Carolina.
- Jan Kreh: Director of Care Ministries, Grace Fellowship Church, Timonium, Maryland.
- Jeremy Lelek: President, Association of Biblical Counselors, Bedford, Texas.
- Randy Patton: Executive Director, National Association of Nouthetic Counselors, Indianapolis, Indiana.
- Sister Olivia S. Pilson: Servant Leader of the Lay Encouragement and Discipleship Ministry, Mount Pleasant Baptist Church, Alexandria, Virginia.
- Pastor Deepak Reju: Pastor of Biblical Counseling and Families, Capitol Hills Baptist, Washington, DC.
- Mark Shaw: President, Truth in Love Ministries, Clay, Alabama.
- Pastor Dan Taylor: Associate Pastor, Bridgeway Community Church, Columbia, Maryland.
- Dr. Wayne A. Vanderwier: Executive Director, Overseas Instruction in Counseling, Chesterton, Indiana.
- Pastor Steve Viars (Senior Pastor) and Pastor Rob Green (Pastor of Counseling and Seminary Ministries): Faith Baptist Church/ Faith Biblical Counseling Ministries, Lafayette, Indiana.
- Pastor Mike Wilkerson: Pastor of Biblical Living, Mars Hill Church, Seattle, Washington.

Appendix 2.1

Congregational SWORD Heart Exam

LEAD Biblical Counseling Ministry

L	Life
E	Encouragers
A	And
D	Disciplers

Changed People Changing Lives with Christ's Changeless Truth

"Speaking the truth in love" (Ephesians 4:15)
"Encourage one another daily" (Hebrews 3:13)

Congregational SWORD Heart Exam

S	Strengths
W	Weaknesses
O	Opportunities
R	Risks
D	Diagnosis

"The word of God is living and active. Sharper than any double-edged sword" (Hebrews 4:12)

Congregational SWORD Heart Exam

Our church is committed to being a *loving place to grow in grace.* One of the ways we seek to fulfill our commitment is by being a church *of* biblical counseling, not simply a church *with* biblical counseling. We want informal one-another ministry to saturate our entire congregation so that we all speak the truth in love to one another. We are also considering launching a formal biblical counseling ministry where specially gifted and trained persons are equipped to change lives with Christ's changeless truth.

In light of this vision, our congregation is taking a serious look at our capacity to provide quality, distinctively Christian care for our congregation and community. This congregational survey seeks to help us to assess our congregation's current informal one-another ministry (mutual encouragement, spiritual friendship) and our formal biblical counseling ministry (offered by pastors and members). This questionnaire also seeks to assess our potential for and commitment to growth in these ministry areas.

This Congregational SWORD Heart Exam takes, on average, one hour. It will be time well spent both personally and congregationally. We ask that you prayerfully and thoughtfully complete this survey by _____ (one month from now), and return it to _____ either electronically at _____, or by snail mail at _____. Or you can place your completed questionnaire in the collection box placed at the Welcome Center kiosk in the church foyer.

Our LEAD (Lay Encouragers And Disciplers) biblical counseling launch team, along with the church leadership, will thoroughly review all returned questionnaires—we will do the "D" of "Diagnosis" in the SWORD exam. Your input (about Strengths, Weaknesses, Opportunities, and Risks) will make a significant difference in our ministry development.

Because ministry is relational, we prefer that you include your name below, rather than completing the survey anonymously. However, we will leave the final decision to you.

Name: _____

Date: _____

APPENDIX 2.1

Present Strengths and Weaknesses

Please respond to the following questions using a 1 to 10 rating. A "1" would indicate a very low level of effectiveness, confidence, or desire in this area. A "10" would indicate a very high level of effectiveness, confidence, or desire in this area. Please feel free to use any number from 1 to 10. Also, feel free to provide any comments you would like, or simply to provide the numerical rating.

___ 1. How well are we encouraging our congregation to care like Christ: to be spiritual friends, to practice informal one-another ministry?

___ 2. How well are we equipping our congregation for biblical counseling: to relate God's Word to people's lives, to change lives with Christ's changeless truth, to speak the truth in love so people mature in Christ?

___ 3. How confident are you in your ability to offer informal spiritual friendship and to come alongside a friend who is suffering or struggling with a sin issue?

___ 4. How confident are you in your ability to provide formal biblical counseling to a person who is suffering or is struggling with a sin issue?

5. How would you assess our congregation's current ability to provide biblical counseling for people in need of (please rate each area below using the 1 to 10 scale):

____ a. Individual biblical counseling

____ b. Pre-marital biblical counseling

____ c. Marital biblical counseling

____ d. Family/parental biblical counseling

____ e. Adolescent biblical counseling

Please answer the following questions based upon the informal one-another ministry and the formal biblical counseling ministry provided both by our pastoral staff and by our equipped members.

1. What are some of the strengths of our current biblical counseling ministry?
2. What are some of the weaknesses of our current biblical counseling ministry that you would like to see us address?
3. What are specific ways that our church could improve the provision of informal one-another care?
4. What are specific ways that our church could improve the provision of formal biblical counseling?
5. What patterns or mindsets might be making it difficult for our church to become a place where we speak the truth in love to one another?
6. When formal biblical counseling is needed, how long does it take to receive it? Have you or someone you know ever requested biblical counseling here but been unable to receive it?
7. Do you believe that we have a sufficient number of trained biblical counselors (pastors and members) to meet the needs of our *congregation*? Why or why not? How many would be sufficient?
8. Do you believe that we have a sufficient number of trained biblical counselors (pastors and members) to meet the needs of our *community*? Why or why not? How many would be sufficient?

Future Opportunities and Risks

Please respond to the following questions using a 1 to 10 rating. A "1" would indicate a very low level of effectiveness, confidence, or desire in this area. A "10" would indicate a very high level of effectiveness, confidence, or desire in this area. Please feel free to use any number from 1 to 10. Also, feel free to provide any comments you would like, or simply to provide the numerical rating.

___1. What impact might more intentional, formal, structured equipping in biblical counseling have on our ministry to people in our *congregation*?

__2. What impact might more intentional, formal, structured equipping in biblical counseling have on our ministry to people in our *community*?

__3. What level of interest and commitment would you have in being further equipped as a spiritual friend who could help others in an informal, friend-to-friend manner when they are suffering or struggling with a sin issue?

__4. What level of interest and commitment would you have in being equipped as a biblical counselor who could help others in a more formal way by relating God's truth to their lives when they are suffering or struggling with a sin issue?

Please answer the following questions based upon the informal one-another ministry and the formal biblical counseling ministry provided both by our pastoral staff and by our equipped members.

1. What obstacles might stand in the way of healthy informal one-another ministry in our church? Where do we need to change or grow if we are to move forward as a church where every member speaks the truth in love?

2. In the past, how has our church responded to change and to the launch of new ministries? How might similar responses hinder or help a renewed focus on equipping in formal biblical counseling?

3. If we launched a formal biblical counseling training ministry, who and what might stand in the way? What apple carts might we upset? What objections might people raise? How could we respond?

4. Read Ephesians 3:20 and dream as if we could not fail. What do you think God will do with our biblical counseling ministry in the future? In one year? Five? Ten? Twenty?

5. What areas of counseling are you aware of that are the greatest need for people in our *congregation*? Of the list below, rank the top ten needs, with 1 being the greatest need.

_____ Addiction: Drugs/Alcohol	_____ Grief
_____ Addiction/Pornography/Sexual	_____ Guilt
_____ Anger	_____ Habitual Sin
_____ Anxiety/Fear/Phobia/Worry	_____ Infertility
_____ Blended Family/Step-Parenting	_____ Infidelity/Affair
_____ Christ-Esteem/Identity in Christ	_____ Loneliness
_____ Christian Growth	_____ Marital
_____ Cutting	_____ Parenting
_____ Death and Dying	_____ Peer Pressure
_____ Depression	_____ Physical Abuse
_____ Divorce/Remarriage	_____ Post-Abortion
_____ Doubt	_____ Prayer Life/Spiritual Disciplines
_____ Eating Disorders	_____ Pre-marital
_____ Educational	_____ Purposelessness/Failure
_____ Emotional Abuse	_____ Self-Harm/Suicidal
_____ Emotional Control/Maturity	_____ Sexual Abuse
_____ Financial	_____ Sexual Identity
_____ Forgiveness	_____ Vocational

_____ Other: _____

_____ Other: _____

_____ Other: _____

6. Were we to provide biblical counseling by trained members of our congregation, for any/all of the above, would you utilize that counseling? Please explain your answer.

7. How could we turn our community upside down for Christ through biblical counseling?

8. What are the five greatest concerns of the residents of our community? Five greatest struggles? How could we address these issues biblically?

9. How responsive do you think our community would be if we offered them biblical counseling?

10. What areas of counseling are you aware of that are the greatest need for people in our *community*? Of the list below, rank the top ten needs, with 1 being the greatest need.

_____ Addiction: Drugs/Alcohol	_____ Grief	
_____ Addiction/Pornography/Sexual	_____ Guilt	
_____ Anger	_____ Habitual Sin	
_____ Anxiety/Fear/Phobia/Worry	_____ Infertility	
_____ Blended Family/Step-Parenting	_____ Infidelity/Affair	
_____ Christ-Esteem/Identity in Christ	_____ Loneliness	
_____ Christian Growth	_____ Marital	
_____ Cutting	_____ Parenting	
_____ Death and Dying	_____ Peer Pressure	
_____ Depression	_____ Physical Abuse	
_____ Divorce/Remarriage	_____ Post-Abortion	
_____ Doubt	_____ Prayer Life/Spiritual Disciplines	
_____ Eating Disorders	_____ Pre-marital	
_____ Educational	_____ Purposelessness/Failure	
_____ Emotional Abuse	_____ Self-Harm/Suicidal	
_____ Emotional Control/Maturity	_____ Sexual Abuse	
_____ Financial	_____ Sexual Identity	
_____ Forgiveness	_____ Vocational	
_____ Other: _____		
_____ Other: _____		
_____ Other: _____		

11. What else would you like to share with us or ask us?

Thank you so much for giving of your valuable time to this valuable project.

Appendix 3.1

A Church-Wide MVP-C Statement

Our Uniontown Bible Church MVP-C Statement

Our Mission Statement

According to the Bible, the mission of Uniontown Bible Church is to make disciples who love Christ, love the body of Christ, and love the world on behalf of Christ.

Therefore, the five-fold purpose of our church is to fulfill the Great Commandment and the Great Commission through:

Discipleship: Equipping God's People
Worship: Exalting and Enjoying God
Fellowship: Encouraging God's People
Stewardship: Empowering God's People
Ambassadorship: Evangelizing the Unsaved

Our Vision Statement

It is our DREAM to be a dynamic family, creatively and relevantly sharing Christ's grace with our neighbors in Carroll County and beyond.

We will skillfully equip one another through small group and one-another discipleship ministries that empower us to build loving relationships that last through all the storms of life.

Our Passion Statement

A Loving Place to Grow in Grace

Our Commission Statement

We will seek to fulfill our MVP through mutually overseeing the equipping of God's family as servant leaders, modeling maturity, mentoring disciple-makers, managing ministers and ministries, and mending the flock.

We will mutually equip one another to lovingly evangelize the community for Christ; we will encourage the congregation toward vital connection with Christ and the body of Christ; and we will empower one another to become makers of disciple-makers.

Appendix 3.2

A Biblical Counseling Ministry-Specific MVP-C Statement

Our LEAD Biblical Counseling Ministry MVP-C Statement

Our Ministry Mission Statement

According to the Bible, LEAD exists to equip encouragers and disciplers who lovingly, wisely, and powerfully relate God's truth to human relationships.

We will apply Christ's grace to the evils we have suffered and to the sins we have committed. Through the personal ministry of the Word, we will empower one another to grasp the truth that:

> It's normal to hurt (Romans 12:15; 2 Corinthians 1:3–9);
> It's possible to hope (Romans 8:28; 2 Corinthians 1:8–11);
> It's horrible to sin, but wonderful to be forgiven (Romans 1–6);
> It's supernatural to mature (Romans 7–15).

Our Ministry Vision Statement

It is our DREAM to be a dynamic family of soul care-givers and spiritual directors who encourage one another through the personal ministry of the Word to turn upward in worship of our Father to find grace to help in our suffering and sin, and to turn outward in fellowship with our brothers and sisters to give and receive Christ's grace.

337

Our Ministry Passion Statement

Sharing Christ's Grace Face-to-Face

Our Ministry Commission Statement

We will seek to fulfill our LEAD MVP through the 4Es of envisioning, enlisting, equipping, and empowering a congregation of spiritual friends, biblical counselors, and small group ministers.

We will comprehensively equip soul care-givers and spiritual directors in the 4Cs of biblical content, Christlike character, counseling competence, and Christian community so they can sustain, heal, reconcile, and guide individuals, couples, and families in our congregation and community to know Christ, grow in Christ, and become Christlike disciple-makers.

Appendix 3.3

An Elder Ministry Team MVP-C Statement

Our Elder Ministry Team MVP-C Statement

Our Mission Statement

According to God's Word, our elder ministry team exists to disciple one another as servant leaders who oversee, empower, and equip our Father's family to reproduce in themselves and others Christlike love for Christ, Christians, and those who do not yet know Christ.

Our Vision Statement

It is God's dream for us to be a team of humble, caring, loving leaders united in Christ and committed to prayerfully discerning our Father's will for His family.

We will mentor faithful disciple-makers, coach committed ministers, and shepherd God's flock.

Our Passion Statement

Servant Leaders Serving Our Leader

Our Commission Statement

God is calling and equipping us to fulfill our Elder Ministry Team MVP *through* ad-ministrating the ministry, organizing the organism, and overseeing the equipping of our church family by modeling maturity, mentoring disciple-makers, and mending the flock.

Appendix 4.1

A Personal Ministry MVP-C Statement

My Congregational Discipleship Pastor MVP-C Statement

My Pastoral Mission Statement

According to God's Word, my fundamental mission as a pastor-teacher is to oversee the equipping of God's people (discipleship) to live out His truth in love so that the body of Christ matures in Christlike love for Christ (worship), Christians (fellowship and stewardship), and those who do not yet know Christ (ambassadorship).

My Pastoral Vision Statement

It is my dream to provide our congregational family with visionary leadership anchored in God's truth and love in order to skillfully oversee the equipping of God's forever family to live out His truth in mature love by building loving relationships that last through all the storms of life with Christ, Christians, and those who do not yet know Christ.

Through God's grace stirring up the gift of God within me to stir up the gift of God within our congregational family, I will creatively feed and dynamically lead Uniontown Bible Church toward becoming God's maturing masterpiece.

My Pastoral Passion Statement

Leaving a Legacy of Loving Leaders

My Pastoral Commission Statement

I am called and commissioned by Christ to oversee that our congregational family is equipped through the Spirit's empowerment to help people grow from spiritual birth to spiritual maturity.

Christ is calling me to oversee that we are equipped to evangelize our community for Christ, encourage the crowd toward vital relationship with the body of Christ, exhort the congregation toward Christlike maturity, enable the committed to minister lovingly in the body of Christ, and empower the core to equip others also all for the purpose of exalting and enjoying Christ.

Appendix 4.2

A Sample Discussion Guide: Discovering Our Biblical Counseling Mission

Discovering Our Biblical Counseling Mission

In groups of three or four, respond to these questions. Then we'll share as a larger group.

1. According to Matthew 22:34–40 and Matthew 28:16–20, what is the end goal or mission of all life and ministry?

2. According to Ephesians 4:11–16, what is our calling from God in the body of Christ?

3. According to Hebrews 3:7–16 and Hebrews 10:19–25, what is the purpose of the personal ministry of the Word—of our one-another spiritual conversations?

4. According to Ephesians 4:15, Philippians 1:9–11, and 1 Thessalonians 2:8, what is the relationship between truth and love in biblical counseling?

5. According to Colossians 2:1–10, 2 Timothy 3:16–17, and 2 Peter 1:3–4, what is the nature and role of God's Word in biblical counseling?

6. Compare and contrast 2 Corinthians 1:3–11, 1 Thessalonians 5:14, and 2 Timothy 2:24–26 regarding the "focus" of biblical counseling—what different types of life situations and struggles does it address?

7. According to Romans 15:14 and Galatians 6:1–5, what are some of the qualifications and characteristics of a mature biblical counselor?

8. Based upon your study so far:

   a. What preliminary definition of biblical counseling would you craft?

   b. What list of biblical counseling values would you develop?

9. Finish the following sentence based upon the verses you've studied: According to the Bible, the mission of a biblical counseling ministry is to . . .

10. Looking at our church mission statement, how would you rewrite your answer to question 9 so that it fully supports and advances the mission of our church?

Appendix 4.3

A LEAD Biblical Counseling MVP-C Statement

Our Church of the Open Door LEAD Biblical Counseling MVP-C Statement

Our Mission Statement

According to the Bible, the mission of LEAD is to equip biblical counselors and small group leaders to speak the truth in love to people struggling with suffering and sin, in order to promote Christlike maturity in the body of Christ.

LEAD exists to assist our church to become an equipping center (Ephesians 4:11–14), a fully functioning family (Matthew 22:34–40), a Christ-centered community (Hebrews 3:7–16; 10:19–25), a healthy body (Ephesians 4:15–16), and a "teaching hospital" for soul physicians healing hurting and hardened hearts (Matthew 23:23–26).

Our Vision Statement

It is the DREAM of our LEAD ministry to be a maturing team of loving encouragers and dynamic disciplers equipped to make God's house a home.

We will be empowered toward personal maturity, encouraged by biblical community, and equipped for relational ministry to God's family and our community.

Through spiritual maturity, biblical wisdom, and relational skillfulness, we will speak the truth in love so that we all may mature in Christ.

Our Passion Statement

Changed People Changing Lives with Christ's Changeless Truth

Our Commission Statement

We will seek to fulfill our LEAD MVP through the 4Es of envisioning, enlisting, equipping, and empowering a congregation of spiritual friends, biblical counselors, and small group ministers.

We will comprehensively equip soul caregivers and spiritual directors in the 4Cs of biblical content, Christlike character, counseling competence, and Christian community so they can sustain, heal, reconcile, and guide individuals, couples, and families in our congregation and community to know Christ, grow in Christ, and care like Christ.

Appendix 4.4

Vision-Catching Probes

Vision-Catching Probes

What's the DNA of Our Congregation and Community?

In each area (past, present, future), select three or four questions to discuss with your group.

Probing Our Past

1. In what unique ways has our congregation provided one-another ministry to each other?

2. What stories do we tell about special times of one-another ministry in our church's history?

3. How have we spoken the truth in love to one another in the past?

4. What words describe the ways in which we've offered biblical counseling in the past, either formally or informally?

5. Have we ever attempted a ministry like this before? If so, what was it like? If not, why not?

6. How have we significantly impacted our community through speaking the truth in love?

Probing Our Present

1. What amazing work is God doing in our church through the personal ministry of the Word?

2. What are you excited about in how we currently provide one-another ministry?

3. What are some of the strengths and weaknesses in the way we provide biblical counseling?

4. Where is biblical counseling already occurring effectively?

5. What persons in our church seem to "embody" speaking the truth in love? How?

6. What special "gift-mix" does our congregation have, and what biblical counseling focus would those gifts best support?

7. Where do we ache for other people?

8. What other churches are offering biblical counseling? How would our ministry be different?

9. How could our biblical counseling vision advance our congregation-wide vision?

10. What are some of the biblical counseling issues faced by people in our congregation?

11. What are some of the biblical counseling issues faced by people in our community?

12. When people in our community think of how we provide biblical counseling, what comes to mind? What stories might they tell—positively or negatively?

Probing Our Future

1. What are our dreams for the biblical counseling ministry in one year? Five? Ten? Twenty?

2. Read Ephesians 3:20 and dream as if we could not fail. What do you think God will do with our biblical counseling ministry in the future?

3. If time, training, and money were no objects, what would our biblical counseling ministry look like?

4. If we were to create a cover page for our biblical counseling brochure, what words might capture the essence of the ministry?

5. What words picture how we want our biblical counseling ministry described in five years?

6. What would "success" look like for our biblical counseling ministry?

7. How could we turn our community upside down for Christ through biblical counseling?

What other questions would you ask or information would you share?

Appendix 5.1

A Formal Congregational Vote

Congregational Vote

Our church leadership [pastors, and/or elders, and/or deacons] is recommending the formal establishment of the LEAD (Life Encouragers And Disciplers) Biblical Counseling [or Spiritual Friendship] Ministry.

The mission of LEAD is to equip biblical counselors [or spiritual friends] and small group leaders to speak the truth in love to people struggling with suffering and sin, in order to promote Christlike maturity in the body of Christ. LEAD exists to assist our church to become an equipping center (Ephesians 4:11–14), a fully functioning family (Matthew 22:34–40), a Christ-centered community (Hebrews 3:7–16; 10:19–25), a healthy body (Ephesians 4:15–16), and a "teaching hospital" for soul physicians healing hurting and hardened hearts (Matthew 23:23–26).

We will seek to fulfill our LEAD mission through envisioning, enlisting, equipping, and empowering a congregation of biblical counselors [or spiritual friends] and small group ministers. We will comprehensively equip soul caregivers and spiritual directors in biblical content, Christlike character, counseling competence, and Christian community so they can sustain, heal, reconcile, and guide individuals, couples, and families in our congregation and community to know Christ, grow in Christ, and become Christlike disciple-makers.

The initial budget for the next fiscal year is _____. For the launch budget, see _____ [reference the appropriate document].

We have consulted the appropriate outside counsel to establish best practice protocol regarding legal and ethical issues. For a summary of these policies and procedures, see _____ [reference the appropriate document].

Appendix 6.1

LEAD Information Packet

LEAD Biblical Counseling Ministry

L   Life
E   Encouragers
A   And
D   Disciplers

INFORMATION AND APPLICATION PACKET

Changed People Changing Lives with
Christ's Changeless Truth

"Speaking the truth in love" (Ephesians 4:15)
"Encourage one another daily" (Hebrews 3:13)

Cover Letter

Dear _____,

Thank you for your interest in our LEAD (Life Encouragers And Disciplers) Biblical Counseling Ministry. We're excited about equipping God's people to change lives with Christ's changeless truth.

Our prayer is that we could mutually discern whether the LEAD ministry is the right fit and match for you and your calling and giftedness from God. As you read the enclosed material and complete the enclosed forms, please pray with us that together we would discern God's will.

In the packet you will find:

- Our LEAD Biblical Counseling MVP-C Statement
- Our LEAD Philosophy of Biblical Counseling
- A Profile of a Nurtured LEAD Graduate
- God's Calling: Who God Is Calling to Minister in LEAD
- God's Equipping: How LEAD Will Minister to You
- Your Future Ministry: How You Will Minister through LEAD
- Your LEAD Personal Cost and Commitment Inventory
- Your LEAD Personal Commitment Form
- The LEAD Biblical Counseling Ministry Application Form
- The Redeemed Personality Inventory

Because the process is mutual, the first step is yours. After reading the information portion of the packet, you should prayerfully decide if you want to complete the application process. If you do, then you need to turn in your signed Personal Commitment Form, your Application Form, and your Redeemed Personality Inventory to _____ by _____ (due date). You then need to contact _____ at _____ to arrange a personal interview (which follows up on your written application).

At that point, the next step is ours. After we read everyone's application, check with the people everyone listed as ministry references, and conduct all the personal interviews, our LEAD team meets to pray and decide who we believe are the best fit for this round of training (in this training sequence we are able to select _____ trainees). We will then contact you to welcome you into this training group, ask you to consider waiting until the next training sequence, suggest that perhaps there might be a better ministry fit in another ministry, or discuss areas that we believe you may want to address in order to be better prepared for a ministry in biblical counseling.

If you have any questions, please feel free to contact _____ at _____. We are praying for you. Please pray for us.

In Christ's Grace,

Your LEAD Biblical Counseling Ministry Team

Our LEAD Biblical Counseling MVP-C Statement

Our Mission Statement

According to the Bible, the mission of LEAD is to equip biblical counselors and small group leaders to speak the truth in love to people struggling with suffering and sin, in order to promote Christlike maturity in the body of Christ.

LEAD exists to assist our church to become an equipping center (Ephesians 4:11–14), a fully functioning family (Matthew 22:34–40), a Christ-centered community (Hebrews 3:7–16; 10:19–25), a healthy body (Ephesians 4:15–16), and a "teaching hospital" for soul physicians healing hurting and hardened hearts (Matthew 23:23–26).

Our Vision Statement

It is the DREAM of our LEAD ministry to be a maturing team of loving encouragers and dynamic disciplers equipped to make God's house a home.

We will be empowered toward personal maturity, encouraged by biblical community, and equipped for relational ministry to God's family and our community.

Through spiritual maturity, biblical wisdom, and relational skillfulness, we will speak the truth in love so that we all may mature in Christ.

Our Passion Statement

Changed People Changing Lives with Christ's Changeless Truth

Our Commission Statement

We will seek to fulfill our LEAD MVP through the 4Es of envisioning, enlisting, equipping, and empowering a congregation of spiritual friends, biblical counselors, and small group ministers.

We will comprehensively equip soul caregivers and spiritual directors in the 4Cs of biblical content, Christlike character, counseling competence, and Christian community so they can sustain, heal, reconcile, and guide individuals, couples, and families in our congregation and community to know Christ, grow in Christ, and care like Christ.

OUR LEAD PHILOSOPHY OF BIBLICAL COUNSELING: WHAT MAKES BIBLICAL COUNSELING TRULY BIBLICAL

The various approaches to biblical/Christian counseling are numerous and diverse. Below, you will find a definition of biblical counseling as we see it, and a description of our convictions about what makes biblical counseling truly biblical. If your philosophy and theology of counseling differs noticeably from what you are about to read, then we likely will not be a good ministry training match. The idea is not to force anyone to walk in lock-step with everything we teach. We desire you to be Bereans (Acts 17:11), not Corinthians (1 Cor. 1:10–17). As a Berean, based upon your understanding of God's Word, test what we teach. At the same time, our team can't function biblically if any member has a Corinthian attitude of negativity, biting criticism, and againstness.

Our Summary Working Definition of Biblical Counseling

Christ-centered, church-based, comprehensive, compassionate, and culturally informed biblical counseling depends upon the Holy Spirit to relate God's Word to suffering and sin by speaking and living God's truth in love to equip people to love God and one another (Matt. 22:35–40). It cultivates conformity to Christ and communion with Christ and the body of Christ, leading to a community of one-another disciple-makers (Matt. 28:18–20).

Biblical Counseling Is Scriptural

Biblical counseling clings tenaciously to the supremacy, sufficiency, and profundity (depth of wisdom) of the Scriptures. God has provided us with all that we need for godly living (2 Peter 1:3). The Scriptures, rightly interpreted and carefully applied, offer us all-encompassing insight for living. The Bible provides us with the interpretive categories for making sense of life from God's perspective. By building our counseling approach on Christ's gospel of grace, we obtain wisdom for bringing people healing hope, the stimulus for change (God's glory), and the understanding of human motivation that energizes these God-honoring changes (2 Tim. 3:15–16).

Biblical Counseling Is Theological

Biblical counseling unites creation, fall, and redemption. In studying a biblical theology of *creation*, biblical counseling examines *people*—God's original design for the soul. In probing the *fall*, biblical counseling examines *problems*—how sin brought personal depravity and suffering. In investigating the Bible's teaching on *redemption*, biblical counseling examines *solutions/cures*—the gospel of Christ's grace, which offers eternal salvation and provides us with daily victory in our ongoing battle against the world, the flesh, and the devil (Matt. 4:1–11).

Biblical Counseling Is Historical

The church has always helped hurting and hardened people. Biblical counseling respects that "great cloud of witnesses" (Heb. 12:1–3) who have gone before us. Biblical counselors appreciate the legacy of Christian soul care and spiritual direction, seeking to apply for today that ancient legacy and consensual wisdom for living found in the writings of the great historic Christian soul physicians.

Biblical Counseling Is Positive

Biblical counseling is "Berean counseling" (Acts 17:11). Biblical counselors have a *critical mind minus a critical spirit*. Biblical counselors seek to focus positively on rightly understanding the Word (2 Tim. 2:15) and on graciously interacting with those with whom they disagree.

Biblical Counseling Is Relational

Because the God of the Bible is the eternal Community of intimate Oneness (John 1 and 17), biblical counselors discard aloofness in favor of "real and raw counseling." While techniques, skills, and tools of competent counseling are not ignored, soul-to-soul relating is emphasized (1 Thess. 2:8). Biblical counseling highlights neither directive nor non-directive counseling. Rather, it practices collaborative counseling where the counselor, the counselee, and the Divine Counselor form a three-way relationship shaped by God's Word and led by God's Spirit.

Biblical Counseling Is Relevant

It is not enough to promote the sufficiency of the Word if we do not also minister in such a way that demonstrates the relevancy of God's Word. Problems in living are seen by biblical counselors as spiritual, relational, mental, volitional, and emotional issues addressed in the Book of Life by the Author of Life so that we can live the abundant life (John 10:10) to glorify the Creator of Life.

Biblical Counseling Is Transformative

Biblical counseling applies the principles of *progressive sanctification* to the daily lives of believers (2 Cor. 3:16–18). It does so *through spiritual formation,* which cultivates *communion with Christ* and *conformity to Christ* through the practice of the biblical/historical individual and corporate spiritual disciplines. Transformative biblical counseling highlights *the inner life* through its emphasis on forming the character of Christ in us—*our inner life increasingly mirroring the inner life of Christ.* It focuses on the *body of Christ* by encouraging the corporate spiritual disciplines and by equipping believers in the individual spiritual disciplines.

Biblical Counseling Is Comprehensive in Theory

Biblical counseling focuses on the full range of human nature created in the image of God (Gen. 1:26–28). A comprehensive bib-

357

lical understanding sees human beings as relational beings who desire (spiritual, social, and self-aware capacities), rational beings who think, volitional beings who choose, emotional beings who experience, and physical beings who act. Biblical counseling models of change focus on each of these areas, seeing the human personality as united. Biblical counseling does not deny the interplay or the complexity of our mind/brain and body/soul connection (Gen. 2:7). It takes seriously the role of the brain (in a fallen world in an un-glorified body) and its impact on healthy human functioning (Rom. 8:19–25).

Biblical Counseling Is Comprehensive in Methodology

Biblical counseling *treats both suffering and sin* by recognizing that God's Word is profitable for dealing with the evils we have suffered as well as with the sins we have committed (2 Cor. 1:3–11; 2:5–11). Biblical counselors offer comfort for the hurting as well as confrontation for the hardened. They provide sustaining and healing for those battered by life as well as reconciling and guiding for those ensnared by Satan.

Biblical Counseling Is Comprehensive in Equipping

Biblical counseling training unites equipping in biblical content, Christlike character, counseling competence, and Christian community (Rom. 15:14). Scriptural insight is learned in the context of close Christian community and applied to the spiritual character development of the counselor-in-training. It results in the relational competency to interact soul-to-soul and to impact others deeply for Christ (Eph. 4:11–16).

Biblical Counseling Is Universal

The apostle Paul insists that all mature, equipped believers are competent to counsel (Rom. 15:14). Therefore, biblical counseling is universal—it is what God's people do informally as spiritual friends and formally as biblical counselors, what pastors do as soul physicians, and what professional Christian counselors do as caregivers.

Biblical Counseling Is Culturally Informed

The fact that biblical counseling is universal in no way excludes the truth that biblical counseling should be culturally informed. It blends into its universal worldview the *unique biblical perspectives* of both genders and all ethnicities (Rev. 7:9–10).

A PROFILE OF A NURTURED LEAD GRADUATE

God's Calling: Whom God Is Calling to Minister in LEAD

We believe that God calls every Christian to become competent to encourage and disciple one another (Rom. 15:14; 2 Cor. 1:3–11). In LEAD we will stir up each other's God-given gifts (2 Tim. 1:5–7) so that we become equipped with biblical content, Christlike character, and counseling competence in the context of Christian community. We will become spiritual friends and soul physicians who dispense Christ's grace to heal our disgrace. LEAD may be for you if:

- You long to know what to do after the hug by becoming a *caregiver* who cares like Christ (Phil. 2:1–5).
- You dream of being the sort of *friend* who can deeply weep with your friend who weeps and who can heartily rejoice with your friend who rejoices (Rom. 12:15).
- You sense that Christ is calling you to be a *soul physician* who can listen well and wisely and lovingly guide others through their problems to the Father's heart (Gal. 6:1–2).
- You sense God leading you to be a *people helper* (a one-to-one encourager) or to be a *people healer* (a small group discipler) (Heb. 10:19–25).
- God is stirring up within you a passion to be the sort of *Christian* who engages in soul stirring encouragement and spirit-shaping discipleship—a Christian who really makes a difference because you really love deeply (Eph. 4:15).
- God is calling you to be a *spiritual friend* who offers *soul care* and *spiritual direction* to sustain, heal, reconcile, and guide others along their journey of faith.
- You desire to be the sort of *son or daughter* of God who connects so deeply with your heavenly Father in your suffering and sin that He empowers you to offer His goodness and grace to others during their struggles with suffering and sin (Heb. 3:12–14).

God's Equipping: How LEAD Will Minister to You

Through LEAD you will be equipped for relational ministry to God's family by speaking God's truth in love (Eph. 4:11–16). You will learn how to care like Christ. In LEAD, we will mature together in four areas that we call the 4Cs: character, content, competence, and community. We derive these four dimensions of counseling from many passages, including Romans 15:14: "I myself am convinced, my brothers, that you yourselves are full of goodness, complete in knowledge and competent to instruct one another."

The Four Dimensions of Comprehensive Biblical Counseling Equipping

Christlike Character	"Full of Goodness"	Heart/Being
Biblical Content/Conviction	"Complete in Knowledge"	Head/Knowing
Counseling Competence	"Competent to Instruct One Another"	Hands/Doing
Christian Community	"Brothers/One Another"	Home/Loving

Christlike Character: "Full of Goodness"—Heart/Being

Throughout our training, we will apply God's Word to our own suffering and struggles with sin by relating truth to our lives. Through Christ's grace we will grow in grace—progressive sanctification. This personal application process will occur in our interactive lecture time, but even more so in our small group lab time. Through our small group relationships, we will experience mutual one-another encouragement and discipleship. In other words, we will experience biblical counseling so that we become more mature Christians who therefore are more effective biblical counselors.

You will meet twice per month with your encouragement partner/ spiritual friend for mutual one-another ministry, and twice per month with your mentor for encouragement and discipleship. During these meetings, not only will you work on counseling competencies, but you will have the opportunity to address issues of suffering and struggles with sin in your own life so you can grow in grace.

Biblical Content/Conviction: "Complete in Knowledge"— Head/Knowing

Throughout our training, we will focus on what God's Word says about biblical encouragement and discipleship—biblical counseling. Through in-depth instruction in God's Word, we will discover a practical, relational, biblical theology of the Bible, God, people, problems, solutions, suffering, salvation, and sanctification—we will develop biblical insight and wisdom for biblical counseling.

In addition to these interactive, applicational lectures, you will also carefully read, study, and reflect on biblical passages, Christian books, and teaching manuals. Through our primary text, *Soul Physicians*, you will learn biblical answers to life's six ultimate questions: What is truth? Who is God? Who am I? What went wrong? How do people change? Where am I headed?

Counseling Competence: "Competent to Instruct One Another"—Hands/Doing

Through your reading and application of our biblical counseling training workbook *Spiritual Friends*, and through our lab times together, you will develop twenty-two biblical counseling relational competencies. You will be trained in the art of soul care for suffering through sustaining and healing and in the art of spiritual direction for sin through reconciling and guiding. Our small group lab times will include opportunities to develop the relational skills necessary to be a competent biblical counselor. We will relate deeply with one another, practice counseling skills, engage in role-plays, discuss case studies, observe live counseling, and counsel one another.

Your monthly meetings with your encouragement partner/spiritual friend and trainer/mentor will empower you to develop the relational skills necessary to be a true soul friend. Halfway into our training, you will have the opportunity for on-the-job-training—providing one-to-one encouragement (biblical counseling/spiritual friendship) or small group discipleship.

Christian Community: "Brothers/One Another"— Home/Loving

LEAD provides intimate fellowship with God's people. It has the potential to become one of the most powerful small group experiences you have ever enjoyed. Our weekly study of God's Word will allow us to interact about and relate God's truth to our daily lives. Our weekly small group sharing and skill-building time will allow us to experience firsthand what it means to share Christ's grace to heal our suffering and sin. We will experience, as past trainees have described it, "real and raw relating." It is going to be intense and intimate as we speak the truth in love to one another.

Every member of our LEAD small group will pair up with an encouragement partner/spiritual friend. If past experience comes true, then your encouragement partner will become one of your most cherished spiritual friends. During our LEAD training, each member will meet twice monthly with our trainer or apprentice leader for one-to-one shepherding and discipleship. Through these means, you will find mending for your hurts, mentoring to find Christ's victory in your struggle with sin, and motivation to develop your spiritual gifts.

Your Future Ministry: How You Will Minister through LEAD

Relational Ministry: Informal One-Another Ministry

Our primary desire in LEAD is to promote relational maturity that leads to relational ministry: the capacity to love God and others out of a pure heart (1 Tim. 1:5) in the muck and mess of daily relationships. So each of us can immediately use the equipping we received in LEAD to grow in love.

Love for God: Worship—To Exalt and Enjoy Our Father

We are interested in promoting a deeper passion for God, a greater enjoyment of God, and a growing dependency upon God. We are interested in daily worship during the daily routines of life.

Love for Our Neighbor: Ministry—To Encourage and Disciple Our Brothers and Sisters

We long to see one another grow in caring for our friends, spouses, parents, children, co-workers, and neighbors. We're interested in spouses who love each other more, parents who encourage their kids better, friends who care more, and Christians who love their unsaved friends better. We're interested in daily relationships during all the storms of life.

Congregational Ministry: Formal Encouragement and Discipleship

As we grow in relational maturity, God increases our power for congregational ministry. LEAD graduates, in addition to the daily worship and ministry in natural life settings, will minister in our congregation and to our community through the following:

Biblical Encouragement: Biblical Counseling/Spiritual Friendship

Some of you have special gifts and passions to relate one-to-one with a brother or sister who is hurting and needs the mending help of soul care (sustaining and healing). You will use your LEAD training to provide biblical counseling that helps people to taste and see that God is good even when life is bad.

Some of you have special gifts and passions to relate one-to-one with a brother or sister who is hardening his or her heart and needs the mentoring help of spiritual direction (reconciling and guiding). You will use your LEAD training to provide biblical counseling that helps people taste and see that God is gracious even when they are sinful.

Small Group Biblical Discipleship: Coaching

Some of you have special gifts and passions to facilitate mending small groups that provide support and recovery for people struggling with suffering and sin. You might use your LEAD training to facilitate a Beauty for Ashes Group (Sexual Abuse Redemption Group), a New Hope Fellowship Group (Addiction Redemption Group), a Parenting Adolescents Group, or another group you are passionate about.

Some of you have special gifts and passions to facilitate mentoring small groups that provide focused biblical discipleship for specific life issues. You might use your LEAD training to facilitate a Men's Iron Sharpeners Group, a Women Mentoring Women Group, a Pre-Marital Preparing for Oneness Group, a Marriage Builders Group, a Parental Home Improvement Group, or another group you are passionate about.

YOUR LEAD PERSONAL COST AND COMMITMENT INVENTORY

Jesus taught us to "count the cost" (Luke 14:25–35) to determine if we have what it takes to complete the commitments we are about to make. LEAD involves a high cost on your part (and promises many benefits). Please prayerfully weigh these costs.

Training Time Commitment

1. In-Class Training Time

LEAD is a two-year training ministry. LEAD will meet every week (except holidays) for two hours from September to May (approximately 36 weeks each of the two years). Consistent attendance is vital—it will be necessary for you to be in attendance at least 90 percent of the time that we meet.

2. Out-of-Class Training Time

You can expect to commit the following time outside of class:

- One hour per week reading/responding to workbook questions
- Two hours per month meeting with your encouragement partner
- Two hours per month meeting with your mentor
- During the second year, two hours per month meeting with a protégé (your meeting time with your encouragement partner will be just once per month the second year)

Ministry Time Commitment

Everyone trained for two years will be asked to serve for the next two years.

1. Biblical Counseling

If you choose to serve as a biblical counselor, you would:

- Counsel one to two hours per week.

- Meet with your trainer/mentor one to two hours per month (may be individual and/or group supervision).
- Spend one hour per week in prayer, study, and preparation for your counseling.

2. Small Group Leadership/Discipleship

If you choose to serve as a small group leader, you would:

- Lead one ninety-minute-to-two-hour small group per week or every other week.
- Meet with your mentor/trainer one to two hours per month (may be individual and/or group supervision).
- Spend one hour per week in prayer, study, and preparation for your group leadership.

Your LEAD Personal Commitment Form

As you ponder whether you can commit to LEAD, we would ask you to evaluate yourself carefully, prayerfully, and honestly. We would also encourage you to gain feedback from others who know you. If you are married, please have your spouse read your LEAD information as he or she will need to weigh the costs and benefits.

If, after careful cost counting, you decide that you want to be considered for our LEAD equipping ministry, then the next steps in your process toward becoming a LEAD member will be to:

1. Sign and date this Personal Commitment Form.
2. Complete the LEAD Biblical Counseling Ministry Application Form.
3. Complete the Redeemed Personality Inventory.

Return these three documents to _____ by _____ (due date).

4. Arrange a personal interview with _____ by contacting _____ at _____.

My Commitment to LEAD

I have carefully read all the LEAD information. Having weighed the benefits and costs, I am willing to commit to fulfilling all LEAD responsibilities. Therefore, I would ask you to prayerfully consider me for selection as a LEAD trainee.

_____   _____
(Signature)   (Date)

I also grant the LEAD Biblical Counseling Ministry my approval to perform a background check.

_____   _____
(Signature)   (Date)

The LEAD Biblical Counseling Ministry Application Form

Personal Information

Name: _____

Age: _____   Marital Status: _____

Church Membership (Where/How Long): _____

How Long You Have Been a Christian: _____

Application Questions: In the space under each question, please share concise and candid responses. If you need more space, please use the back of each sheet.

1. How did you come to know Christ?

2. Who and what has contributed most to your growth in Christ over the years?

3. As you review our LEAD MVP-C Statement:

   a. What questions do you have?
   b. What aspects resonate/connect with you most?
   c. Which aspects least resonate/connect with you?

4. As you review our LEAD Philosophy of Biblical Counseling:

   a. How would you word differently your working definition of biblical counseling (please do not respond with, "I would not change it at all")?

   b. Which of the twelve areas regarding what makes biblical counseling truly biblical do you think are most important? Why? Least important? Why?

5. Consider the "4Cs" in the Profile of a Nurtured LEAD Graduate:

   • Christlike Character: "Full of Goodness"—Heart/Being

369

- Biblical Content/Conviction: "Complete in Knowledge"—Head/Knowing

- Counseling Competence: "Competent to Instruct One Another"—Hands/Doing

- Christian Community: "Brothers/One Another"—Home/Loving

a. What further growth do you need to experience in the area of Christlike character?

b. What biblical content do you think is most important for a biblical counselor to know and apply?

c. In terms of counseling skills/competence, how would you rate yourself at this point in your life?

d. What are examples in your life that demonstrate how highly you value Christian community—connecting deeply with others in Christ?

6. What are the primary reasons you are interested in being a part of LEAD?

7. Describe any of your previous long-term (two years or more) ministry commitments.

8. What is your definition of sin?

9. What is your definition of maturity?

10. Having read our commitment inventory:

a. Which area of commitment do you feel will be most difficult for you to keep? Why?

b. Describe how comfortable you are with the openness and vulnerability required (being "real and raw" and "intense and intimate" and speaking the truth in love to each other).

11. Discuss your strengths, particularly as they may affect your readiness for LEAD.

12. Discuss your weaknesses, particularly as they may affect your readiness for LEAD.

13. Do you have a model/approach to counseling that you are most comfortable with? If so, please describe it and share how you learned it.

14. What authors, articles, and books have most significantly shaped your views and practice of counseling?

15. In counseling and discipleship, what would you tend to focus upon more, people's suffering or their sin? Why? How?

16. What future ministry do you hope to fulfill as a result of your LEAD equipping?

17. Comment on the encouragement that you have received from family members, church leaders, and significant friends concerning your giftedness for a ministry in biblical counseling and discipleship.

18. A friend comes up to you and says, "I'm about ready to give up on Christianity." Describe how you would interact with your friend.

19. What questions do you have for us?

20. Please list the names and contact information of two people you give us permission to talk to about your preparation for LEAD.

The Redeemed Personality Inventory

Name: _____

    This inventory is based upon your candid assessment of where you currently are in your process toward mature Christlikeness. Evaluate your progress toward growth into the image of Christ using a 10 for "Most like Christ" and a 1 for "Least like Christ."

____ Like Jesus, I increasingly exalt, enjoy, love, and find satisfaction in God more than any other.

____ I increasingly cling to God, running home to Him as my Father, like a faithful son or daughter.

____ I increasingly enjoy Christ more than any other joy in life.

____ I increasingly depend upon the Holy Spirit to sanctify me, make me holy, beautify me, empower and equip me.

____ I increasingly love others deeply and sacrificially from the heart with grace.

____ I increasingly rest confidently in who I am in and to Christ.

____ Like Jesus, I increasingly view life from the Father's eternal, gracious, and good perspective.

____ I increasingly, together with all the saints, grasp the holy love of God.

____ I increasingly allow God's eternal story to invade my earthly story.

____ I increasingly renew my mind and stir up wholesome thinking.

____ Like Jesus, I increasingly die to self and live for God and others.

____ I increasingly trust Christ courageously and take risks to minister to others.

____ I increasingly find my life by dying to myself, taking up my cross, and following Christ.

____ I increasingly live to shepherd and minister to others.

____ I increasingly serve Christ and others out of a pure heart, a good conscience, and a sincere faith.

____ I increasingly develop emotional self-awareness: understanding my moods.

____ I increasingly develop emotional self-mastery: soothing my soul in my Savior.

____ I increasingly develop emotional maturity: managing my moods with a ministry focus.

____ I increasingly develop emotional empathy: recognizing emotions in others.

____ I increasingly develop emotional savvy: handling my relationships well.

Appendix 7.1

Biblical Counseling 4C Equipping Goals

Biblical Counseling 4C Equipping Goals

We commit to implementing best practice local church equipping by following Christ's disciple-making model of intentionally equipping the whole person: the heart (being—Christlike character), the head (knowing—biblical content), and the hands (doing—counseling competence), in the context of God's home (loving—Christian community) (Romans 15:14).

1. Christlike Character: "Full of Goodness"—Heart/Being

Spiritual Goal: Love—Equipped to Be (Enriching the Heart to Manifest Godly Love)

- Christlike love
- Soft heart for godliness: spiritual fruitfulness
- Spiritual formation: spiritual maturity through intimacy with Christ

Since personal maturity is the foundation for powerful spiritual ministry, Christlike disciple-makers must be enriched to be "full of goodness"—to love more like Jesus (*reflecting* Christ).

2. Biblical Content/Conviction: "Complete in Knowledge"— Head/Knowing

Educational Goal: Truth—Equipped to Know (Educating the Head to Apply God's Truth)

- Christlike thinking
- Sharp mind for biblical truth: biblical wisdom
- Spiritual foundation: changing lives with Christ's changeless truth

Since powerful ministry requires biblical wisdom, Christlike disciple-makers must be educated to know and apply God's Word deeply ("complete in knowledge")—to think more like Jesus (*renewed* in Christ).

3. Counseling Competence: "Competent to Instruct One Another"—Hands/Doing

Ministry Goal: Service—Equipped to Do (Empowering the Hands to Serve God's People)

- Christlike ministry
- Serving hands that impact lives: relational skillfulness
- Spiritual friendship: relating God's truth to human relationships

Since relational ministry requires relating Christ's grace to human hurts, Christlike disciple-makers must be empowered to skillfully do ("competent to instruct")—to serve more like Jesus (*reproducing* Christ in others).

4. Christian Community: "Brothers/One Another"— Home/Loving

Relational Goal: Connecting—Equipped to Connect (Encouraging God's House to Become a Home)

- Christlike relationships
- Sensitive home that connects people: biblical community
- Spiritual fellowship: relational maturity through intimacy with Christians

375

Since effective ministry requires Christian community, Christlike disciple-makers must be equipped to encourage the Christian community to meaningfully address the needs of people in the great tradition of soul care and spiritual direction where discipleship, counseling, and Christian community are united ("brothers")—to build community in Jesus (*reconnected* through Christ).

Appendix 10.1

LEAD Biblical Counseling Trainee Assessments

LEAD Year One 4C Assessment

Trainee's Name: _____

Name of Person Completing the Assessment: _____

Assessments of the Trainee by Others

- The Redeemed Personality Inventory and the Biblical Counseling Competency Evaluation Form should be completed in writing by each trainee, by the trainee's encouragement partner, and by the trainee's supervisor/mentor.
- Attach these two assessment forms to this cover sheet, place them in a sealed envelope, and turn them in to _____ by _____ [due date].

Christlike Character: "Full of Goodness"—Heart/Being

- Complete the attached Redeemed Personality Inventory for this trainee [see Appendix 6.1].

Counseling Competence: "Competent to Instruct One Another"—Hands/Doing

- Complete the attached Biblical Counseling Competency Evaluation Form for this trainee.
- The "C" of Counseling Competence is also covered through small group lab verbal feedback.

Trainee Exam Assessment and Self-Assessment

- The LEAD Year One Final Exam and the Personal Spiritual Workout Routine Self-Assessment should be completed in writing by each trainee.
- Attach all four assessment forms to this cover sheet, place them in a sealed envelope, and turn them in to _____ by _____ [due date].

Biblical Content/Conviction: "Complete in Knowledge"—Head/Knowing

- Trainee, complete the attached LEAD Year One Final Exam.

Christian Community: "Brothers/One Another"—Home/Loving

- Trainee, complete the attached Personal Spiritual Workout Routine Self-Assessment.
- The "C" of Christian Community is also covered through small group lab verbal feedback.

LEAD Biblical Counseling Competency Evaluation Form

Trainee's Name: _____

Name of Person Completing the Assessment: _____

Using the scale below, evaluate the trainee in the following biblical counseling competency areas:

1. I disagree strongly
2. I disagree
3. I am not sure
4. I agree
5. I agree strongly

____1. Sustaining: Listens to and senses people's suffering and hurts.

____2. Sustaining: Climbs in the casket with people, empathizing with and embracing their pain, communicating that it's normal to hurt.

____3. Healing: Encourages people to find God in their pain even when they can't find answers.

____4. Healing: Encourages people to see God's perspective on their suffering, helping them to know that it's possible to hope.

____5. Reconciling: Lovingly, humbly, wisely, and courageously exposes areas of sin, helping people to understand that it's horrible to sin.

____6. Reconciling: Shares God's grace, showing people how wonderful it is to be forgiven.

____7. Guiding: Equips and empowers others to grow in grace.

____8. Guiding: Enlightens people to God's supernatural work of maturity.

____9. Love/Compassion: Compassionately identifies with people, engaging them with deep personal involvement and relating to them with Christlike love.

____10. Truth/Discernment: Uses biblical principles to understand the root causes and spiritual dynamics at work in people's lives.

____11. Relational: Helps people to assess their desires—exposing thirst for Christ and false idols of the heart.

____12. Rational: Helps people to assess their images and beliefs—exposing foolish beliefs and helping people to renew their mind in Christ.

____13. Volitional: Helps people to assess the goals and purposes behind their behaviors and relationships—helping them to put off the old self and to put on the new person in Christ.

____14. Emotional: Helps people to assess their moods—assisting people to become more emotionally self-aware and better able to manage their moods with a ministry focus.

____15. Overall: I would recommend this person to others as a competent biblical counselor.

LEAD YEAR ONE FINAL EXAM

Trainee's Name: _____

Short Answer/Essay Questions

- Of the ten questions below, answer any *seven* of your choice. You may use your notes, but this exam seeks to assess how well you have grasped what has been taught—so simply repeating the notes will be insufficient. This is an open-Bible exam.
- Each answer should be approximately one page in length.
- Staple your answers to this cover page.

1. How do the issues of the sufficiency of Scripture, the purpose of Scripture, and the relevancy of Scripture make a difference in how you actually counsel someone?
2. Someone comes to you with the "presenting problem" of feeling lonely and disconnected. How does the nature of God and the doctrine of the Trinity impact the way you help this person?
3. How do Satan and spiritual warfare impact the biblical counseling process?
4. Explain a comprehensive biblical understanding of people as if you were teaching it to a group of high school students.
5. How could you use a biblical model of suffering (biblical sufferology) in a way that would be an encouragement to someone who had just experienced a life loss?
6. Using the case study of Bill from *Spiritual Friends*, how could you help Bill see his relational, rational, volitional, and emotional sin (diagnosing sin biblically)?
7. How does an understanding of our complete salvation (justification, regeneration, reconciliation, and redemption) make a difference in the progressive sanctification process with someone struggling with the besetting sin of lust?
8. What is the role of the church in Christian growth?

9. How does knowing the end of the story impact the way coun-selees handle their current life story?
10. Imagine that you have three to five minutes to explain the sus-taining, healing, reconciling, and guiding model of biblical counseling. How would you do it?

LEAD Personal Spiritual Workout Routine Self-Assessment

Trainee's Name: _____

- Respond to each question below with one to three paragraph answers.
- Staple your answers to this cover page.

1. Summarize your sense of your growth in terms of depth of engagement and involvement with the rest of the LEAD group.

   a. How "real and raw," "intense and intimate," "open and connected" have you been?

   b. In your life, where do you see more room for growth in this area of Christian community/connection?

2. Summarize the horizontal spiritual disciplines (communion with the body of Christ) that you chose as part of your spiritual workout routine.
   a. Which disciplines did you choose and why?

   b. How well and how consistently have you been implementing these disciplines?

   c. What growth are you seeing as a result of your practice of these spiritual disciplines?

3. Summarize the vertical spiritual disciplines (communion with Christ) that you chose as part of your spiritual workout routine.
   a. Which disciplines did you choose and why?

   b. How well and how consistently have you been implementing these disciplines?

   c. What growth are you seeing as a result of your practice of these spiritual disciplines?

LEAD YEAR TWO 4C ASSESSMENT

Trainee's Name: _____

Name of Person Completing the Assessment: _____

Assessments of the Trainee by Others

- The Redeemed Personality Inventory and the Biblical Counseling Evaluation Competency Form should be completed in writing by each trainee, by the trainee's encouragement partner, and by the trainee's supervisor/mentor.
- Attach these two assessment forms to this cover sheet, place them in a sealed envelope, and turn them in to _____ by _____ [due date].

Christlike Character: "Full of Goodness"—Heart/Being

- Complete the attached Redeemed Personality Inventory for this trainee [see Appendix 6.1].

Counseling Competence: "Competent to Instruct One Another"—Hands/Doing

- Complete the attached Biblical Counseling Competency Evaluation Form for this trainee [see above for the same form used at the end of year one].
- The "C" of Counseling Competence is also covered through small group lab verbal feedback.

Trainee Final Exam Assessment Final Research Project

- The LEAD Year Two Final Exam should be completed in writing by each trainee.
- The LEAD Final Research Project should be turned in with your final exam.

- Attach all four assessment forms to this cover sheet, place them in a sealed envelope, and turn them in to _____ by _____ [due date].

Biblical Content/Conviction: "Complete in Knowledge"— Head/Knowing

- Trainee, complete the attached LEAD Year Two Final Exam.
- Trainee, turn in the LEAD Final Research Project per the instructions distributed in class.

Christian Community: "Brothers/One Another"—Home/ Loving

- For year two, the "C" of Christian Community is covered through small group lab verbal feedback.

LEAD YEAR TWO FINAL EXAM

Trainee's Name: _____

Short Answer/Essay Questions

Of the five questions below, answer any *four* of your choice. You may use your notes, but this exam seeks to assess how well you have grasped what has been taught—so simply repeating the notes will be insufficient. This is an open-Bible exam.

Each answer should be approximately one to two pages in length. Staple your answers to this cover page.

1. Summarize your growth as a Christian and as a biblical counselor. How have you grown in the 4Cs of biblical content, Christlike character, counseling competence, and Christian community? In other words, what have you learned, how has it impacted you personally, and how is it helping you as a biblical counselor?

2. Summarize individual counseling. Describe what you think the keys are to sustaining, healing, reconciling, and guiding individuals. This is your chance to review and synthesize individual counseling. Be sure to include core LEAD concepts: grace, truth, the Word, the Trinity, creation, the fall, redemption, consummation, relational, rational, volitional, emotional, physical, sustaining, healing, reconciling, and guiding.

3. Summarize marriage counseling. Describe what you think the keys are to sustaining, healing, reconciling, and guiding couples. This is your chance to review and synthesize marriage counseling. Be sure to include core LEAD concepts related to a theology of marriage and the methodology of marriage counseling.

4. Summarize family/parental counseling. Describe what you think the keys are to sustaining, healing, reconciling, and guiding families/parents. This is your chance to review and synthesize family/parental counseling. Be sure to include core LEAD concepts

related to a theology of family life and the methodology of family/parental counseling.

5. Summarize your "embryonic" model. Assume that you are preparing for an interview for a position in our church as a LEAD trainer. The leadership wants you to submit a summary of your model of biblical counseling and your method of equipping biblical counselors. What would you submit? Throughout your training, you have been encouraged to think what *you* would do differently, how *you* would teach various principles, and what *your views* are on individual, marital, and family counseling. Share *your* model of biblical counseling and equipping biblical counselors.

LEAD Final Research Project

Trainee's Name: _____

Instructions

In our second year of LEAD, we studied biblical teaching about biblical counseling for depression and anxiety. We examined a Creation/Fall/Redemption understanding of each of these mood disorders. We used academic theology, spiritual theology, practical/pastoral theology, and historical theology to develop a theory and methodology for understanding and counseling people struggling with depression or anxiety.

For your final project, you are to follow the process we modeled in class to develop your embryonic understanding of and approach to a counseling issue such as (but not limited to) the following: anger, eating disorder, grief/loss, besetting sin, sexual abuse recovery, and "addictive" behavior.

You should use the Scriptures, as we did in class with anxiety and depression (but use Scriptures pertinent to the issue you are studying), to outline the following:

- Creation/Understanding People: What is God's original design related to this issue? In other words, before the fall, what did healthy functioning look like in this area?
- Fall/Diagnosing Problems: What went wrong? What contributes to this problem relationally (in a spiritual, social, or self-aware manner), rationally, volitionally, emotionally, physically, and circumstantially?
- Redemption: How do people change? What does the Bible teach about how people can overcome this area of suffering and/or overcome this area of besetting sin?
- Interaction/Intervention: What does sustaining, healing, reconciling, and guiding look like for this issue? What is a biblical counseling approach to helping someone who struggles in this area?

Your paper should be eight to twelve pages, double-spaced. Staple your paper to this cover page.

Appendix 10.2

LEAD Sample Lesson Objectives and Lesson Outline

How to Change Lives with Christ's Changeless Truth

Note: This is a three-hour, two-part interactive, introductory lesson. PowerPoint slides with numerous images are used throughout.

Lesson Objectives: Through active participation and engagement in this learning experience, students will be able to:

1. Share God's answers to life's six ultimate questions in order to relate Christ's changeless truth to our changing times.
2. Understand people biblically in order to discover how God designed us to live, love, and relate.
3. Diagnose problems scripturally in order to uncover what went wrong—why we do the things we do.
4. Prescribe God's solutions effectively in order to apply Christ's answers for daily life problems.

How to Change Lives with Christ's Changeless Truth

*Sharing the Story of Our Soul Physicians' Journey—
The Tale of Two Counselors*

1. After listening to "The Tale of Two Counselors," connect with a few partners and interact about the following questions:

   a. Do you tend to be more on the truth/Scripture side or more on the love/soul side? Why?

   b. Has anyone ever interacted with you like either of Tim's counselors? What did it feel like? What were the results?

   c. What view of the Bible and of people helping might have motivated Tim's counselors?

2. What content does a person need to know to be a biblical counselor, pastoral counselor, lay counselor, spiritual friend, soul physician, mentor, discipler, or people helper?

Introduction: Scripture and Soul

- How do we make our counseling truly Christian?
- Knowing how the Bible should shape our counseling can feel like a maze.
- We need to think and care like Christ: counsel with Scripture and soul—1 Thessalonians 2:8.

Overview: Why We Are Here/My Promise to You

Everyone talks about biblical counseling, but how do we make counseling truly biblical?

We are here to learn how to use God's Word accurately, powerfully, and lovingly. We are here to be equipped to become artful soul physicians by developing a Christ-centered, church-based, comprehensive, compassionate, and culturally informed biblical model of counseling that values and applies the sufficiency, supremacy, authority, profundity (profound insight), and relevancy of Scripture to change lives with Christ's changeless truth.

Preview: The Great Soul Physician and the "SPDR"

Addressing Life's Six Ultimate Questions

- The Word: "What is truth?" "Where can I find answers?"
- The Trinity: "Who is God?"
- Creation: "Who am I?"
- Fall: "What went wrong?"
- Redemption: "Can I change?" "How do people change?"
- Glorification: "Where am I headed?"

I. Nourish the Hunger of the Soul: Preventive Medicine—God's Word (Matthew 4:4)

   A. _____ on the Word of God: *Coram Deo Sola Scriptura*—Colossians 2:3–10; 2 Peter 1:3

   B. Make truth and love _____—Ephesians 4:15; Philippians 1:9–10; 1 Thessalonians 2:8

   C. Read the Bible as the _____ of _____ offered, rejected, and fought for: Genesis 1–3

   D. Relate God's truth to human _____ through Trialogues: Matthew 18:20

   E. How does this apply to your relationships? To your ministry?

So what? What difference should nourishing the hungry soul with God's Word make? In how you live and in how you minister, what difference could it make if you:

- Feasted on and helped others feast on God's Word?
- Made truth and love kiss as you ministered to hurting and hardened people?
- Read and shared the Bible as the story of the battle for our hearts?
- Related God's truth to human relationships through trialogues—personally relating truth to life?

II. Know the Creator of the Soul: the Great Physician—the Trinity

   A. Begin before the _____: John 1:1—soul contact

   B. Build your life and ministry on the _____: John 1; John 17

     1. Relate _____ to _____ because God is Trinitarian: John 1:18—Perichoresis

     2. Make spiritual friendships all about _____: John 17

     3. Know the _____ _____ personally to be a soul physician: John 17:20–26

   C. How does this apply to your relationships? To your ministry?

So what? What difference should knowing the Trinitarian Creator of our soul make? In how you live and in how you minister, what difference could it make if you:

- Began before the beginning where God related before He created—soul contact?
- Built your life and ministry on the Trinity—deep connecting?
- Related soul-to-soul because God is Trinitarian?
- Made spiritual friendships all about Him—spreading His fame?
- Knew the Soul Physician personally, not just academically?

III. Understand People: Examine the Spiritual Anatomy of the Soul—Creation
   A. Value the CFR narrative: _____, _____,
      _____

     1. Creation: understand _____—examine the spiritual anatomy of the soul
     2. Fall: diagnose _____—diagnose the fallen condition of the soul
     3. Redemption: prescribe God's _____—dispense God's cure for the soul
   B. Pursue God's _____—the image of God—God's design of the soul

Our inner life increasingly reflecting the inner life of _____!

     1. We are relational: designed to love _____—
     Matthew 22:35–40
      a. We are _____: designed for relationship with God—worship
      b. We are _____: designed for relationships with one another—ministry
     2. We are rational: designed to think _____—
     Romans 12:1–2 (spiritual eyes)
     3. We are volitional: designed to choose _____
     —Joshua 24:15
     4. We are emotional: designed to feel _____—
     1 Thessalonians 4:13
     5. We are physical: designed to live _____—
     Genesis 2:7; Romans 6:12–13
   C. How does this apply to your relationships? To your ministry?

So what? What difference should understanding the spiritual anatomy of the soul make? What would be *missing* in our ministry to one another if we omitted the following:

- The relational/spiritual affections—our longing for communion with God?
- The relational social affections—our longing for connection with one another?
- The relational/self-aware affections—our longing for personal peace and wholeness?
- The thinking/mindsets—our beliefs?
- The choosing/pathways/purposes—our behaviors and choices?
- The feeling/mood states—our emotions?
- The physical body—our complex mind/body connection?

IV. Diagnose Problems: Diagnose the Fallen Condition of the Soul—
   The Fall

The Grand Canyon: "This ain't the way it's supposed to be!"

A. We must _____ reality or we make ourselves irrelevant: Genesis 3:1–24

The fall is the only explanation for _____ and _____

B. We must diagnose suffering _____ and
   _____

C. We must diagnose sin biblically
   1. Diagnose sin _____: our descent into the abyss of sin—Ephesians 4:17–24
   2. Diagnose sin _____: why we do what we do—James 4
      The sin in our _____ (human relationships) is always ultimately due to the sin in our _____ (relationship with God)
   3. Diagnose sin _____: Jeremiah 2:1–5, 13, 19, 20
      The sin in our heart is always due to _____ God (relational—spiritual adultery) because we have lost our _____ of God (rational—foolish thinking), and

_____ (volitional—selfish motivation) to love
   false gods (god-substitutes)
D. How does this apply to your relationships? To your ministry?

So what? What difference should diagnosing the fallen condition of the soul make? In how you live and in how you minister, what difference could it make if you:

- Faced the reality that "this ain't the way it's supposed to be"?
- Diagnosed suffering biblically and compassionately?
- Had a biblical theology of suffering—understanding that our world is fallen and it often falls on us?
- Had a model of God's healing for life's losses?
- Diagnosed sin comprehensively—our relating to God/others, thinking, choosing, and feeling?
- Diagnosed sin spiritually—the sin in our heart?

V. Prescribe God's solution: dispense God's cure for the soul—redemption
   A. Grasp the big _____: the Bible is _____, not _____
   B. Apply our complete _____ to our daily lives and relationships: Romans 5–15
      1. _____: new pardon/not guilty—Judge
      2. _____: new peace/family—Father
      3. _____: new person/purity—Creator
      4. _____: new power/victory—Champion
      - *Coram Deo Sola Gratia*: Face-to-face with God by
         _____ _____
      - Dispense _____!
   C. How does this apply to your relationships? To your ministry?

So what? What difference should prescribing God's cure for the soul make? In how you live and in how you minister, what difference could it make if you:

- Grasped the big picture that the Bible is comedy, not tragedy?
- Applied justification: our new pardon/forgiveness?
- Applied reconciliation: our new peace/family/new nurture?
- Applied regeneration: our new person/purity/heart/new nature?
- Applied redemption: our new power/victory?

VI. Envision the final healing of the soul: home—glorification
   A. Live today in light of _____: Revelation 21–22
      How does our future destiny impact our present _____?: Romans 8:17–18
   B. Read the end of the _____
   C. How does this apply to your relationships? To your ministry?

So what? What difference should envisioning the final healing of the soul make? In how you live and in how you minister, what difference could it make if you:

- Lived today in light of eternity?
- Saw your present suffering in light of your future glory?
- Allowed your future destiny to impact your present reality?
- Read the end of the story?

Conclusion: Scripture and Soul for Life and Ministry

1. Of everything we covered in this lesson, what one or two points do you most want to start applying to your *life*? Why? How will you begin doing that?

2. Of everything we covered in this lesson, what one or two points do you most want to start applying to your *ministry*? Why? How will you begin doing that?

Appendix 11.1

LEAD Ministry Policy and Procedure Manual

LEAD Biblical Counseling Ministry

L	Life
E	Encouragers
A	And
D	Disciplers

POLICY AND PROCEDURE MANUAL

*Changed People Changing Lives with
Christ's Changeless Truth*

"Speaking the truth in love" (Ephesians 4:15)
"Encourage one another daily" (Hebrews 3:13)

LEAD Biblical Counseling Ministry Intake Procedures

Preliminary Matters

1. The LEAD AA and Pastor Kellemen meet every Monday morning to review:
   a. Pastor Kellemen's pastoral counseling schedule.
   b. LEADers' biblical counseling schedules.
   c. Biblical counseling intakes.
   d. The biblical counseling waiting list.

2. We will determine on a weekly basis whether or not we can take new counselees. If Pastor Kellemen, other staff pastors, and all LEADers are booked, then individuals will be referred to the appropriate outside resource persons.

Intake Procedures

1. When a call for biblical counseling is transferred to our office, the LEAD AA will complete the Biblical Counseling Initial Intake Form and:
   a. Record all information.
   b. Explain the type of ministry we offer: lay biblical counseling through biblical encouragement and discipleship.
   c. Gain a brief summary of the reason for the call. Some callers will prefer not to summarize the issue with an AA. Be gracious, but firm. Assure them of confidentiality (within the limits of our confidentiality policy).
   d. Determine whether they desire ongoing meetings or one appointment.
   e. If there appears to be a "crisis" need, immediately contact Pastor Kellemen or the on-call pastor.

2. The LEAD AA plays a vital role in assessing the nature and urgency of the call and caller. He or she must determine what help is needed and being requested. If there are any questions, the LEAD AA will contact Pastor Kellemen or the on-call pastor immediately.

Referral Procedures

1. For a caller who wants one immediate (non-crisis) meeting:
   a. Complete the Initial Intake Form.
   b. Ask if there is a specific pastor the person would like to speak to. If not, go to point c.

c. Select the next available pastor on the pastoral rotation schedule. Tell the caller that this pastor will call within 24 hours.

d. Contact that pastor and give him a copy of the Initial Intake Form. Request that he contact the caller.

e. Within 24 hours, double-check with that pastor. Then give a copy of the Initial Intake Form to Pastor Kellemen.

2. For a caller who wants ongoing biblical counseling:

a. Referral options include referral to Pastor Kellemen, to another pastor, to a LEADer, or to an outside agency.

b. Therefore, do not promise that a certain person will see the caller. Pastor Kellemen will determine this.

c. Have the caller complete the Initial Intake Form, and explain that he or she will need to come in for an initial ninety-minute meeting—forty-five minutes to complete necessary forms and forty minutes to meet with Pastor Kellemen so he can appropriately assign the person.

d. Arrange the appointment based upon Pastor Kellemen's schedule.

e. Inform Pastor Kellemen of the appointment.

f. Explain and have the caller complete the following forms:
   (1) LEAD Biblical Counseling Ministry Personal Information Form
   (2) LEAD Biblical Counseling Ministry Goals Form
   (3) LEAD Biblical Counseling Ministry Consent Form
   (4) LEAD Biblical Counseling Ministry Welcome Sheet
   (5) LEAD Biblical Counseling Ministry Permission to Record and Review Form

g. Pass the forms to Pastor Kellemen, who will review them and meet with the person to make an appropriate assignment.

LEAD Biblical Counseling Ministry Initial Intake Form*

Personal Information

Name: _____

Date: _____ Time: _____

Address: _____

_____

Home Phone: _____

Cell Phone: _____

E-mail: _____

Age: _____ Gender: _____

Church Membership/Attending: _____

Work Schedule: _____

Work Phone: _____

Marital Status: _____ Referred by: _____

Open to Lay Encouragement and Discipleship with a Biblical Counselor:
_____ Yes _____ No

Brief Summary of Why the Person Desires Biblical Counseling

Personnel Assignment

_____ 1. Referred to _____
    because/for: _____

    _____.

_____ 2. Scheduled with _____ for one
    immediate meeting on _____.

_____ 3. Appointment scheduled to complete forms and have initial
    meeting with _____ on _____

    _____.

Homework Assignment

Use the back of this sheet to provide a brief description of the assignment given to the caller to complete before the first meeting.

* Developed from materials in Robert Kellemen, *Spiritual Friends: A Methodology of Soul Care and Spiritual Direction* (Winona Lake, IN: BMH Books, 2007), 67.

LEAD Biblical Counseling Ministry Guidelines

1. LEAD biblical counselors are not permitted to accept assignments from anyone except Pastor Kellemen.
2. No meeting records (notes, test results, or tapes) are to be taken out of the church building. All records are to be kept in locked files maintained by the LEAD Administrative Assistant (AA).
3. All biblical counseling meetings are to be conducted at the church in rooms reserved in advance through the LEAD AA.
4. Biblical counseling meetings should normally last no more than 50 to 60 minutes.
5. All people assigned to LEADers should complete the Personal Information Form and sign all release forms prior to the beginning of the first meeting. These should be kept in the person's files in the LEAD office.
6. Following each meeting, the LEADer should immediately complete the Biblical Counseling Record Sheet and include it in the file before leaving the office.
7. When an assignment is made, the LEAD Biblical Counseling Ministry Department is responsible for contacting the person and arranging the first appointment. If the person fails to make an appointment, fails to reschedule, or decides to terminate, the LEADer should attempt to initiate at least one follow-up session with the person to clarify the reasons for the decision.
8. A LEADer may or may not give out his/her home phone number to the disciplee. If in doubt, discuss this with Pastor Kellemen.
9. Under no circumstances should the LEADer discuss biblical counseling meetings with anyone except Pastor Kellemen.
10. The LEADer should plan to audio record all meetings. Tapes are to be listened to only by the LEADer and the supervisor. They are to be protected with the utmost confidentiality. They are to be kept in the LEAD office files.

11. During the commencement meeting, the person should complete the LEAD Biblical Counseling Evaluation Form and discuss it with the LEADer. The LEADer should complete the Biblical Counseling Commencement Summary.
12. In case of a crisis situation, immediately contact Pastor Kellemen or the on-call pastor.

LEAD Biblical Counseling Ministry "Welcome!"*

We welcome you to the LEAD Biblical Counseling Ministry of
_____ Church. We desire to be used by God to "speak His
truth in love." We know that the path to maturity is often steep and rough
and at times filled with pain and confusion. However, there are answers.
We believe that the Bible is *God's all-sufficient guide for relational living*.
There is a route to life. Our Lord is that *way*. Christ is the *truth* who frees
us to love. He is the *life* who satisfies the deepest thirsts of our soul.

Ministries Offered

As a *ministry* of _____ Church, our services are *free*. As a
discipleship ministry of a *local church*, we offer to you:

- Individual biblical counseling regarding spiritual and personal issues.
- Pre-marital biblical counseling.
- Marital biblical counseling.
- Family/parental biblical counseling: with children under the age
  of thirteen we work primarily with the parents and/or with the
  parents and children.
- Adolescent biblical counseling: with parental consent and involvement.
- Small group discipleship: see our brochure on our various groups.
- A referral network.

Confidentiality

Confidentiality is an important aspect of the biblical counseling relationship, and we will carefully guard the information you entrust to us.
All communications between you and our LEAD Biblical Counseling
Ministry offices will be held in strict confidence, unless you (or a parent
in the case of a minor) give authorization to release this information.
The exceptions to this would be: (1) if a person expresses intent to harm
himself/herself or someone else; (2) if there is evidence or reasonable
suspicion of abuse against a minor child, elder person, or dependent
adult; (3) if a subpoena or other court order is received directing the
disclosure of information; (4) if/when LEAD biblical counselors consult
with their supervision; or (5) if a person persistently refuses to renounce
a particular sin (habitual unrepentant rebellion against the Word of God)
and it becomes necessary to seek the assistance of others in the church to

* Developed from materials in *Spiritual Friends*, 174–75.

encourage repentance, restoration, and reconciliation (see Matt. 18:15–20 and our *Church Discipline Policy*). Please be assured that our counselors strongly prefer not to disclose personal information to others, and that they will make every effort to help you find ways to resolve a problem as privately as possible.

Appointments

Our biblical counselors work by scheduled appointments. Of course, in emergencies, exceptions are made. We need your prompt and consistent participation in your scheduled meetings. Please contact our office 24 hours in advance if you must cancel an appointment. This will allow us to schedule another individual during this time.

Arriving forty-five minutes early for your first appointment will allow you to complete all necessary forms. During your initial meeting, you will determine the goals you would like to work toward. After five sessions, you and your biblical counselor will evaluate your progress toward those goals and together determine what further action needs to be taken.

Our Commitments to You in Biblical Counseling

You have read our term "biblical counseling." We would like to explain what we mean by it. Biblical counselors are spiritual friends who commit to the historic roles of *soul care* and *spiritual direction* through:

- *Sustaining:* Empathizing with your suffering, helping you to understand that *"It's normal to hurt."*
- *Healing:* Encouraging you to see life from a biblical perspective, helping you to know that *"It's possible to hope."*
- *Reconciling:* Examining and exposing your current responses to life and suggesting new ways of handling problems, helping you to see that *"It's horrible to sin, but wonderful to be forgiven."*
- *Guiding:* Exploring how and empowering you to mature through Christ, helping you to grasp that *"It's supernatural to mature."*

Because we care about *you*, our desire is for you to be drawn closer to Christ and to become more like Christ, which we see as *your inner life increasingly reflecting the inner life of Christ*.

- *Relational Maturity:* Loving God wholeheartedly and loving others sacrificially.

- *Rational Maturity:* Wisely living according to the truth of Christ's gospel of grace.
- *Volitional Maturity:* Courageously choosing to pursue God's purposes in your life through the Spirit's power.
- *Emotional Maturity:* Deeply and honestly experiencing life with integrity, fully open to God while managing your moods for God's glory and with a ministry focus.

Your Commitments to Christ, to Yourself, and to Us in Biblical Counseling

We ask that you commit to:

- Sharing your hurts and struggles honestly and openly.
- Evaluating your own emotions, actions, motivations, beliefs, and relationships.
- Actively participating in the growth of renewed emotions, actions, convictions, and affections.
- Coming to each meeting prepared to review your progress throughout the last week (including the completion of personalized "homework" assignments) and prepared to share your goals for the present meeting.

Because the Scriptures teach that growth in Christ requires all the resources of the body of Christ (not only biblical counseling, but also discipleship, worship, fellowship, stewardship, and ambassadorship), we believe that it is essential that those seeking biblical counseling at our church commit themselves to the following:

- Regular church attendance (at your church or our church)
- Active participation in Adult Bible Fellowship/Sunday school
- Participation in at least one small group (we'll discuss the appropriate group for you)

We ask that you sign below to indicate your understanding of, agreement with, and commitment to our Biblical Counseling Ministry focus as described on these three pages.

_____   _____
(Signature)   (Date)

_____   _____
(Parent if Minor)   (Date)

LEAD Biblical Counseling Ministry Consent Form

I have been informed that the spiritual care I will be receiving from
_____ at _____
  (Name of Biblical Counselor)   (Name of Church)
is Christian and biblical in nature. I have also been informed that
_____ is an encourager and discipler trained at
(Name of Biblical Counselor)
_____ as a biblical counselor and spiritual friend
      (Name of Church)
in the church's LEAD (Life Encourager And Discipler) Biblical
Counseling Ministry. Under supervision from one of the LEAD trainers,
_____ offers to provide biblical encouragement
  (Name of Biblical Counselor)
and discipleship on personal and relational matters from a spiritual perspective guided by biblical principles. He/she is *not* trained,
authorized, or licensed to provide professional counseling, psychological treatment, or psychological diagnosis. I understand that if
and when I desire and request professional counseling, then I will
be encouraged to seek such outside assistance. I give my consent to
_____ to discuss any and all of the
      (Name of Biblical Counselor)
information that I talk about in our meetings with his/her supervisor(s) in
the LEAD Biblical Counseling Ministry.

_____   _____
          (Signature)   (Date)

LEAD Biblical Counseling Ministry Consent to Minister to a Minor Child

I have been informed that the spiritual care that my child
_____will be receiving from _____
      (Name of Child)   (Name of Biblical Counselor)
at _____ is Christian and biblical in nature.
           (Name of Church)
I have also been informed that_____
                              (Name of Biblical Counselor)
is an encourager and discipler trained at _____
                                 (Name of Church)
as a biblical counselor and spiritual friend in the church's LEAD (Life Encourager And Discipler) Biblical Counseling Ministry. Under supervision from one of the LEAD trainers, _____ offers to provide biblical encouragement
(Name of Biblical Counselor)
and discipleship on personal and relational matters from a spiritual perspective guided by biblical principles. He/she is *not* trained, authorized, or licensed to provide professional counseling, psychological treatment, or psychological diagnosis. I understand that if and when I desire and request professional counseling for my child, then I will be encouraged to seek such outside assistance for my child. I give my consent to _____ to discuss any and all of the information
      (Name of Biblical Counselor)
that my child talks about in his/her meetings with his/her supervisor(s) in the LEAD Biblical Counseling Ministry.

_____   _____
       (Name of Child)   (Age of Child)

_____   _____
       (Signature)   (Date)

LEAD Biblical Counseling Ministry Goals Form*

Name: _____   Date: _____

1. How did you get the idea of coming for biblical counseling meetings? When did you get the idea? Why now?

2. How will you know that your biblical counseling meetings have been helpful? How will you know that you no longer need to meet?

3. Suppose that one night while you were asleep, this problem was solved. How would you know?

4. What will be different in your life when your biblical counseling meetings are successful?

5. Have you had other situations similar to this? What have you learned from these situations that might be helpful to you now?

6. What are things like when you are not having this problem? What are you doing differently when you do not have this problem?

7. How will you and God keep these times of victory going?

* Developed from materials in *Spiritual Friends*, 68.

APPENDIX 11.1

LEAD Biblical Counseling Ministry Personal Information Form*

Identification Information

Name: _____

Home Phone: _____ Cell: _____

Address: _____

_____

E-mail: _____

Birth Date: _____ Gender: _____

Education in Years: _____ Occupation: _____

Work Phone: _____

Marital Status: ____ Single ____ Married ____ Separated
                ____ Divorced ____ Widowed ____ Engaged

Referred Here By: _____

Reason for Seeking Biblical Counseling

Why do you desire to meet with a biblical counselor? _____

_____

_____

_____

How long has this issue existed? _____

_____

Were there any significant events occurring in your life/family's life when this issue began?_____

_____

_____

_____

* Developed from materials in *Spiritual Friends*, 69–72.

What have you done about this issue? _____

_____

_____

_____

How would things be different for you if the issue were remedied? _____

_____

_____

What results are you expecting in coming here for biblical counseling?

_____

_____

_____

Marriage and Family Information

Spouse's Name: _____

Home Phone: _____ Cell: _____

Spouse's Address: _____

_____

Spouse's E-mail: _____

Birth Date: _____ Gender: _____

Spouse's Education in Years: _____ Occupation: _____

Work Phone: _____

Date of Marriage: _____

Age When Married: Husband: _____ Wife: _____

Is your spouse willing to come for counseling? Yes: _____ No: _____

Uncertain: _____

Give brief information about any previous marriages: _____

_____

_____

Information about Children

PM*	Name	Age	Sex	Education (Grade)	Marital Status

*Check this column if child is by previous marriage.

What type of instruction in Christian living is given in your home and by whom? _____

Who disciplines in your home? _____

For what behaviors are your children disciplined? _____

What methods of discipline are currently being used? _____

How do you and your family members communicate that you love each other? _____

How much time do you spend with your family members each week?
Spouse: _____
Children: _____

Personality Data

Circle any of the following words that best describe you now:

Active	Shy	Hardworking	Leader	Compulsive
Nervous	Likable	Impulsive	Follower	Excitable
Impatient	Self-conscious	Often-blue	Sarcastic	Serious
Moody	Jealous	Calm	Self-confident	Easy-going
Imaginative	Ambitious	Good-natured	Persistent	Quiet
Introverted	Extroverted	Fearful	Loner	Stubborn

Others: _____

Complete the following sentences:

People who know me think that I am: _____
_____

If they knew the "real me," they would know that I am: _____
_____

What I desire more than anything else in life is: _____
_____

What I fear most in life is: _____
_____

The person I admire most in life is: _____
_____

Because: _____
_____

Is there any other information that you would like us to know? _____
_____
_____
_____
_____

APPENDIX 11.1

Health Information

Rate your health: Very Good: ___ Good: ___ Average: ___ Poor: ___
Weight changes recently: None: ___ Lost: ___ Gained: ___
List all important present or past illnesses, injuries, or disabilities: _____
_____
_____
_____
_____

Date of last medical exam: _____
Report: _____
_____
Physician's name: _____ Address: _____
_____
Are you presently taking medication? Yes: ___ No: ___
Type: _____
_____
_____

Have you used drugs for other than medical purposes? Yes: ___ No: ___
If yes, explain: _____
_____
Have you ever had any counseling before? Yes: ___ No: ___
When: _____
For: _____
Are you willing to sign a release so that your counselor may write for medical or counseling reports? Yes: ___ No: ___

Religious Background

What church do you attend? _____
_____
How often do you attend church? _____
Are you saved? Yes: ___ No: ___ Not sure what you mean: ___
What ministries/activities are you involved in at church? _____
_____
How often do you read the Bible? _____
Describe your prayer life: _____
Describe your relationship with Christ: _____

LEAD Biblical Counseling Ministry Permission to Record and Review Form

I give my permission for _____ to

(Name of Lay Biblical Counselor)

audio/video record any and all of our biblical counseling meetings and to review these recordings with his/her supervisor and fellow trainees in the LEAD Biblical Counseling Ministry. I understand that these recordings will be used only for evaluation and training purposes. I understand that they will be destroyed when they are no longer needed for these purposes or when I cease meeting with my biblical counselor (whichever comes first).

_____   _____
                (Signature)   (Date)

Authorization for Release of Information*

To:
Pastor Robert W. Kellemen, Ph.D., LCPC
_____ Church
Address: _____
_____
Church Phone: _____ Cell Phone: _____
E-mail: _____

From:
Name/Address of Facility/Counselor: Counselee's Address at Time of
                                        Service:

_____   _____

_____   _____

_____   _____

_____   _____

Re:
Name: _____
DOB: _____   SS #: _____

This signed release authorizes you to furnish Pastor Robert W. Kellemen
the following: _____
_____
_____

Please forward the requested information to Pastor Kellemen at the address
listed above. It is understood that this is confidential information and that it will
not be released without the written permission of the counselee or guardian.

I understand that I may revoke this authorization, except for the action
already taken, at any time. Expiration date, event, or condition after which
consent is no longer valid:

_____   _____
(Signature of Counselee or Guardian)   (Date)

_____
                        (Witness)

* Developed from materials in *Spiritual Friends*, 73.

414

Authorization to Release Information*

From:

Pastor Robert W. Kellemen, Ph.D., LCPC

_____ Church

Address: _____

_____

Church Phone: _____

Cell Phone: _____

E-mail: _____

To:

Name/Address of Facility/Counselor: Counselee's Address at Time of Service:

_____   _____

_____   _____

_____   _____

_____   _____

Re:

Name: _____

DOB: _____   SS #: _____

This signed release authorizes Pastor Robert W. Kellemen to furnish the following: _____

_____

_____

The requested information will be forwarded to the address listed above. It is understood that this is confidential information and that it will not be released without the written permission of the counselee or guardian.

I understand that I may revoke this authorization, except for the action already taken, at any time. Expiration date, event, or condition after which consent is no longer valid:

_____   _____

(Signature of Counselee or Guardian)   (Date)

_____

(Witness)

* Developed from materials in *Spiritual Friends*, 74.

LEAD BIBLICAL COUNSELING RECORD SHEET*

Counselee's Name: _____

Session Number: _____ Date: _____

Pre-Meeting Information

Counselee's Review/Update/Report:
Your Review/Summary:
Counselee's Goals:
Your Goals/Focus:

Biblical Counseling Meeting Notes

Biblical Counseling Post-Session Homework Assignment(s)

Next Meeting Date and Time: _____

* Developed from materials in *Spiritual Friends*, 176–77.

Biblical Counseling Post-Meeting Assessment and Planning

- Sustaining: "It's Normal to Hurt."
  - Biblical Assessment: I discerned . . .
  - Biblical Planning: We need to work on . . .
- Healing: "It's Possible to Hope."
  - Biblical Assessment: I discerned . . .
  - Biblical Planning: We need to work on . . .
- Reconciling: "It's Horrible to Sin, but Wonderful to Be Forgiven."
  - Biblical Assessment: I discerned . . .
  - Biblical Planning: We need to work on . . .
- Guiding: "It's Supernatural to Mature."
  - Biblical Assessment: I discerned . . .
  - Biblical Planning: We need to work on . . .
- Relationally: Affections—Spiritual, Social, Self-Aware
  - Biblical Assessment: I discerned . . .
  - Biblical Planning: We need to work on . . .
- Rationally: Mindsets—Images, Beliefs
  - Biblical Assessment: I discerned . . .
  - Biblical Planning: We need to work on . . .
- Volitionally: Purposes/Pathways—Goals, Motivations, Actions
  - Biblical Assessment: I discerned . . .
  - Biblical Planning: We need to work on . . .
- Emotionally: Singers, Mood States—Awareness, Management
  - Biblical Assessment: I discerned . . .
  - Biblical Planning: We need to work on . . .

LEAD Biblical Counseling Tape Self-Evaluation*

LEAD Tape Self-Evaluation Part I: Interaction Log

1. Record the number of times your interactions focused upon:

   a. Sustaining: *"It's normal to hurt."*   _____

   b. Healing: *"It's possible to hope."*   _____

   c. Reconciling:

      (1) Part A: *"It's horrible to sin."*   _____

      (2) Part B: *"It's wonderful to be forgiven."* _____

   d. Guiding: *"It's supernatural to mature."* _____

2. Record the number of times your interactions focused upon:

   a. Creation: God's Design   _____

   b. Fall: Person's Depravity   _____

   c. Redemption: Renewed Dignity   _____

3. Record the number of times your interactions focused upon:

   a. Relational Longings (Affections):

      (1) Spiritual   _____

      (2) Social   _____

      (3) Self-Aware   _____

* Developed from materials in *Spiritual Friends*, 178–79.

b. Rational Concepts (Mindsets):

    (1) Images   _____

    (2) Beliefs   _____

c. Volitional Choices (Purposes/Pathways):

    (1) Goals   _____

    (2) Actions   _____

d. Emotional Responses (Mood States):   _____

e. Physical Issues (Habituated Tendencies):   _____

LEAD Tape Self-Evaluation Part II: Personal Assessment

Using the scale below, evaluate yourself in the following biblical counseling areas:

1. I disagree strongly
2. I disagree
3. I'm not sure
4. I agree
5. I agree strongly

____1. Sustaining: I listened to and sensed my spiritual friend's hurts.

____2. Sustaining: I climbed in the casket with my spiritual friend, empathizing with and embracing my spiritual friend's pain.

____3. Healing: I encouraged my spiritual friend to embrace God.

____4. Healing: I trialogued (spiritual conversations and scriptural explorations) with my spiritual friend, encouraging him/her to see God's perspective on his/her suffering.

____5. Reconciling: I exposed the horrors of my spiritual friend's sin.

____6. Reconciling: I shared God's grace, showing how wonderful it is to be forgiven.

____7. Guiding: I enlightened my spiritual friend to God's supernatural work of maturity.

____8. Guiding: I equipped and empowered my spiritual friend to grow in grace.

____9. Relational: I effectively used the concept of "affections" to assess and expose the relational motivations in my spiritual friend's soul.

____10. Rational: I effectively used the concept of "mindsets" to assess and expose the rational direction (images and beliefs) in my spiritual friend's heart.

____11. Volitional: I effectively used the concept of "purposes/pathways" to assess and expose the volitional interactions (styles of relating, goals, purposeful behaviors) in my spiritual friend's will.

____12. Emotional: I effectively used the concept of "mood states" to assess and expose the emotional reactions in my spiritual friend's moods.

____13. Truth/Discernment: I used theological insight to understand the spiritual dynamics and root causes related to my spiritual friend's actions and motivations.

____14. Love/Compassion: I compassionately identified with my spiritual friend—I was engaged, was involved, and related from my soul.

____15. Overall: I would go to myself for biblical counseling/spiritual friendship.

LEAD Individual Biblical Counseling Evaluation*

As biblical counselors, we desire to grow in our ability to speak God's truth in love. Your honest feedback is very helpful to us. Please evaluate your biblical counselor based upon the following scale:

1. I disagree strongly
2. I disagree
3. I'm not sure
4. I agree
5. I agree strongly

___1. My biblical counselor listened to and sensed my hurts.

___2. My biblical counselor empathized with and embraced my pain.

___3. My biblical counselor encouraged me to embrace God in my pain.

___4. My biblical counselor encouraged me to see God's perspective on my suffering.

___5. My biblical counselor lovingly, courageously, and humbly exposed areas of sin in my heart.

___6. My biblical counselor helped me to see the wonders of God's grace so I could experience God's forgiveness.

___7. My biblical counselor helped me to see that I can mature only through Christ's resurrection power.

___8. My biblical counselor equipped and empowered me to love like Christ.

___9. My biblical counselor helped me to assess the longings of my soul, exposing the false idols of my heart as well as my soul's thirst for Christ.

___10. My biblical counselor helped me to assess beliefs, which exposed foolish beliefs and helped me to renew my mind in Christ.

___11. My biblical counselor helped me assess the motivations behind my behaviors, which helped me put off the old self and put on the new person in Christ.

___12. My biblical counselor helped me assess my moods, which assisted me to become more emotionally self-aware and better able to manage my moods.

___13. My biblical counselor used biblical principles to understand the spiritual dynamics and root causes at work in my life.

* Developed from materials in *Spiritual Friends*, 180.

___14. My biblical counselor compassionately identified with me, engaging me with deep personal involvement and relating to me with Christlike love.

___15. The goals that we set for biblical counseling were successfully met.

___16. Because of our biblical counseling relationship, I love Christ more.

___17. Because of our biblical counseling relationship, I love other people more.

___18. Because of our biblical counseling relationship, I more readily accept my identity in Christ.

___19. I would go to my biblical counselor again for biblical counseling.

___20. I would recommend my biblical counselor to others for biblical counseling.

Please use the back to share any additional suggestions, thoughts, questions, or comments.

Your Name: _____

Biblical Counselor's Name: _____

LEAD Marital Biblical Counseling Evaluation

As biblical counselors, we desire to grow in our ability to speak God's truth in love. Your honest feedback is very helpful to us. Please evaluate your biblical counselor based upon the following scale:

1. Poor
2. Fair
3. Good
4. Superior
5. Excellent

___1. Our biblical counselor helped us clarify the key issues we needed to face and work on in our marriage.

___2. The goals that we set for biblical marriage counseling were successfully met.

___3. Our biblical counselor spoke the truth (God's Word) in love (in a caring manner).

___4. Our biblical counselor empathized (related to, accepted) with our hurt and pain.

___5. Our biblical counselor encouraged us to see our relationship from God's perspective, giving us hope.

___6. Our biblical counselor helped us see where sinful/selfish issues in our hearts led to issues in our relationship.

___7. Our biblical counselor helped us grant forgiveness to each other and reconcile with each other.

___8. Our counselor helped us examine our marital relationship and apply biblical principles for facing problems in our marriage.

___9. Our counselor helped us to understand better and meet each other's God-created desires and biblical marital expectations.

___10. Our counselor helped us to understand better and implement the biblical roles of husband and wife.

___11. Our biblical counselor helped us to see how our deepest thirsts are quenched in Christ (and not in each other).

___12. As a result of our biblical counseling relationship, we love our Lord more.

___13. As a result of our biblical counseling relationship, we love each other more.

___14. As a result of our biblical counseling relationship, we love others more.

____15. We would recommend our biblical counselor to others.

Please share any additional suggestions, thoughts, questions, or comments.

Your Names: _____

Biblical Counselor's Name: _____

LEAD Family Biblical Counseling Evaluation

As biblical counselors, we desire to grow in our ability to speak God's truth in love. Your honest feedback is very helpful to us. Please evaluate your biblical counselor based upon the following scale:

1. Poor
2. Fair
3. Good
4. Superior
5. Excellent

___ 1. Our biblical counselor helped us clarify the key issues we needed to face and work on in our family.

___ 2. The goals that we set for biblical family counseling were successfully met.

___ 3. Our biblical counselor spoke the truth (God's Word) in love (in a caring manner).

___ 4. Our biblical counselor empathized (related to, accepted) with our hurt and pain.

___ 5. Our biblical counselor encouraged us to see our family relationship from God's perspective, giving us hope.

___ 6. Our biblical counselor helped us see where sinful/selfish issues in our hearts led to issues in our family relationship.

___ 7. Our biblical counselor helped us grant forgiveness to each other and reconcile with each other.

___ 8. Our biblical counselor helped us examine our family relationship and apply biblical principles for facing problems in our family.

___ 9. Our biblical counselor helped us to understand better and meet each other's God-created longings and family expectations.

___ 10. Our counselor helped us to understand better and implement the biblical roles of parents and children.

___ 11. Our biblical counselor helped us understand how our deepest thirsts are quenched in Christ (and not in each other).

___ 12. As a result of our biblical counseling relationship, we love God more.

___ 13. As a result of our biblical counseling relationship, we love each other more.

___ 14. As a result of our biblical counseling relationship, our family loves others more.

___ 15. We would recommend our biblical counselor to others.

Please share any additional suggestions, thoughts, questions, or comments.

Your Names: _____

Biblical Counselor's Name: _____

LEAD Biblical Counseling Commencement Summary*

Counselee's name: _____

Date first seen: _____ Date last seen: _____

Today's date: _____ Your name: _____

Summary of initial issue(s), major goal(s), biblical assessment, and biblical plans

Summary of growth/maturity resulting from biblical counseling meetings

Insight concerning any unresolved areas and suggestions for growth

Reason(s) for commencement:

* Developed from materials in *Spiritual Friends*, 339.

Appendix 11.2

LEAD Biblical Counseling Ministry Evaluation Form

The LEAD Biblical Counseling Ministry Evaluation Form

Name: _____

Date: _____

In the LEAD ministry we are committed to being as effective as possible in equipping encouragers and disciplers for biblical counseling and small group leadership. You have been evaluated throughout the training process. Now it is your turn to evaluate your trainers. We appreciate your candid evaluations so that we can improve our LEAD equipping ministry and grow personally.

Section One: 4C Ratings

- Please rate your LEAD equipping in the following areas using the following scale.

    0 = Not Applicable   1 = Poor   2 = Fair
    3 = Average   4 = Good   5 = Excellent

- Please circle your rating.
- Please include comments with each rating. Use the back side if you need more space.

Category	Rating	Comments
1. Character: Contribution of LEAD toward my growth in Christlikeness	0 1 2 3 4 5	_____
2. Content: Contribution of LEAD toward my biblical and theological understanding	0 1 2 3 4 5	_____
3. Content: Contribution of LEAD toward my biblical counseling and discipleship insight	0 1 2 3 4 5	_____
4. Competency: Contribution of LEAD toward my biblical counseling relational competencies	0 1 2 3 4 5	_____

5. Community:
Contribution of
LEAD toward my
development of
deep connection
with Christ and
the body of Christ

0 1 2 3 4 5

_____
_____
_____
_____
_____
_____

6. My LEAD trainers'
evidence of
Christlike
character

0 1 2 3 4 5

_____
_____
_____
_____
_____
_____

7. My LEAD trainers'
mastery of biblical
content

0 1 2 3 4 5

_____
_____
_____
_____
_____
_____

8. My LEAD trainers'
mastery of coun-
seling competency

0 1 2 3 4 5

_____
_____
_____
_____
_____
_____

9. My LEAD trainers'   0 1 2 3 4 5
   practice of Chris-
   tian community

   _____
   _____
   _____
   _____
   _____
   _____

10. My confidence   0 1 2 3 4 5
    level for initial
    LEAD ministry

    _____
    _____
    _____
    _____
    _____
    _____

Section Two: Discussion of Your LEAD Equipping Experience

Use the back side if you need more space.

1. What have you appreciated most about your LEAD equipping experience?

2. Do you have suggestions for enhancing the LEAD equipping experience?

3. How did your LEAD equipping compare to your original expectations?

4. What other questions, comments, suggestions would you like to share?

Appendix 12.1

Church Discipline Policy

Church Discipline Policy: Restoring the Purity of the Body of Christ

- Officially adopted as part of the Church Constitution on
  _____.
- To be read, explained, and discussed at membership classes.
- To be signed and dated by every new member.
- To be read each year in the annual meeting.
- This is the Short Form. The Long Form (available to all members and prospective members) was officially adopted as part of the Church Constitution on _____.

We, the members of _____,
believe that church discipline includes the loving, biblical corrective measures taken by an individual, church leaders, or the congregation regarding a matter of sin in the life of a believer.

We further believe that the following biblical passages are the foundation for our church discipline policy: Matthew 5:23–24; Matthew 18:15–20; Acts 5:1–11; Acts 15:1–35; 1 Corinthians 6:1–11; 2 Corinthians 2:1–11; 2 Corinthians 6:11–7:13; Galatians 1:6–8; Galatians 2:11–14; Galatians 6:1–10; Philippians 3:18–4:2; Colossians 2:16–23;

2 Thessalonians 3:6–15; 1 Timothy 1:3–20; 1 Timothy 5:19–20; 2 Timothy 2:14–26; 2 Timothy 4:1–5; Titus 1:10–13; Titus 3:10–11; Hebrews 12:1–17; Hebrews 13:17; 2 John 7–11; Jude 1–20; Revelation 2:1–3:22.

We further believe that the purpose of church discipline includes reconciliation, righteousness, repentance, return to God, restoration, peace, and purity.

We further believe that church discipline must be invoked when habitual unrepentant rebellion arises in the areas of unbiblical public teaching, and/or unreconciled personal relationships, and/or unrepentant practice of sin.

We further believe that those administering church discipline must demonstrate spiritual integrity, personal purity, loving motivation, gentle strength, humility, and the desire to be a burden bearer.

We further believe that the biblical procedure for church discipline involves the Spirit-led, situation-specific, flexible implementation of the following principles:

- Awareness and identification of the discipline issue
- Personal confrontation
- Private conference
- Consultation with church leaders
- First warning by pastoral representative
- Second warning by pastoral representative
- Public announcement to the church
- Exclusion from body-life relationships
- Expulsion from church
- Re-admittance to church upon fruits of repentance

We further believe that every person who unites with our church, therefore, vows to submit to the discipline of this church as described both in this Short Form and in the Long Form. And we covenant as members of _____ not to pursue legal action or to sue the pastors, elders, deacons, or church staff in connection with the performance of their official duties relative to this church discipline policy.

We further believe that church membership and the related covenant agreements are both granted and removed only by the action and consent of the church leadership. Thus, all members agree that once the church discipline process has started, "resignation from church membership" does not void the church's responsibility to carry on the church discipline process.

Bibliography

Sources Cited and Consulted

Adams, Jay. *The Christian Counselor's Manual.* Grand Rapids: Zondervan, 1973.

———. *Competent to Counsel.* Phillipsburg, NJ: Presbyterian & Reformed, 1970.

———. *How to Help People Change: The Four-Step Biblical Process.* Grand Rapids: Zondervan, 1986.

———. *A Theology of Christian Counseling: More than Redemption.* Grand Rapids: Zondervan, 1979.

Aden, L. "Comfort/Sustaining" In *The Dictionary of Pastoral Care and Counseling,* edited by R. J. Hunter, 193–95. Nashville: Abingdon Press, 1990.

American Association of Christian Counselors. *AACC Christian Counseling Code of Ethics.* Forest, VA: AACC, 2001.

Barna, George. *The Power of Vision.* Ventura, CA: Regal Books, 1992.

———. *Turning Vision into Action.* Ventura, CA: Regal Books, 1996.

Beers, Mark, ed. *The Merck Manual of Diagnosis and Therapy.* 17th ed. Chicago: Merck, 2003.

Begley, Sharon. "A World of Their Own." *Newsweek,* May 8, 2000, 52–56.

Behm, J. *"noeo"* In *The Theological Dictionary of the New Testament,* edited by G. Bromiley, 636-46. Abr. ed. Grand Rapids: Eerdmans, 1992.

———. *"parakletos"* In *The Theological Dictionary of the New Testament,* edited by G. Bromiley, 782–84. Abr. ed. Grand Rapids: Eerdmans, 1992.

Berman, J. S., and N. C. Norton. "Does Professional Training Make a Therapist More Effective?" *Psychology Bulletin* 98, no. 2 (1985): 401–407.

Broger, John. *Self-Confrontation: A Manual for In-Depth Discipleship*. Nashville: Thomas Nelson, 1994.

Bromiley, Geoffrey, ed. *Theological Dictionary of the New Testament*. Abr. ed. Grand Rapids: Eerdmans, 1992.

Brown, Francis, S. Driver, and C. Briggs. *The New Brown, Driver, and Briggs Hebrew and English Lexicon of the Old Testament*. Lafayette, IN: Associated Publishers, 1981.

Bullis, Ronald. *Sacred Calling, Secular Accountability: Law and Ethics in Complementary and Spiritual Counseling*. Philadelphia: Brunner-Routledge, 2001.

Burck, J. R. "Reconciliation." In *The Dictionary of Pastoral Care and Counseling*, edited by R. J. Hunter, 1047–48. Nashville: Abingdon Press, 1990, 1047–1048.

Clebsch, William, and Charles Jaekle. *Pastoral Care in Historical Perspective*. New York: Harper, 1964.

Clinton, Tim, and Ron Hawkins. *Biblical Counseling: The Quick-Reference Guide*. Grand Rapids: Baker Books, 2009.

Crabb, Larry. *Understanding People*. Grand Rapids: Zondervan, 1987.

Croft, Brian. *Test, Train, Affirm & Send into Ministry: Recovering the Local Church's Responsibility in the External Call*. Leominster, UK: Day One, 2010.

Deckard, Mark. *Helpful Truth in Past Places: The Puritan Practice of Biblical Counseling*. Ross-shire, UK: Mentor, 2010.

Durlak, J. "Comparative Effectiveness of Paraprofessional and Professional Helpers." *Psychological Bulletin* 86, no. 1 (1979): 80–92.

Earle, Ralph. *Word Meanings in the New Testament*. Peabody, MA: Hendrickson, 2000.

Edwards, Jonathan. *Religious Affections: How Man's Will Affects His Character before God*. Portland, OR: Multnomah, 1984.

Emlet, Michael. *CrossTalk: Where Life & Scripture Meet*. Greensboro, NC: New Growth Press, 2009.

Eyrich, Howard, and William Hines. *Curing the Heart: A Model for Biblical Counseling*. Ross-shire, UK: Christian Focus Publications, 2002.

Faith Biblical Counseling. *Starting a Counseling Ministry*. Seminar notes presented at Faith Baptist Church, Lafayette, IN, 2009.

Fitzpatrick, Elyse. *Idols of the Heart: Learning to Long for God Alone*. Phillipsburg, NJ: P&R Publishing, 2001.

Fitzpatrick, Elyse, and Dennis Johnson. *Counsel from the Cross: Connecting Broken People to the Love of Christ*. Wheaton, IL: Crossway Books, 2009.

Graham, L. K. "Healing." In *The Dictionary of Pastoral Care and Counseling*, edited by R. J. Hunter, 497–501. Nashville: Abingdon Press, 1990.

Grudem, Wayne. *Systematic Theology: An Introduction to Biblical Doctrine*. Grand Rapids: Zondervan, 1994.

Hattie, J. A., H. J. Rogers, and C. F. Sharpley. "Comparative Effectiveness of Professional and Paraprofessional Helpers." *Psychological Bulletin* 95, no. 3 (1984): 534–41.

Haugk, Kenneth. *Christian Caregiving: A Way of Life*. Minneapolis: Augsburg Publishing, 1984.

Haugk, Kenneth, and McKay, William. *Christian Caregiving: A Way of Life—Leader's Guide*. New ed. Minneapolis: Augsburg Publishing, 1994.

Henderson, John. *Equipped to Counsel: A Training Program in Biblical Counseling—Leader Notebook*. Mustang, OK: Dare 2 Dream Books, 2008.

———. *Equipped to Counsel: A Training Program in Biblical Counseling—Leader Resource Book*. Mustang, OK: Dare 2 Dream Books, 2008.

———. *Equipped to Counsel: A Training Program in Biblical Counseling—Student Notebook*. Mustang, OK: Dare 2 Dream Books, 2008.

Herman, Keith. "Reassessing Predictors of Therapist Competence." *Journal of Counseling and Development* 72 (September/October 1993): 29–32.

Holifield, E. Brooks. *A History of Pastoral Care in America: From Salvation to Self-Realization*. Nashville: Abingdon Press, 1983.

Hughes, Barbara. *Disciplines of a Godly Woman*. Wheaton, IL: Crossway Books, 2006.

Hughes, R. Kent. *Disciplines of a Godly Man*. Wheaton, IL: Crossway Books, 1991.

Hull, Bill. *Jesus Christ Disciple Maker: Rediscovering Jesus' Strategy for Building His Church*. Grand Rapids: Revell, 1984.

———. *The Disciple Making Church*. Grand Rapids: Revell, 1990.

———. *The Disciple Making Pastor*. Grand Rapids: Baker Books, 1999.

Huntford, Roland. *Shackleton*. London: Hodder & Stoughton, 1985.

Kellemen, Robert. *God's Healing for Life's Losses: How to Find Hope When You're Hurting*. Winona Lake, IN: BMH Books, 2010.

———. "Hebrew Anthropological Terms as a Foundation for a Biblical Counseling Model of Humanity." Master's thesis, Grace Theological Seminary, 1985.

———. *Soul Physicians: A Theology of Soul Care and Spiritual Direction*. Winona Lake, IN: BMH Books, 2007.

———. "Spiritual Care in Historical Perspective: Martin Luther as a Case Study in Christian Sustaining, Healing, Reconciling, and Guiding." Ph.D. diss., Kent State University, 1997.

———. *Spiritual Friends: A Methodology of Soul Care and Spiritual Direction*. Winona Lake, IN: BMH Books, 2007.

Kellemen, Robert, and Karole Edwards. *Beyond the Suffering: Embracing the Legacy of African American Soul Care and Spiritual Direction*. Grand Rapids: Baker Books, 2007.

Kellemen, Robert, and Susan Ellis. *Sacred Friendships: Celebrating the Legacy of Women Heroes of the Faith*. Winona Lake, IN: BMH Books, 2009.

Keller, Timothy. *Ministries of Mercy*. 2nd ed. Phillipsburg, NJ: P&R Publishing, 1997.

———. "Puritan Resources for Pastoral Counseling." *Journal of Pastoral Practice* 9, no. 3 (1988): 11–44.

Lake, Frank. *Clinical Theology*. London: Darton, Longman & Todd, 1966.

Lane, Tim, and Paul Tripp. *How People Change*. Greensboro, NC: New Growth Press, 2008.

Levicoff, Steve. *Christian Counseling and the Law*. Chicago: Moody Press, 1991.

MacArthur, John. *Counseling: How to Counsel Biblically*. Nashville: Thomas Nelson, 2005.

MacArthur, John, and Wayne Mack, eds. *Introduction to Biblical Counseling: A Basic Guide to the Principles and Practice of Counseling*. Dallas: Word Publishing, 1994.

Mack, Wayne. *A Homework Manual for Biblical Living: Personal and Interpersonal Problems*. Vol. 1. Phillipsburg, NJ: P&R Publishing, 1979.

———. *A Homework Manual for Biblical Living: Family and Marital Problems*, Vol 2. Phillipsburg, NJ: P&R Publishing, 1980.

Mallory, Sue. *The Equipping Church: Serving Together to Transform Lives*. Grand Rapids: Zondervan, 2001.

———. *The Equipping Church Guidebook*. Grand Rapids: Zondervan, 2001.

Malphurs, Aubrey. *Advanced Strategic Planning: A New Model for Church and Ministry Leaders*. 2nd ed. Grand Rapids: Baker Books, 2005.

Marshall, Colin. *Passing the Baton: A Handbook for Ministry Apprenticeship*. Kingsford, Australia: Matthias Media, 2007.

Marshall, Colin, and Tony Payne. *The Trellis and the Vine: The Ministry Mind-Shift That Changes Everything*. Kingsford, Australia: Matthias Media, 2009.

McNeil, John. *A History of the Cure of Souls*. New York: Harper, 1951.

Medical Economics Staff, eds. *The Physician's Desk Reference*. Boston: Medical Economics, 2002.

Meiburg, A. "Care of Souls." In *The Dictionary of Pastoral Care and Counseling*, edited by R. J. Hunter, 122. Nashville: Abingdon Press, 1990.

Mills, L. "Pastoral Care: History." In *The Dictionary of Pastoral Care and Counseling*, edited by R. J. Hunter, 836–44. Nashville: Abingdon Press, 1990.

Oden, Thomas C. *Care of Souls in the Classic Tradition*. Philadelphia: Fortress Press, 1983.

———. *Classical Pastoral Care*. 4 vols. Grand Rapids: Baker, 1987.

Ohlschlager, George, and Peter Mosgofian. *Law for the Christian Counselor: A Guidebook for Clinicians and Pastors*. Dallas: Word, 1992.

Osborne, Grant. *The Hermeneutical Spiral: A Comprehensive Introduction to Biblical Interpretation*. Downers Grove, IL: InterVarsity, 1991.

Peugh, Roger, and Tammy Schultz. *Transformed in His Presence: The Need for Prayer in Counseling*. Winona Lake, IN: BMH Books, 2005.

Piper, John. *Brothers, We Are Not Professionals: A Plea to Pastors for Radical Ministry*. Nashville: B&H Books, 2009.

———. *Desiring God: Meditations of a Christian Hedonist*. Rev. and expanded ed. Sisters, OR: Multnomah, 2003.

Plantinga, Cornelius. *Not the Way It's Supposed to Be: A Breviary of Sin*. Grand Rapids: Eerdmans, 1995.

Powlison, David. *Seeing with New Eyes: Counseling and the Human Condition through the Lens of Scripture*. Phillipsburg, NJ: P&R Publishing, 2003.

———. *Speaking Truth in Love: Counsel in Community*. Winston-Salem, NC: Punch Press, 2005.

Priolo, Lou. *The Heart of Anger: Practical Help for Prevention and Cure of Anger in Children*. Amityville, NY: Calvary Press, 1998.

Quine, Jay. "Court Involvement in Church Discipline." Parts 1 and 2. *Bibliotheca Sacra*, January–March 1992.

———. *Legal Issues for Christian Workers and the Church*. Seminar notes presented at Lancaster Bible College, Lancaster, PA, 1998.

———. "Legal Issues Related to Confidentiality and Pastoral Counseling." *Bibliotheca Sacra*, January–March 1997.

Rainer, Thom, and Eric Geiger. *Simple Church: Returning to God's Process for Making Disciples*. Nashville: B&H Books, 2006.

Richards, Lawrence, and Gary Bredfeldt. *Creative Bible Teaching*. Rev. and expanded ed. Chicago: Moody, 1998.

Robertson, A. T. *Word Pictures in the New Testament*. Concise ed. Nashville: Holman, 2000.

Robinson, Haddon. *Biblical Preaching: The Development and Delivery of Expository Messages*. Grand Rapids: Baker Books, 1982.

Sande, Ken. *The Peacemaker: A Biblical Guide to Resolving Personal Conflict*. Rev. and expanded ed. Grand Rapids: Baker Books, 2004.

Shaw, Mark. *Strength in Numbers: The Team Approach to Biblical Counseling*. eEpanded ed. Bemidji, MN: Focus Publishing, 2010.

Smith, Robert. *The Christian Counselor's Medical Desk Reference*. Stanley, NC: Timeless Texts, 2000.

Southerland, Dan. *Transitioning*. Grand Rapids: Zondervan, 1999.

Stetzer, Ed, and Thom Rainer. *Transformational Church: Creating a New Scorecard for Congregations*. Nashville: B&H Books, 2010.

Stott, John. *The Cross of Christ*. Downers Grove, IL: InterVarsity, 1986.

Strauch, Alexander. *Biblical Eldership: An Urgent Call to Restore Biblical Church Leadership*. Rev. ed. Littleton, CO: Lewis & Roth Publishers, 1992.

Tan, Siang-Yang. *Lay Counseling: Equipping Christians for a Helping Ministry*. Grand Rapids: Zondervan, 1991.

Tan, Siang-Yang, and Yiu-Meng Toh. "The Effectiveness of Church-Based Lay Counselors: A Controlled Outcome Study." *Journal of Psychology and Christianity* 16, no. 3 (1997): 260–67.

Tautges, Paul. *Comfort Those Who Grieve: Ministering God's Grace in Times of Loss*. Leominster, UK: Day One, 2009.

———. *Counsel One Another: A Theology of Personal Discipleship*. Leominster, UK: Day One, 2009.

———. *Counsel Your Flock: Fulfilling Your Role as a Teaching Shepherd*. Leominster, UK: Day One, 2009.

Tripp, Paul David. *Instruments in the Redeemer's Hands*. Phillipsburg, NJ: P&R Publishing, 2002.

———. *A Quest for More: Living for Something Bigger than You*. Greensboro, NC: New Growth Press, 2007.

Viars, Stephen. *Putting Your Past in Its Place: Moving Forward in Freedom and Forgiveness*. Eugene, OR: Harvest House, 2011.

Walker, Clarence. *Biblical Counseling with African-Americans*. Grand Rapids: Zondervan, 1992.

Warren, Rick. *The Purpose Driven Church: Growth without Compromising Your Message and Mission*. Grand Rapids: Zondervan, 1995.

Welch, Ed. *Addictions—A Banquet in the Grave: Finding Hope in the Power of the Gospel*. Phillipsburg, NJ: P&R Publishing, 2001.

———. *Blame It on the Brain? Distinguishing Chemical Imbalances, Brain Disorders, and Disobedience*. Phillipsburg, NJ: P&R Publishing, 1998.

———. *When People Are Big and God Is Small*. Phillipsburg, NJ: P&R Publishing, 1997.

Whitney, Donald. *Spiritual Disciplines for the Christian Life*. Colorado Springs: NavPress, 1991.

Wiersbe, Warren. *Preaching and Teaching with Imagination*. Wheaton, IL: Victor Books, 1994.

Wilkerson, Mike. *Redemption: Freed by Jesus from the Idols We Worship and the Wounds We Carry*. Wheaton, IL: Crossway Books, 2011.

Equipping Resources from Dr. Kellemen and RPM Ministries

Dr. Kellemen wants his ministry to you to continue even after you've turned the last page of this book. He desires to equip you further as you change lives with Christ's changeless truth.

4E Consulting

If you would like to learn more about Dr. Kellemen's 4E Consulting where he walks step-by-step with churches through the envisioning, enlisting, equipping, and empowering process, contact him at rpm .ministries@gmail.com. For free resources related to *Equipping Counselors for Your Church*, visit Bob's website and blog at www.rpmministries.org.

Written Resources for Changing Lives

Equipping Counselors for Your Church is Dr. Kellemen's sixth book. Be equipped as a biblical counselor through "Doc K's" other books on Christ-centered, church-based, comprehensive, compassionate, and culturally informed biblical counseling. Order from www.rpmministries.org.

- *Soul Physicians: A Theology of Soul Care and Spiritual Direction*
- *Spiritual Friends: A Methodology of Soul Care and Spiritual Direction*

- *God's Healing for Life's Losses: How to Find Hope When You're Hurting*
- *Sacred Friendships: Celebrating the Legacy of Women Heroes of the Faith*
- *Beyond the Suffering: Embracing the Legacy of African American Soul Care and Spiritual Direction*

Changing Lives Seminars

Dr. Kellemen offers life-changing seminars around the country and the world. Learn more about the following seminars at www.rpm ministries.org.

- The 4E Ministry Training Strategy: A one-day, hands-on, next-step seminar that builds upon *Equipping Counselors for Your Church*.
- How to Care Like Christ: A one-day, interactive, practical seminar that equips God's people to change lives with Christ's changeless truth (based upon *Soul Physicians* and *Spiritual Friends*).
- God's Healing for Life's Losses: A three-quarter-day seminar sensitively presented for grieving persons and caregivers (based upon *God's Healing for Life's Losses*).
- Heroes of the black church: A moving, life-changing one-day seminar that applies life lessons from the black church to our lives and ministries today (based upon *Beyond the Suffering*).
- Celebrating the Legacy of Women Heroes of the Faith: An inspiring, life-changing one-day seminar that applies life lessons from women in church history to our lives and ministries today (based upon *Sacred Friendships*).

Robert W. Kellemen (Ph.D., LCPC), in his three pastoral ministries, has equipped hundreds of people as biblical counselors and spiritual friends. As founder and CEO of RPM Ministries, Bob is known for his Christ-centered, church-based, comprehensive, compassionate, and culturally informed approach to equipping God's people to change lives with Christ's changeless truth. Bob served for more than a dozen years as the founding Chairman of the Master of Arts in Christian Counseling and Discipleship Department at Capital Bible Seminary. He is now Professor of Counseling and Discipleship in that department. Bob is also the executive director of the Association of Biblical Counselors' Center for Church Equipping, and he is the executive director of the Biblical Counseling Coalition.